The Narrative Study of Lives

The purpose of this Series is to publish studies of actual lives in progress, studies that use qualitative methods of investigation within a theoretical context drawn from psychology or other disciplines. The aim is to promote the study of lives and life history as a means of examining, illuminating, and spurring theoretical understanding. *The Narrative Study of Lives* will encourage longitudinal and retrospective in-depth studies of individual life narratives as well as theoretical consideration of innovative methodological approaches to this work.

Guidelines for authors:

The editors invite submissions of original manuscripts of up to 40 typed pages in the areas described above. As a publication of an interdisciplinary nature, we welcome authors from all disciplines concerned with narratives, psychobiography, and life-history. In matters of style, we encourage any creative format that best presents the work. Long quotations in the protagonists' voice are desirable as well as discussion of the author's place in the study.

References and footnotes should follow the guidelines of the *Publication Manual of the American Psychological Association* (3rd ed.). A separate title page should include the chapter title and the author's name, affiliation, and address. Please type the entire manuscript, including notes and references, double-spaced, and submit three copies to:

Ruthellen Josselson, Ph.D., Co-Editor
The Narrative Study of Lives
Department of Psychology
Towson State University
Towson, MD 21252

THE NARRATIVE STUDY OF LIVES
Volume 5

The Narrative Study
▪ of Lives ▪

Amia Lieblich
Ruthellen Josselson
editors

The Narrative Study of Lives ▪ Volume 5

SAGE Publications
International Educational and Professional Publisher
Thousand Oaks London New Delhi

For information:

SAGE Publications, Inc.
2455 Teller Road
Thousand Oaks, California 91320
E-mail: order@sagepub.com

SAGE Publications Ltd.
6 Bonhill Street
London EC2A 4PU
United Kingdom

SAGE Publications India Pvt. Ltd.
M-32 Market
Greater Kailash I
New Delhi 110 048 India

Printed in the United States of America

Library of Congress Cataloging-in-Publication Data

ISBN 0-7619-0324-0 (cloth); ISBN 0-7619-0325-9 (paper)

ISSN 1072-2777

This book is printed on acid-free paper.

97   98   99   00   11   10   9   8   7   6   5   4   3   2   1

Acquiring Editor:	C. Deborah Laughton
Editorial Assistant:	Eileen Carr
Production Editor:	Sanford Robinson
Production Assistant:	Karen Wiley
Typesetter:	Janelle LeMaster
Indexer:	Will Ragsdale
Cover Designer:	Candice Harman
Print Buyer:	Anna Chin

Contents

Introduction

The present volume of *The Narrative Study of Lives* consists of contributions received from 1994 to 1996 and is, like the first three volumes, jointly edited by Ruthellen Josselson in Baltimore, Maryland, and Amia Lieblich in Jerusalem, Israel. It also resembles the first three volumes of our Annual in that it is based on the flow of articles submitted for publication, without a specific call for papers on a defined subject within the broad area of narrative studies of lives. Whereas Volume 4, *Ethics and Process in the Narrative Study of Lives*, invited authors and researchers to address specifically the issue of ethical dilemmas and solutions in the process of conducting and writing about narrative research, the present volume presents a variety of current theoretical contributions and empirical studies.

In the past, we tried to indicate by the title of the volume what was the central theme of the articles within it. Volume 2 bore the title *Exploring Identity and Gender*, and Volume 3, the more general title *Interpreting Experience*. However, these titles proved not entirely adequate in describing at least one or two chapters. In the future, unless the editors decide to solicit papers with a special focus, as in Volume 4, all academic contributions that approach human life from a narrative perspective will be considered for publication, in accordance with their quality and not their topic.

The flow of submissions for *The Narrative Study of Lives* has remained fairly stable during the last 7 years (from the time we started the collection of material for the annual), and in the present volume we have published 9 of the 25 papers that were submitted for review. It is still not easy to describe what makes a good piece of narrative work. What we are usually looking for is a combination of original story and intellectual perspective. In other words, we try to select contributions for the quality and originality of narratives and for their capacity to shed light on some meaningful issue in psychology, sociology, anthropology, or other academic fields. Furthermore, such selections are embedded in theoretical questions and demonstrate how to analyze or use stories for the study of human lives. Although some traditions seem to have emerged in the field, with powerful influences of older scholars in North America and Europe who provide models for younger researchers, the area can still be characterized by its fertile ambiguities. It allows individual thinking and writing a great amount of freedom and creativity. There is still no set of ground rules for this new methodology and style of reporting narrative work (as even the style of reporting traditional scientific work in psychology is under debate—see, for example, Josselson & Lieblich, 1996; Madigan, Johnson, & Linton, 1995); It is perhaps easier to define what we are trying to change or avoid. Yet, although there are as yet very few places that publish this kind of work, allowing enough space for longer quotations to represent the real flavor of the narrative, the relatively slow flow of papers of high quality to our series, and the great amount of revision and editorial work required before publication, indicate the persisting difficulty of performing narrative work in an academic setting, writing about it in an ethical and revealing fashion, and drawing meaningful conclusions from such projects. We hope that the present volume provides more viable models of this sort for researchers who are considering the fascinating choice of narrative studies in their academic work.

Regarding the nine chapters that make up the present volume, their variety of content yet their nearly common language and converging conceptual framework seem to reflect the development of the area of the narrative study of lives in the last few years. We see researchers from various disciplines choosing to explore many topics, yet coming aboard the ship of narrative studies with a common denominator in their work. This common quest, which is expressed, directly or indirectly, by almost all the authors, is to uncover, describe, and interpret the meaning of experience. Several chapters use narratives to point out how identical events are experienced as having different meaning for individuals (e.g., Sered regarding Jewish bath rituals [Chapter 3] and Wilson regarding African Americans' and whites' memories of growing up in the 1950s [Chapter 7]). Others point to the common matrix of meaning underlying experience (e.g. Bennett and Detzner in depicting loneliness among female elderly refugees [Chapter 6]). All, however, deal with meanings: the way people construct and reconstruct their life history and experience to convey meanings (e.g., Rosenthal in Chapter 2) or their conceptions of meaning in telling their lives (e.g., Maruna in Chapter 4).

Through their various routes to realizing this common quest, the chapters of Volume 5 can be grouped into those with strongly theoretical lessons to teach and those using narrative methods to explore specific subjects within their domain of scholarship. Furthermore, the empirical studies form two groups: Four present work that is entirely qualitative, based on individuals' stories, whereas two have used narrative research to enrich and lead to further insight in their quantitative research. The chapters of this volume will be ordered according to this general classification.

Alasuutari (Chapter 1) and Rosenthal (Chapter 2) make contributions to the epistemology of life-story research. Both have been conducting narrative research for many years, and both write about it extensively as part of a theory-building process. Moreover, both enlarge our understanding of the concepts of identity, personality, and individuality through the use of life narratives.

Pertti Alasuutari's Chapter 1 focuses on how the complex construct *personality* can be read out of a life story. Beginning with a broad theoretical and historical review of the field of life-story research, Alasuutari presents life-story narration within a discursive approach, focusing on its functions for the individual. Compared to older approaches, in which life stories were simply considered pictures of the lives led by the interviewees, or were used to make inferences about the teller's "real" personality, the current approach studies life-story narrating as an everyday phenomenon in its own right, whose function is to construct a person's individuality. Central to this approach is the concept of *face*, the expectation that the teller should be consistent, that self-presentation should follow life events as told in the story. In an intriguing example, the author says that notwithstanding the truth of an autobiography, "as job interviewers know, if a person is able to tell a life story in which the new job can be believably presented as the realization of a career development, he or she will probably adjust well to the new task" (p. 10). Personality can therefore be considered as an accounting strategy, that is, to account for the behavior of individuals who have many, often contradictory, roles. Thus, the creation of consistency—or of continuity—is not only a means to the end of telling a good story, but a central feature in our adjustment to changing, demanding, personal and historical circumstances.

Gabriele Rosenthal (Chapter 2) takes up similar themes regarding the development of multicultural identity as a dynamic process. People have a nationality stamped in their passport, but, in fact, national identity is shaped and reshaped by their personal history, as well as by the history of the world during their lifetime. People's identity is based on their life story, in the sense that by presenting an autobiography, they come to terms with the various components and conflicts of this national identity, in parallel to the actual lifelong process of becoming what they are. Postmodern identities are in many cases multicultural, yet not diffuse, and their best representations are in their narrators' autobiographical constructions. The life histories of Israeli Jews of European descent are particularly revealing in this respect, insofar as historical events during their lifetimes required frequent moves and changes in their national identities. In comparing the life histories of two women who grapple with their identities as Jews, Germans, Hungarians, Europeans, Israelis, and so on, Rosenthal demonstrates how autobiographies not only achieve a sense of continuity in complicated lived-through experiences but also contribute to actual choices and actions in the present.

Both of these chapters deal with the achievement of coherence in the face of complexity. It is perhaps not surprising that they both come from a European background, with its 20th-century history of shifting boundaries and identities on so many levels.

Susan Starr Sered's Chapter 3 is a bridge between the theoretical and the empirical. Although studying a particular cultural phenomenon—the feminine Jewish ritual of purification—she seems less interested in the phenomenon per se than in the intriguing differences between various observers' views of the world, including the ritual in question. In this volume, her chapter represents the field of anthropology, where narrative studies have been employed for many years. In respecting the subjectivity of the teller, such studies enable the scholar to freely explore a culture that is foreign and unknown. In this chapter, Sered reports on her study of the menstrual rites in contemporary Jerusalem, through accounts of two women, each invested with the authority to provide the services needed for these rituals. The women tell her about their lives, beliefs, and choice of occupation, as well as describing their understanding of the significance of the rites. By using their different voices, Sered interprets the practice as jointly produced by cultural and historical traditions, on the one hand, and the personalities of those involved in the ritual at a particular moment, on the other. The different versions, which are both presented as fully legitimate, undermine the illusion that rituals have "a meaning." Rather, the versions stem from the interaction of the particular teller, the context of her setting, and her power position within it. Polyphonic narratives are thus used to prove the richness and complexity of cultural practices.

The fertilization of ideas coming from theoretical perspectives about narratives as they encounter new questions leads to fascinating, original, and innovative research. The next chapters (4 through 7) present empirical studies that take narrative theory and methodology to be givens, allowing them to explore their chosen subjects, rather than developing claims for narrative per se.

Shadd Maruna (Chapter 4) deals with life narratives of reform, namely the transition away from delinquent behavior, or "going straight"—a fairly neglected, yet socially highly significant area of research. In agreement with Bakan's (1996) call for the use of published materials rather than research interviews to avoid ethical problems in narrative studies, Maruna selects published autobiographies of reformed criminals and attempts to encode the key elements of these stories for the understanding of desistance from crime. Guided mainly by McAdams's (1985, 1993) conceptual framework for narrative analysis, Maruna is able to point to the similarity of these life stories and reach general conclusions that may have practical implications for rehabilitation practices.

Narrative research seems to be the most natural method of studying phenomena of great rarity, where sampling is not an option and researchers aspire to go beyond description into deeper levels of individual judgment and meaning. The place of moral deviance in one's life story, and the way narrators present or justify their antisocial behavior, is also the topic of Ruth Linn's Chapter 5. However, whereas Maruna explores criminal histories, Linn studies the moral resistance of soldiers who refuse to serve in the army—either totally, or selectively, namely only when ordered to use power against other humans. This is also a form of law breaking, but it is usually recognized as a nonviolent declaration of high individual morality. How do refusers explain their decision to assume this unconventional and deviant moral position? This, argues Linn, is the function of the moral narrative, which serves to demonstrate the major moral concerns of the resisters. Her analysis suggests that in spite of their antisocial behavior, moral resisters display a struggle for connectedness in their narratives.

Loneliness and race relations, the subjects of the next two chapters, are much more universal than the topics studied in the previous two. The power of Jane A. Bennett and Daniel F. Detzner's Chapter 6 on loneliness lies in its touching quotations from interviews with old Southeast Asian refugee women. With these short excerpts, the writers are able to convey a sense of the aching loneliness in the lives of the refugees they interviewed. It is known and documented that having lived the majority of their lives in a radically different culture than their host society, refugees, especially the elderly, experience tremendous losses and live lives of extreme loneliness. What this narrative study is able to contribute concerns the meaning of the experience of loneliness in the lives of these refugee women, and it shows very concretely how the entire system of meaning of their lives has disintegrated. Following this, the chapter demonstrates the importance of cultural continuity for understanding loneliness in everyday life.

In studying individual recollections of the 1950s, Janelle Wilson (Chapter 7) also stresses that her work looks for the meaning of the decade in which her interviewees came of age. Focusing on the topic of race relations, she interviews "ordinary" African American and white individuals who grew up in the 1950s and finds that the memories of whites and African Americans are systematically different. Through their recollections, Wilson arrives at a more complex picture of the decade than that offered by the generalized concept of "collective memory." Individual memories, she concludes, may be inconsistent with collective memory, as well as much richer and more selective or personalized. Thus, Wilson's conclusion repeats the theoretical claims of Sered's Chapter 3, about having to listen to the different voices in one's culture in order to arrive at a more comprehensive picture of reality.

As qualitative studies in various disciplines gain greater acceptance, some quantitative researchers have found it worthwhile to supplement their method with narrative work, in order to enrich their more traditional "scientific" approaches and provide deeper understanding of the investigated domain. The final two chapters of this volume present work of combined methodology, of narrative work as an additional approach within a larger quantitative project of research. These researchers also seem to have reached the conclusion that whereas quantitative work may lead to general results, conveying the meaning of *personal* experience requires the narrative approach. We are hoping that this kind of study may lead to wider teaching and application of narrative perspectives to the study of lives within the broader spectrum of research methods.

Phame M. Camarena, Pamela A. Sarigiani, and Anne C. Petersen's Chapter 8 applies this joint methodology to the study of adolescence and gender in an attempt to shed light on the question of why adolescent girls are at high risk for depression. Analyzing stories of well-being for their quality and for particular gender-typed themes enables the researchers to propose an integration of the participants' subjective reflections with their objective longitudinal assessments, suggesting that psychological well-being has different meanings for adolescent boys and girls.

Jacquelyn Boone James, Joan Huser Liem, and Joan Gateley O'Toole's Chapter 9 presents a similar approach. Within a large study of resilience among survivors of childhood sexual abuse, in-depth interviews were conducted with four women who belong to this sample, in order to explore the meaning and experience of resilience in their lives. The authors hypothesize that finding socially acceptable outlets for the victims' power motive may be an important source of their resilience as adults. The individual stories gathered for the narrative study support this claim yet prove to be richer in meaning— showing how former victims of sexual abuse applied deliberate and focused efforts toward overcoming their hardships and finding their individual avenue for feeling powerful rather than powerless.

It is obvious that the chapters cover a large spectrum of topics, concerning women, men, humans, races, gender, deviance, suffering, and transcending. The narrative approach proves relevant and enriching to the study of the rare, the unusual, the common, and the prevalent. It is always concerned with the creation of and the search for meaning in people's lives.

As I compare the introductions of the four general volumes of this annual, and particularly the one I wrote for Volume 2 about 3 years ago, I am deeply impressed with the growing confidence we have developed both in theory and method, which are part of the narrative approach to human lives. In my frequent conversations with Ruthellen Josselson regarding this annual, we keep discovering wider circles that use these terms and do this kind of work, as evidenced not only by the growing number of published books and articles or academic theses written by graduate students, but by Internet sites dedicated to literature and course materials on narrative psychology. Conferences of scholars on narrative psychology, using various titles, also mark the growing interest and confidence in the field. Let me mention just one of these significant events, inspired by Carol Gilligan of Harvard University, who is among the leading authorities of the field and a member of the editorial board of *The Narrative Study of Lives* since its beginning.

The conference was titled The New Psychologies Conference and took place in Tarbert, Scotland, in June 1996. The original invitation said,

> We have called the conference "new psychologies" to signal what we see as a break in this research from the mainstream tradition that has been so unsuccessful in making sense of our social world. . . . We see the new psychologies as work which has often employed what others see as improper methods, that does not respect traditional disciplinary boundaries and avoids the twin pitfalls of reductionism or essentialism.

The conference was organized around relational topics—for example, the mother-infant dyad, fatherhood, sexuality, and relational development of women. All speakers presented innovative research approaches and results, most of them narrative, which emphasized subjectivity, listening to the personal voice, and—last but not least—portraying a researcher who is human, self-aware, and concerned. For me, as a participant in this beautiful setting, the most moving aspect of the conference was the coming together of an international group of people from distant locations and fields, yet all speaking a new common language, as well as the fertile relationship between older and younger generations of scholars discussing and studying together how to do this kind of work. Whereas the older generation may be perceived as the pioneers of the area, it is the younger who pave the way with much more confidence and zeal. Clearly, *The Narrative Study of Lives* is an important component in this worldwide progress, which, as our various papers indicate, encompasses other fields beside psychology.

In closing this introduction, I would like to thank our two loyal assistants, without whom this work could have never been completed. In Jerusalem, Yael Oberman, our editorial associate, has done much of the editing of the chapters for the volume, and in Towson, Diana Buck has corresponded with authors and overseen most of the technical work.

AMIA LIEBLICH

References

Bakan, D. (1996). Some reflections about narrative research and hurt and harm. In R. Josselson (Ed.), *Ethics and process in the narrative study of lives* (Vol. 4, pp. 3-8). Thousand Oaks, CA: Sage.

Josselson, R., & Lieblich, A. (1996). Fettering the mind in the name of "science." *American Psychologist, 51,* 651-652.

Madigan, R., Johnson, S., & Linton, P. (1995). The language of psychology: APA style as epistemology. *American Psychologist, 50,* 428-436.

McAdams, D. (1985). *Power, intimacy and the life story: Personological inquiries into identity*. New York: Guilford.

McAdams, D. (1993). *The stories we live by*. New York: William Morrow and Company.

❦ 1 ❦

The Discursive
Construction of Personality

Pertti Alasuutari

*I*n the social sciences, life stories have traditionally been approached from two alternative but often combined perspectives. Either they have been used as material in studying lives in their social contexts (Bertaux & Bertaux-Wiame, 1981; Roos, 1985), or they have been viewed as texts that reflect individuals' personality or identity construction (Alasuutari, 1986; Burgos, 1988; Gubrium, 1993; Gubrium & Holstein, 1994; Linde, 1987, 1993; Weintraub, 1978). Bertaux and Kohli (1984) have named these two viewpoints the *sociostructural* and the *sociolinguistic* approaches.

A wide unanimity about a proper definition of a life story also reflects and supports the idea that there are basically only two ways of approaching life stories. According to Lejeune (1989), autobiography is "retrospective prose narrative written by a real person concerning his [sic] own existence, where the focus is his individual life, in particular the story of his personality" (p. 4). Linde (1987, p. 344) broadens the definition by saying that a life story is all the stories told by an individual during his or her lifetime that (a) make a point about the speaker, not about the way the world is, and (b) "have extended reportability"—that is, they are tellable over the course of a long period of time. In other words, these definitions distinguish two main components in a proper life story: In it, a person tells about his or her life, and the focus is on the individual's character, as it is reflected in and substantiated by the life events told.

This view of two alternative approaches to a life story in social sciences and humanities is limited in one respect. The studies about the role and meaning of *biographical work* (Gubrium & Holstein, 1995a, 1995b; Gubrium, Holstein, & Buckholdt, 1994) or *biographical reasoning* (Alasuutari, 1986, 1992) as a phenomenon that takes place in everyday life cannot really be applied to either of the two approaches. Although the sociolinguistic trend emphasizes that life-story narration has a function in constructing self and identity, it approaches the phenomenon from the perspective of an already available story, using it as evidence about self-construction. By discussing recent developments in life-story research, this chapter points to life-story narration as seen from the other end of the chain. What can be learned by analyzing the everyday life situations in which individuals give accounts about aspects of their personal past? What are the functions of life-story narration? Because it is obvious that life stories can be seen as a means of personality or identity construction, what are the particular situations in which the "personality" or "disposition" of an individual is invoked? What is the social function of personality in social interaction?

In the following sections, I first discuss the two older approaches to life stories and then show how developments, especially in the sociolinguistic approach, already point in the direction of the third, discursive approach. Then I give an outline and a case example of the new approach, where personality is seen as an accounting strategy for maintaining continuity and saving face. Finally, I discuss the new agenda this approach sets for sociological research.

Sociostructural and Sociolinguistic Approaches

Bertaux and Bertaux-Wiame's (1981) study of life stories in the Parisian bakers' trade is an example of the sociostructural trend. On the basis of the life stories and other data they gathered, Bertaux and Bertaux-Wiame constructed a picture of the set of sociostructural relationships that form the institution of artisanal bakery in France. By drawing primarily upon life stories as evidence, they could explain why, in France, more than 90% of the bread is still produced by small bakers, whereas in most other industrial countries, artisanal bakery disappeared long ago, bread being manufactured in large factories and delivered by trucks all over the land. The answer lay in a continuous flow of bakery workers from the countryside and in the particular way in which the young apprentices organized their and their wives' lives around the family business of the bakery and bakery shop.

In this approach, the life stories are simply considered pictures of the lives the interviewees have led. The data are approached from what I have elsewhere (Alasuutari, 1995) called the *mechanistic variant of the factist* perspective; they are seen as consisting of statements that give us information about the reality outside the data.[1] If this kind of reading of the life stories adds up to a picture of the personality traits of the narrators, it is based on inferences of the facts we get from their lives and behavior, not on the way they tell their stories or what they tell about their experiences.

The sociolinguistic approach is more interested in the subjectivity of the narrators. Bertaux and Kohli (1984) use Burgos's approach to life stories as an example of this trend. In her analysis of oral life stories as narratives, as a genre, she has employed Bakhtin's distinction between *epic* and *romanesque* forms of narration. In the epic form, the world and personages are taken as given, whereas in the romanesque form—whose ideal type is the *Bildungsroman*—the world is problematic, the self is unstable, and life (and the life story) takes the shape of a search for meaning and identity. In her view, the usefulness of the life story in sociological or historical research is in the fact that—through the narrative form it takes—it reflects the individual's self-image. As Burgos (1988) puts it, "Thus, autobiography is a valuable method of investigation which yields information about life experiences, subjectivity, individual choices, the rational and conscious motives for actions, etc., but it is nonetheless a means, rather than a finished statement of the truth" (p. 12).

The sociolinguistic trend acknowledges and makes use of the linguistic and narrative form taken by autobiography in order to make inferences about the personality of the subject. This has implications for data collection. To be valid as autobiographical testimonies, the analyzed life stories must not be too much affected by the characteristics of the interaction between the interviewer and the interviewee

—or by later use of the original material. Burgos (1988), for instance, discusses the trickery of commercially produced life stories, which are not "authentic" (p. 17). They, for instance, find their inspiration "in the training in essay-writing given in schools." Furthermore, the final products have been "coauthored" by editors. "The reader is led to believe that he has bought a genuine local product (usually the life story of a peasant or an artisan); whereas what he has really got is a counterfeit which has practically nothing to do with the original."

In this approach, one assumes that every person has a genuine personality that can be grasped by studying the person's life story. This, of course, requires that the story be also genuine, unaffected by the data collection situation or by the storyteller's or researcher's literary influences.[2]

Historians of the autobiography describe much the same approach. A number of scholars have studied the rise and history of autobiographies as a reflection or indicator of the rise of individualism. For instance, Delany (1969) notes that the emergence of autobiographies in Italy was preceded by family histories. And the same goes for Britain: "In early British autobiographies we often find similar transitions from genealogy to autobiography; by placing his own story in the context of family tradition the writer could avoid giving the appearance of an unseemly egotism" (Delany, 1969, p. 12). The histories of autobiography also suggest that individuality is a specifically modern form of self-conception, which began in the Renaissance and reached full blossom in the time of Goethe (Misch, 1969; Weintraub, 1975, 1978). Weintraub (1975) points out that autobiography is inseparably linked to the problem of self-conception: "The manner in which men conceive of the nature of the self largely determines the form and process of autobiographic writing" (p. 834). Autobiographies reveal the gradual emergence of that form of self-conception called individuality. From the Hellenic and the Roman times onward, there has been, according to Weintraub (1975), an ever sharper turn toward an inner-directed personality. Then, since the time of the Renaissance, "Western man has by a series of complex and gradual developments formed a particular attachment to the ideal of personality we call individuality. This ideal is characterized by its very rejection of a valid model for the individual" (Weintraub, 1975, p. 838).

In the historians' approach, one also assumes that there is an object —personality or self-concept—whose historical transformation the autobiographies reflect. The changes in the genre of autobiographic writing are perceived from this viewpoint: as changing ways of expressing the self and, in that sense, reflecting the changing self-concept.

To sum up, one can say that in the sociolinguistic trend, the textual and literary aspects of the life story are given more attention. Yet, this trend also approaches the data from the factist perspective. Whereas the sociostructural trend conceives of the life story as a picture of a life, the sociolinguistic trend perceives it as a picture of a personality.

Toward a Discursive View

Life stories have also been studied from the other end of the chain: Instead of analyzing the frames or narrative structures evident in the end products of life-story narrating, some researchers have studied life-story narrating as an everyday life phenomenon in its own right. For instance, folklorists have paid attention to oral life stories and life-story narrating as a form of oral tradition, which is of interest as such. These new considerations have meant a gradual move away from the assumption, discussed in the previous section, that each person possesses an authentic self that could be captured in a text where the person honestly tells his or her life story. Instead, it is increasingly emphasized that life-story narrating is always situational and serves a function.

As a discipline, folklore has, of course, always been keen on forms of oral tradition, such as proverbs, jokes, and folktales. However, an increased interest in narrating and in the actual situations where oral tradition is transmitted (Georges, 1969, 1976; Hoppál, 1980) paved the way for paying attention to the personal elements and points of view of orally communicated history (Agar, 1980; Allen, 1979; Robinson, 1981) and to considering life stories as a folklore genre (Pentikäinen, 1980; Stahl, 1977; Titon, 1980).[3] These developments, cross-fertilized with advances in, for instance, narratology and discourse analysis, have established life-story narrating as an independent object of research. Labov and Waletzky's (1973) ethnography of speech approach to oral accounts of personal experience is an early example.

Along with these changes, many researchers began to see life-story narrating as an everyday life phenomenon that obviously serves certain functions. Individuals do not have their readily narrated life stories in their back pockets or the back of their minds, waiting for a researcher to collect them. Any account of one's personal past (also when told to a researcher in a *life-story interview*) makes a point and serves a function. A particular case of life-story narration must be related to its local setting in order to see what it is needed or used for.

Studies following this line of thought show that accounts of a personal past often justify a change of perspective by reconstructing continuity over time. This is illustrated in, for instance, Early's (1982) study of therapeutic narratives in Cairo, Egypt. In the worldview of the *baladi* women she studied, there is a clear-cut dichotomy: *baladi* versus *afrangi*, or honorable, religious, and nationalistic, as opposed to dishonorable, nonreligious, and foreign. The baladi curative system replicates this inside/outside dichotomy: There are "domestic" and "foreign" causes for illnesses, such as benevolent spirits (*baladi asyat*) and malevolent spirits (*afrangi afarit*). Correspondingly, the native healing system and Western medicine live side by side: If the local healers' methods do not seem to work, the patient is taken to see a doctor. However, and this is the point, first the illness narrative has to be changed.

A similar kind of reconstructive work seems to be needed in descriptions of individuals' personal characteristics. The claim of a personality often justifies one's present behavior, but the claim itself is justified by biographical work. For instance, Gergen and Gergen (1984) considered the way people's daily accounts of themselves require a biographical interpretation and, if needed, long-standing story of self: "Suddenly and momentarily to see oneself as 'aggressive,' 'poetic,' or 'male,' for example, might seem mere whimsy unless such concepts could be secured to a series of earlier events" (p. 173). Thus, life stories consist of retrospective accounts of the past, accounts that are given for particular reasons and in particular situations, such as an onset of chronic illness (Williams, 1984).

Although life-story narrating may also take place as an individual's "inner speech" needed for creating a sense of continuity of self in changing conditions and situations, the concepts, discourses, explanatory systems (Linde, 1987) or interpretative repertoires (Potter & Wetherell, 1987, pp. 146-157) used in such accounts are not private language. People always use the interpretive resources available for them, even when it comes to creating a sense of self.

These considerations lead into a discursive theory of self (see Harré & Gillett, 1994). It maintains that to accomplish their plans, projects, and intentions, people have certain linguistic resources or repertoires at their disposal.

> The resources people have available in some roughly de-
> lineated, cultural system have been called an " . . . -ology."
> So an emotionology is a representation of the linguistic and
> other discursive resources people have available for describ-
> ing emotional phenomena. (Harré & Gillett, 1994, p. 98)

The Cultural Premises of Self

Let me now further pursue the implications of the discursive turn in life-story research by introducing an ethnomethodological aspect to the discussion. It is obvious that individuals use life-story narration and autobiographical accounting to construct their individuality, a continuity over time. That is how a sense of self is discursively accomplished.

This leads to the question of what are the cultural premises on which members' understanding of a life story as a story about an individual life, a story of a personality, is based. If self and personality are discursively constructed, how is it done? What implicit frames or cultural premises are required of a reader of a "life story"? I suggest that we can identify two kinds of intertwined premises for the understanding of a life story: the *narrative implicature* and the concept of *face*.

By the narrative implicature, I refer to Grice's (1975, 1978) idea of *conversational implicature*, which means that in ordinary conversations everyone assumes that participants follow the cooperative principle, which is realized in certain maxims of conversations. Geis (1982) lists six such maxims. It is not necessary to go through all these maxims here; let me just say that these maxims we automatically follow require us to avoid unfamiliar language, to be truthful and relevant, and to say no less or no more than is necessary. The point of these maxims is not their being regulative rules; it is rather that people use them in interpreting each other's utterances in conversation (Nofsinger, 1991, p. 40).

Similarly, when a person is telling a long story, we assume that there is a logical and thematic link that connects different sentences of a story together. Van Dijk (1980) actually makes the same point by showing that in addition to semantic macrostructures, we assume that texts have a thematic coherence. He gives an example:

> John was ill, so he called the doctor. But the doctor could not come, because his wife wanted to go to the theater with him. They were playing *Othello*, which she thought they could not miss because Shakespeare is one of the few dramatical authors who. . . . (p. 40)

Each fact is a condition for a next one; participants are also kept identical for a while; but still this fragment has no coherence because a uniting theme is missing. We expect to find a theme or topic in a story, and if we fail to find it, we will soon ask what the point of the story is. In storytelling and listening to stories, we do accept irrelevant details up to a point, but because we follow the cooperative principle, we also try to make sense of the details of, for instance, a life story. Consider the following sentences:

> I was never a good liar. When Paula asked me if I knew how to swim, I said yes.

Formally there is no link between the two sentences, but by following the cooperative principle, we automatically read them as a way of saying or emphasizing the point that the speaker told the truth. However, in addition to such a narrative implicature, the example above also illustrates another, related self-evident frame. We automatically assume, upon hearing that the person was "never a good liar," that he continues to be that way.

This leads us to the concept of face, the expectation that a person should be self-consistent. Although the concept has initially been applied to human interaction, we can assume that it also holds in the telling of longer stories. In the act of storytelling, participants to human interaction are supposed to give a consistent picture of themselves as characters. We are supposed to maintain our face: to successfully and consistently play the role we chose to take when entering the situation. Goffman (1967) argues that a sacred principle prevails in conversation situations whereby the parties to the conversation have a reciprocal system of maintaining and defending each others' faces. This means, among other things, that the people involved in the conversation are considerate toward each other and try to sustain each other's self-image. Brown and Levinson (1987) have, in fact, shown that there is a universal principle of politeness based on avoiding face-threatening acts, which can be of two types: they may threaten our negative or positive face. *Negative face* refers to the wish of every competent adult that his or her actions be unimpeded by others. *Positive face*, in turn, refers to the wish of every adult that her or his needs/wishes be desirable at least to some others (p. 62). When we say "You couldn't, by any chance, tell me the time, could you?" rather than "Tell me the time," we are conforming to conventional expectations of politeness by showing that we are aware of and honor the negative-face wants of the addressee. In face-to-face interaction, maintaining face also means that if I introduce myself as a specialist in a field, it is considered humiliating if my next turn of speech shows that I know very little or nothing about it.

By choosing to tell my life story, I enter an interaction situation by giving a presentation of myself. It may, of course, be that the audience of a written autobiography is unknown to the storyteller, but the story is nonetheless a presentation of self, a character, and as such, the consistency implicature applies.

In a life-story presentation, the consistency principle means that the characteristics by which the storytellers describe themselves are consistent with the life events told in the story. In a sense, this is obvious, because any events included in a life story are there precisely because they make a point about the person. Life-story narrating is usually employed when accounting for possibly face-threatening acts, public acts that might be seen to contradict the public self-image the person has previously claimed for him- or herself.

Consider a job interview or an autobiographical statement required in the application to a vacancy. The events of past life mentioned must be truthful enough not to contradict one's personal records and documents. On the other hand, the story constructed on the basis of these events should convey a long-standing interest in precisely the kind of job for which one is applying. This means that, for instance, previous work in a totally different field should be presented as a mistake finally acknowledged. Another possibility is that one is able to plot an account where the common element between the tasks is pointed out, preferably in such a light that one's personal calling could be better realized in the new job than in the old one.

Are such life-story narratives totally false, and thus useless in trying to get a grasp on an individual's true self? Not really. As job interviewers know, if a person is able to tell a life story in which the new job can be believably presented as the realization of a career development, he or she will probably adjust well to the new task. First, the same account can be given to friends and relatives. Second, biographical reasoning also works as a personal device by which we get a sense of continuity about our own self. If we need to remodel our self-concept in order to better fit the changed role requirements, we can depict our life story anew by these means. Memory and forgetfulness are also both excellent tools is shaping and reshaping the personal self.

Rescuing the Split Character: The "Freudian" Narrative

To sum up what was discussed in the previous section, we can say that the telling and reading of life stories is based on the implicit assumption that there is a coherence in the past actions of the protagonist, that is, that he or she maintains a face. To approach this from the perspective of everyday life interaction, we can say that the function of life-story narrating is to construct a face, or self. Let me now, in this section, argue that the particular conditions of face protection in complex societies result in the modern notion of personality, as it is formulated, for instance, by Freud.

As historical studies have shown, autobiographies are a story genre that developed along with modernization (Delany, 1969; Misch, 1969; Weintraub, 1975, 1978). If we accept the idea that life-story narrating is a means of face protection, it is not that obvious why this should be the case. According to cross-cultural research reported by Brown and Levinson (1987), there seem to be universal rules of politeness based on the notion of face, and thus the requirement of maintaining one's face seems to be a universal phenomenon. So why do autobiographies as a genre emerge along with modernization?

In complex societies, individuals have multiple "roles": one's face changes from one contact to another. As, for instance, Mauss (1979) and Geertz (1973, pp. 360-411; 1983, pp. 62-68) have emphasized, in "premodern" society, people are identified as collective stereotypes, as *personages* rather than persons, or as dramatis personae rather than actors:

> On the one hand the clan is conceived of as constituted by a *certain number of persons*, actually roles; and, on the other, the purpose of all these roles is really to symbolize, each in its own portion, the pre-figured totality of the clan. (Mauss, 1979, p. 65)

In such a social system, the point that one has maintained face throughout one's life would sound like an obvious point to make in a life story, but that is precisely why biographical work became important along with modernization. The simplicity of the role system does not cause face-threatening tensions to the same extent that modern society does. Life-story narrating makes a point in a situation where role expectations radically vary from one social encounter to another one, but one nevertheless holds on to the moral obligation to maintain face. The impossibility to actually maintain face in the traditional sense of the word leads to narrative innovations, a changed conception of characters and personhood, and finally the split image of personality canonized as the Freudian personality theory.

In effect, Freud constructed and gave names to parts of a split self, a self—or personality—that was a solution to the difficulty in accounting for the behavior of the modern individual. The modern individual appears in several, often contradictory roles, but the prevalent cultural notion of self still holds on to the idea that one is supposed to maintain and defend a single face. Now, the popular Freudian and other notions of personality are a resource used in accounting for face-threatening situations or personal histories.

From a narratalogical point of view, modernization has meant ever more complicated figures in popular stories. Consider, for instance, the characters of folktales (Propp, 1975): Each character—a hero or a villain, say—pursues an obvious, simply stated goal with the means of rational action. With modernization, such fictional characters came to be considered and scorned as too "black-and-white," while modern novels introduced more complex characters with ambivalent views and motives hidden from others and even from themselves.[4]

Narratalogically, this *personality structure* is constructed by dividing a self into two or more characters with their separate goals or, to put it another way, by uniting several lines of action into one "self." As a consequence, the otherwise incoherent account of a face is rescued by inscribing an inner structure on the character in question; a personality that includes contradictory lines of action in a single self.

A Case Example in Personality Construction

How is the Freudian reading of life-story narrating as the reflection of a personality structure actually accomplished? What frames are required of a reader who hears the life story as a reflection of the Freudian paradigm of the personality?[5] How is such a picture of the supposed object-like construction called personality made and empirically defended? Let us address these questions in the light of a case example.

Consider an individual telling about and reflecting on his past, like the men interviewed in a study of mine (Alasuutari, 1986, 1992, chapter 4). In many of the life-story interviews, the men expressed an ambivalence toward the schooling phase of their lives. For these men, who were all manual workers (half of them were also alcoholic), school had been an ambiguous experience. The men were first asked to draw a continuous line depicting the ups and downs of their life and then to explain them in an unstructured interview. The ambivalence about schooling could often be seen in the fact that school was drawn as a downturn, but when asked about it, it was described as a jolly good time.

> Q: I understand you were held back a year. What was it like?
>
> A: Actually there was a lot happening that year. I was 16, and it was the last year of my schooling. I, for example, had an affair with my teacher. It was a wild experience.
>
> Q: Was it an upturn in life?
>
> A: I suppose I was held back as a consequence of all this. So it really can't be perceived as a high point.

The ambivalence about such a phase in life comes from the fact that it can be evaluated from two points of view. If the men pay attention to what they liked and wanted at the time, schooling was boring and ending it was a relief, a liberation from a straitjacket. From this perspective, having fun during the school hours was the positive part of that phase. If, on the other hand, they consider how they got on at school and the usefulness of conscientious schooling for a future life, the values are reversed. In reflecting on and assessing a phase in life, the past moods and inclinations conflict with long-term interests as presently perceived. This often leads to remorse, to second thoughts about what one or others should have done.

> I wish I had gone on with my schooling. Not then but now, afterward. I sure would have handled it, even though I wouldn't have liked it then. Father should have forced me, but it was a question of money and the fact that I didn't like school.

The frame within which the narrator reflects upon his past behavior is very close to the Freudian notion of personality, as consisting of a *libido* and an *ego* (Freud, 1978), although he does not use those concepts. However, he does refer to a popular Freudian notion of a tension between desire and self-control.

What are the steps we take to arrive at such a split image of an objectified personality as the character of the narrative? The first step is to abstract different views of personal conduct, to make a typology of them. The lines of action associated with things usually considered pleasures, sins, or socially unacceptable behavior are—as options for future action or as views of past action—named libido or desire. The views of action usually thought to be in accordance with socially esteemed values, with moral codes, or with an individual's long-term interests are named *superego* or self-control. After constructing this typology of separate lines of action into two classes, the next step is to conceive of them as object-like elements in an object-like structure called *personality*.

In the previous extract from a life-story interview, we read the Freudian personality structure from the man's narrative, regardless of his own interpretations. However, often this personality theory is "written into" the life stories themselves as the frame within which narrators interpret their own behavior. Linde's (1987) analysis of explanatory systems in oral life stories is similar. She mentions the "popular Freudian psychology" as one of the explanatory systems people use in accounting for their past life. In a broader perspective, another explanatory system she identifies, *behaviorist psychology*, also falls within the personality structure frame as it is used here. Both of these commonsense theories include a split of the self into parts, which are in conflict.

In perhaps its clearest form, this view of the self as split into contradictory elements can be seen, in everyday usage, in accounts of some socially unacceptable behaviors, such as heavy drinking. Among the alcoholics of the sample of life-story interviews discussed above, drinking often becomes interpreted as an uncontrolled craving, alien from the men themselves: "It was a high point when I got a job and became a sailor, although I drank a lot. Before I went to the army, it got out of control really, I couldn't hold back."[6]

From a narratological point of view, the personality structure solution to a difficulty in preserving face, to maintaining an image of a separate autonomous self pursuing an expressed line of action, is indeed an interesting one. The diverse and often conflicting logics of action identified in one's self are objectified into evidence of parts of an inner structure. In his structural theory of narratives, Greimas (1987) in a sense deconstructed such a notion of character by making a distinction between actors and actants of a story: Actors may consist of several actants.

To return to Freud, who was one of the first to work out a sophisticated theory of such a modern notion of personhood, it is often said that with the invention of the libido and the unconscious, he shattered the self. This is partly true: He did shatter the rational homogeneity of the self by inventing its inner contradictory structure. However, by so doing, he actually rescued the Western object-like notion of the self as distinct from other selves. It was only much later, with the emergence of family-systems theoretical therapeutic models that the conception of the individual self as a center was challenged and surpassed (Gubrium, 1992). It turned out that many families or social networks were best helped, not by treating the identified patient, but by making an intervention to the system (for instance, Haley, 1985; Watzlawick, Weakland, & Fish, 1974).

Biographical Narration and Self

In this chapter, I have contrasted the discursive approach with older trends of life-story research and then pursued the implications of the new trend for the notion of the self. I have come to the conclusion that personality can be considered an accounting strategy. It is used in accounting for the behavior of a person who has appeared in more than one role and, in doing so, followed logics that are contradictory, if one assumes that each person only wears one face.

Does this imply that we should forget about the self or personality, argue that it does not really exist? Such sentiments have indeed been raised in some postmodernist discussions around the issue. I suggest that it is premature to announce the death of the subject. Rather, what we are dealing with is a different view of the ontological status of individual selves—that is, the sense in which we should conceive of the existence of selves. We do have our physical existence, but selves—or personalities—are not objects in the physical world. Rather, they are part of social reality: constructions we live by. For us, selfhood as lived experience is very real, and the discursive view as it is outlined here might seem to be useless philosophical hair-splitting that has no practical value. However, to realize that selves are, after all, constructions we live by enables us, when that is needed, to renew ourselves. It allows us to adopt a view of life and self that better adapts to changed conditions or which, because the conception of oneself is changed, changes the conditions by viewing them in a new light.

Notes

1. In this instance, Silverman (1993) and Holstein and Gubrium (1995) talk about an approach to interviews reflecting Enlightenment sensibilities.

2. I have elsewhere (Alasuutari, 1995, pp. 47-62) discussed this as the *humanistic variant of the factist* perspective. Holstein and Gubrium (1995) refer to it as the *romanticist* view of interviewing. See also Silverman, 1993.

3. The folklorists and anthropologists active in this field have especially been influenced by what became known as a *schema-theoretic* view of producing, reading, and understanding stories (Adams & Collins, 1979; Chafe, 1977a, 1977b, 1980; Kintsch, 1978; Kintsch, Mandel, & Kozminsky, 1977; Rumelhart, 1975; Voss & Bisanz, 1985; for an introduction to the theory, see Mandler, 1984). Later, some of the researchers started to talk about cultural models of language and thought as the object of this line of inquiry (Holland & Quinn, 1987).

4. Elias (1982) links this development with more complex interpersonal relationships, with the outcome that an individual's image of others becomes richer in nuances, freer of spontaneous emotions: It is "psychologized":

> Where the structure of social functions allows the individual greater scope for actions under the influence of momentary impulses than is the case at court, it is neither necessary nor possible to consider very deeply the nature of another person's consciousness and affects, or what hidden motives may underlie his behavior. If at court calculation meshes with calculation, in simpler societies affect directly engages affect. (p. 273)

Elias takes it for granted that along with the "civilizing process," the personality structure of the individual changes, without noticing the fact that the same process gives birth to the *notion* of such a structure.

5. We could also put it this way: What did Freud do to the elements of the life-story narrating he heard from his psychiatrist's couch in order to construct his personality theory? By the latter question, I do not mean that we could or should try to reconstruct what Freud actually did; it is rather that as people living in a post-Freudian culture, we do it all the time.

Freud is known for his crucial role in shattering the Enlightenment view of the rational self, the individual in control of her- or himself. By introducing the concepts of libido, id, and the unconscious, Freud pointed out that the individual self is not the agent of even his or her own mind. It must, of course, be remembered that the Western view of the self did not change just because of the genius of Freud. The idea of the possibility that a person is not her or his own master is definitely older than Freud. It is, for instance, reflected in middle-age Christian asceticism, which included the idea that certain behaviors, especially pleasures, represent *nature* in the individual, and that is why they had to be overcome, controlled by *reason*. Originally the term *personality* only referred to those who were able to control their urges and impulses (Weber, 1971, pp. 118-119), thus implying that the opposite could be true as well. In his uncompleted project, Foucault (1980, 1986, 1988) traced the origins of the "genealogy of the desiring man" (Foucault, 1986, p. 12) to ancient Greece.

Then, what is the significance of Freud? Admittedly, he was just one of the people who formulated the changed and changing conception of the self. Yet, the influence of Freud and psychoanalysis probably cannot be overestimated because Freud has provided the Western world with a popular vocabulary with which to talk about the psyche.

6. This interpretation of an individual's action, often named *addiction*, is real lived experience for many individuals. By analyzing the way this Freudian conception of the self is discursively produced, I do not intend to deny the very real nature of the experience (see Alasuutari, 1992).

References

Adams, M. J., & Collins, A. (1979). A schema-theoretic view of reading. In R. O. Freedle (Ed.), *New directions in discourse processing* (pp. 1-22). Norwood, NJ: Ablex.

Agar, M. (1980). Stories, background knowledge, and themes: Problems in the analysis of life history narrative. *American Ethnologist, 7*(2), 223-239.

Alasuutari, P. (1986). Alcoholism in its cultural context: The case of blue-collar men. *Contemporary Drug Problems, 13*, 641-686.

Alasuutari, P. (1992). *Desire and craving: A cultural theory of alcoholism.* New York: State University of New York Press.

Alasuutari, P. (1995). *Researching culture: Qualitative method and cultural studies.* London: Sage.

Allen, B. (1979). The personal point of view in orally communicated history. *Western Folklore, 38*, 110-118.

Bertaux, D., & Bertaux-Wiame, I. (1981). Life stories in the bakers' trade. In D. Bertaux (Ed.), *Biography and society: The life history approach in the social sciences* (pp. 169-189). Beverly Hills, CA: Sage.

Bertaux, D., & Kohli, M. (1984). The life story approach: A continental view. *Annual Review of Sociology, 10,* 215-237.

Brown, P., & Levinson, C. C. (1987). *Politeness: Some universals in language usage.* Cambridge: Cambridge University Press.

Burgos, M. (1988). *Life stories, narrativity, and the search for the self.* University of Jyväskylä, Finland: Publications of the Research Unit for Contemporary Culture.

Chafe, W. L. (1977a). Creativity in verbalization and its implications for the nature of stored knowledge. In R. O. Freedle (Ed.), *Advances in discourse processes* (Vol. 1, pp. 41-55). Norwood, NJ: Ablex.

Chafe, W. L. (1977b). The recall and verbalization of past experience. In R. W. Cole (Ed.), *Current issues in linguistic theory* (pp. 215-246). Bloomington & London: Indiana University Press.

Chafe, W. L. (1980). The deployment of consciousness in the production of a narrative. In W. L. Chafe (Ed.), *The pear stories: Cognitive, cultural, and linguistic aspects of narrative production* (pp. 9-50). Norwood, NJ: Ablex.

Delany, P. (1969). *British autobiography in the seventeenth century.* London: Routledge & Kegan Paul.

Early, E. A. (1982). The logic of well-being: Therapeutic narratives in Cairo, Egypt. *Social Science & Medicine, 16,* 1491-1497.

Elias, N. (1982). *Power & civility: The civilizing process* (Vol. 2). New York: Pantheon Books.

Foucault, M. (1980). *The history of sexuality: Vol. 1. An introduction.* New York: Vintage Books.

Foucault, M. (1986). *The history of sexuality: Vol. 2. The use of pleasure.* New York: Viking.

Foucault, M. (1988). *The history of sexuality: Vol. 3. Care of the self.* New York: Vintage Books.

Freud, S. (1978). *The standard edition of the complete psychological works of Sigmund Freud: Vol. 21. Civilization and its discontents* (pp. 57-146). London: Hogarth.

Geertz, C. (1973). *The interpretation of cultures.* New York: Basic Books.

Geertz, C. (1983). *Local knowledge: Further essays in interpretive anthropology.* New York: Basic Books.

Geis, M. L. (1982). *The language of television advertising.* New York: Academic Press.

Georges, R. A. (1969). Toward an understanding of storytelling events. *Journal of American Folklore, 82,* 313-328.

Georges, R. A. (1976). From folktale research to the study of narrating. *Studia Fennica, 20,* 159-168.

Gergen, M., & Gergen, K. (1984). The social construction of narrative accounts. In K. J. Gergen & M. M. Gergen (Eds.), *Historical social psychology* (pp. 173-189). Hillsdale, NJ: Lawrence Erlbaum.

Goffman, E. (1967). *Interaction ritual: Essays on face-to-face behavior.* New York: Pantheon.

Greimas, A. J. (1987). *On meaning: Selected writings in semiotic theory.* Minneapolis: University of Minnesota Press.

Grice, H. P. (1975). Logic and conversation. In P. Cole & J. L. Morgan (Eds.), *Syntax and semantics: Vol. 3. Speech acts* (pp. 41-58). New York: Academic Press.

Grice, H. P. (1978). Further notes on logic and conversation. In P. Cole (Ed.), *Syntax and semantics: Vol. 9. Pragmatics* (pp. 113-128). New York: Academic Press.

Gubrium, J. F. (1992). *Out of control: Family therapy and domestic disorder.* Newbury Park, CA: Sage.

Gubrium, J. F. (1993). *Speaking of life: Horizons of meaning for nursing home residents.* New York: Aldine de Gruyter.

Gubrium, J. F., & Holstein, J. A. (1994). Grounding the postmodern self. *The Sociological Quarterly, 35,* 685-703.

Gubrium, J. F., & Holstein, J. A. (1995a). Biographical work and new ethnography. In R. Josselson & A. Lieblich (Eds.), *Interpreting experience: The narrative study of lives* (pp. 45-58). Thousand Oaks, CA: Sage.

Gubrium, J. F., & Holstein, J. A. (1995b). Life course malleability: Biographical work and deprivatization. *Sociological Inquiry, 65,* 207-223.

Gubrium, J. F., Holstein, J. A., & Buckholdt, D. R. (1994). *Constructing the life course.* New York: General Hall.

Haley, J. (1985). *Problem-solving therapy.* New York: Harper Torchbooks.

Harré, R., & Gillett, G. (1994). *The discursive mind.* Thousand Oaks, CA: Sage.

Holland, D., & Quinn, N. (Eds.). (1987). *Cultural models in language & thought.* Cambridge: Cambridge University Press.

Holstein, J. A., & Gubrium, J. F. (1995). *The active interview* (Qualitative Research Methods, Vol. 37). Newbury Park, CA: Sage.

Hoppál, M. (1980). Folk narrative and memory processes. In N. Burlakoff & C. Lindahl (Eds.), *Folklore on two continents: Essays in honor of Linda Dégh* (pp. 293-299). Bloomington, IN: Trickster Press.

Kintsch, W. (1978). Comprehension and memory of text. In W. K. Estes (Ed.), *Handbook of learning and cognitive processes: Vol. 6. Linguistic functions in cognitive theory* (pp. 57-86). Hillsdale, NJ: Lawrence Erlbaum.

Kintsch, W., Mandel, T. S., & Kozminsky, E. (1977). Summarizing scrambled stories. *Memory & Cognition, 5,* 547-552.

Labov, W., & Waletzky, J. (1973). Narrative analysis: Oral versions of personal experience. In J. Helm (Ed.), *Essays on the verbal and visual arts* (pp. 12-44). San Francisco: American Ethnological Society.

Lejeune, P. (1989). *On autobiography.* Minneapolis: University of Minnesota Press.

Linde, C. (1987). Explanatory systems in oral life stories. In D. Holland & N. Quinn (Eds.), *Cultural models in language & thought* (pp. 343-366). Cambridge: Cambridge University Press.

Linde, C. (1993). *Life stories: The creation of coherence.* New York: Oxford University Press.

Mandler, J. M. (1984). *Stories, scripts, and scenes: Aspects of schema theory.* Hillsdale, NJ: Lawrence Erlbaum.

Mauss, M. (1979). A category of the human mind: The notion of person, the notion of "self." In M. Mauss (Ed.), *Sociology and psychology: Essays* (pp. 57-94). London: Routledge & Kegan Paul.

Misch, G. (1969). *Geschichte der autobiografie, I-IV.* Frankfurt Am Main: Verlag G. Schulte-Bulmke.

Nofsinger, R. E. (1991). *Everyday conversation.* Newbury Park, CA: Sage.

Pentikäinen, J. Y. (1980). Life history: A neglected folklore genre. In N. Burlakoff & C. Lindahl (Eds.), *Folklore on two continents: Essays in honor of Linda Dégh* (pp. 150-159). Bloomington, IN: Trickster Press.

Potter, J., & Wetherell, M. (1987). *Discourse and social psychology: Beyond attitudes and behavior.* London: Sage.

Propp, V. (1975). *Morphology of the folktale.* Austin and London: University of Texas Press.

Robinson, J. A. (1981). Personal narratives reconsidered. *Journal of American Folklore, 94,* 58-85.

Roos, J. P. (1985). Life stories of social changes: Four generations in Finland. *International Journal of Oral History, 6,* 179-190.

Rumelhart, D. E. (1975). Notes on a schema for stories. In D. G. Bobrow & A. Collins (Eds.), *Representation and understanding.* New York: Academic Press.

Silverman, D. (1993). *Interpreting qualitative data: Methods for analyzing talk, text, and interaction.* London: Sage.

Stahl, S. K. D. (1977). The personal narrative as folklore. *Journal of the Folklore Institute, 14*(1-2), 9-30.

Titon, J. T. (1980). The life story. *Journal of American Folklore, 93,* 276-292.

van Dijk, T. A. (1980). *Macrostructures: An interdisciplinary study of global discourse, interaction, and cognition.* Hillsdale, NJ: Lawrence Erlbaum.

Voss, J. F., & Bisanz, G. L. (1985). Knowledge and the processing of narrative and expository texts. In B. R. Britton & J. B. Black (Eds.), *Understanding expository text: A theoretical and practical handbook for analyzing explanatory text* (pp. 173-198). Hillsdale, NJ: Lawrence Erlbaum.

Watzlawick, P., Weakland, J. H., & Fish, R. (1974). *Change: Principles of problem formation and problem resolution.* New York: Norton.

Weber, M. (1971). *The Protestant ethic and the spirit of capitalism.* London: Unwin University Books.

Weintraub, K. J. (1975). Autobiography and historical consciousness. *Critical Inquiry, 2,* 821-848.

Weintraub, K. J. (1978). *The value of the individual: Self and circumstance in autobiography.* Chicago: The University of Chicago Press.

Williams, G. (1984). The genesis of chronic illness: Narrative reconstruction. *Sociology of Health and Illness, 6*(2), 175-200.

❧ 2 ❧

National Identity or Multicultural Autobiography

Theoretical Concepts of Biographical Constitution Grounded in Case Reconstructions

Gabriele Rosenthal

Am I Czech, Hungarian, German, or Jewish? What is my mother tongue? To which nation or people do I belong? Are these questions even relevant for people who have grown up among different cultures and whose life history means they have different possibilities of where to locate themselves? How does the course of one's life history and the biographical constellation lead to a national or ethnic sense of belonging or affiliation becoming a central theme? The life histories of Israeli Jews[1] originating from a multicultural area of central and eastern Europe, who were labeled Jewish during the period of Nazi persecution—regardless of their own self-definition—and who are now a part of a multicultural majority, are ideal for reconstructing the conditions required for developing a multicultural identity as well as a multicultural habitus (disposition). These biographers[2] were socialized within the conflict between auto- and heterostereotyping, were mainly raised bilingually, and, at different points in their lives, were members of a minority culture (in Europe) and a majority culture (in Israel).

But what do we mean by a multicultural or even a national identity? And are these types of identity determined by self-definition or by life experiences? As self-definition and life experiences are by no means necessarily compatible—and the current self-definition offers us no clues as to its genesis—we must ask whether the concept of identity is any use to us if we need additional constructions to overcome its static character. The point here is by no means to invalidate attempts to expand the concept with a process-oriented focus. One such attempt is undertaken by Weinreich (1989), based on Erikson (1963) and Laing (1961); an approach that "emphasizes continuity rather than sameness in identity and gives central importance to the process of construal" (p. 50).[3] However, my position on the issue is that by choosing the biography concept, it is possible to avoid the problematic aspects of the identity concept and to empirically enable process-oriented analysis. In contrast to the rather rigid identity concept, the biography concept is genuinely process oriented: "Biography is a concept which takes temporality into account. It both constitutes and processes temporality" (Fischer-Rosenthal, 1995a, p. 258). On the other hand, the identity concept focuses on the following question: What is now making up one's identity, not so much how one became what one is? "Biography refers to an interpretatively open process of 'becoming.' Identity, on the other hand, focuses on a fixed state of 'being' or 'having' " (Fischer-Rosenthal, 1995a, p. 258). Biographies are composed of a series of chronological experiences and informed by the biographer's access to these experiences. Thus the central questions of a biographical analysis become: What did the biographer experience in the course of his/her life, how does he/she view these experiences in the present, and what visions of the past and the future result from his/her perspective?

Apart from the numerous senses of belonging in modern societies, living conditions alter during the course of one's life. Furthermore, the sense of belonging takes on a different relevance, moving between the background and foreground, depending on social and biographical processes. The question "who am I" becomes increasingly difficult to answer. This difficulty is a result of both attributions by the self and by others. Does this then mean that autobiographies characterized by variation and changes of belonging lead to identity diffusion? Do individuals lose their sense of who they are because they can only define their belonging with difficulty? Although in some (especially bureaucratic) situations, an "unambiguous" belonging may indeed be socially demanded—for example, in applying for German citizenship —in modern society, biographical constructions are increasingly being demanded rather than the self-construction "I am so-and-so." Individuals are presented with the task of creating continuity in their life history[4] by informing themselves and others of how they came to be what they are today. By telling others and themselves their life story, the discontinuities within the life history and how they came to be how they are today become understandable and plausible, for themselves as well as for others.

Because migration biographies are increasing in Europe, the idea of belonging to a nation or a people defining "identity" for life is as much outdated by experience as the courses of migration described in the social sciences, mainly in terms of losses (cf. Breckner, 1994; Lutz, 1995). The analysis of biographical courses of migration processes, on the other hand, shows us how little the biographical work of changing living conditions leads to identity problems and/or diffusion, but rather to the formation of a multicultural course of action and a self-confidence independent of macrosocial questions of belonging. "Instead of a 'before and after' perception which treats migration as the missing link, the individual is seen as one who has lived through changes, adapted to them or not, and created strategies of resistance" (Lutz, 1995, p. 305).

In view of these considerations, following Wolfram Fischer-Rosenthal (1995a), I favor the biography[5] concept as more comprehensive, rather than the somewhat static and even normative identity concept. The concept of biography makes the concept of identity redundant. Biography is an empirically more productive, logically multirelational (instead of birelational), and linguistically more narrative (instead of argumentative) concept. Empirical analysis of narrated life stories[6] allows us to reconstruct the lived-through life history of the biographer, as well as to reconstruct the biographers' construction of their life, that is, how their past appears to them today—beyond their conscious interest in presentation—and how it makes sense of their present and future (cf. Rosenthal, 1993, 1995a).[7]

Self-assignment to a culture, nation, or people is constituted from biographical experiences. We are not direct elements of a collective that we represent; rather, we live from the potential for experience and meaning in our own life history, which is embedded in collectives, environments, and nations. People's multifaceted histories are experienced and lived through, acting in concrete biographical terms. Above all, one's own life history should be considered as developing against a backdrop of the family history active over several generations. In our own lives, we not only solve current problems, but also take on family delegations from our parents' generation, and in particular from that of our grandparents (cf. Stierlin, 1982). These delegations are especially effective when we are not aware of them. We are driven on by them without knowing and are often blocked by them. We can thus neither understand the fighting in former Yugoslavia nor the neo-Nazism among young Germans independently of the respective latent family history still in force.[8]

In light of these considerations, the concept of national identity can hardly do justice to the complexity of social belonging. Rather, a sufficiently realistic insight into the social processes of self-definition and action is provided by the reconstruction of the constellation of life and family histories, in which belonging to a collective is actually a subject for the biographer, together with the discovery of the functions of identification with ethnicity or nationality in relation to the life and family histories. Corresponding to an empirically founded development of theory, as required inter alia by the so-called grounded theory (cf. Glaser & Strauss, 1967), in my opinion, concepts should not be developed independently of empirical analysis nor set normatively to begin with and should only be tested empirically. To concretize this further, the empirical questions raised are:

1. In which situations during life—and life always means the interaction between individual and social events—does belonging to a nation, ethnic group, or culture become a subject of importance for an individual?
2. What biographical function does self-definition have? In other words: How does self-definition help one deal with specific biographical problems, such as discontinuity?

3. To what extent does self-definition correspond to actual acting and to the history of acts and events experienced in the life of the biographer?

4. How are actions and self-definition constituted in the course of the biography?

A Contrasting Comparison
Between Two Case Studies[9]

I would now like to contrast the life stories of two women whose biographies are characterized by multicultural experiences but who are differentiated by their self-definitions. Whereas one of the biographers feels part of an ethnic group, the other considers herself bonded to different nations and cultures. According to Jewish law, both women are Jewish, and both grew up bilingually in multicultural Czechoslovakia prior to 1938. Their background allows them different possibilities for locating themselves. This further complicates the question—typical for the Jewish course through life—of belonging to the Jewish people, as well as of association with the culture of one's country of origin or belonging to the country and state where one lives. Both women emigrated to Israel upon their release from concentration camps and so live in a multicultural society. The state of Israel has a national individuality due to the very fact of its cultural and ethnic diversity. In contrast to their children's generation, the two women do not consider themselves to be primarily Israelis, although for 40 years, they have been leading a life devoted to developing Israel. From an Israeli and, in general, a Jewish point of view, these are not particularly unusual biographies.

Hannah Zweig[10] was born in France in the mid-1920s as the daughter of French Jews. Her father died in an accident when she was 3 years old. Two years later, her mother married a Czech Jew, and mother and daughter emigrated to Prague. Both French and Czech were spoken at home. Mrs. Zweig gained Czech citizenship and kept her French nationality. She learned German at school, where classes focused on German culture and history. As was typical in upper-middle-class Jewish families, Mrs. Zweig also received private tutoring in English. The family respected Jewish law, that is, the mother ran a kosher house.

If we assume, in reference to the multicultural viewpoint of her original background, that this socialization was not the norm, then we can ask the following questions: What did Mrs. Zweig consider herself to be at this time? We can also ask whether the girl suffered from this diversity and/or whether she felt herself torn between the different cultures and did not know where she belonged.

Before going into some aspects of Mrs. Zweig's image of herself, I would like to briefly outline some further points in her life history. When Mrs. Zweig was 12, her mother died in childbirth. Mrs. Zweig remained with her stepfather and, at the age of 16, married a Belgian Jew. Following the invasion of Prague by the German army in March 1938, both her husband and her stepfather joined the Czech resistance. Both men were arrested in 1940, and Mrs. Zweig heard of their fate only upon her liberation from the camps in 1945. Mrs. Zweig herself was deported to the concentration camp Theresienstadt in January 1942. She was imprisoned in the camp for 3 years and subjected to medical experiments. At the end of 1944 she was moved to Prague, along with other female prisoners, to build anti-tank weapons. Her release by the Red Army in May 1945 was an unimaginably traumatic experience: She was raped by several members of the Red Army.[11] The Russians became her most feared enemies, and so she fled to the American zone in Germany. In the meantime, she learned that her husband and stepfather had both been murdered. She then worked for the Americans as a translator. Here she met Arieh, the son of a German mother and Jewish Czech father, who had been imprisoned in a concentration camp as a so-called *mischling*.[12] In 1948, Arieh and Hannah were married. Thus, although Mrs. Zweig lived a multinational and multicultural life, she maintained a certain continuity to family tradition in her choice of a partner. In 1948, before the founding of the state of Israel, Mrs. Zweig, like her husband, became a member of the Zionist-Socialist/Marxist youth group Hashomer Hazair (cf. Reinharz, 1986). In 1953, the couple and their two children, who had meanwhile been born in Germany, emigrated to Israel under the auspices of this group.

The whole family entered a kibbutz as followers of the Socialist movement, which also means that they lived in a demonstratively antireligious manner (e.g., pork was eaten on the Sabbath).

Mrs. Zweig has since been divorced and has left the kibbutz. As a conscientious Zionist, she moved to a small town in the Negev Desert, inhabited mainly by Oriental Jews who do not share her European cultural heritage. In her everyday life, alongside Hebrew, she speaks mainly German and English. Her circle of friends contains, among others, Jews from a German background and Ethiopian Jews who have been living in her town for the last few years. She also is friendly with the Bedouins and spent several months living in their tents to learn about their way of life.

To which culture or nation do people who have been multiculturally molded by life history and experience feel they belong? Is this even a subject of discussion for them? Let us see what Mrs. Zweig tells us about this topic. I carried out two biogaphical-narrative interviews in German with her to find out what she thinks.[13] Mrs. Zweig speaks German almost flawlessly, and the analysis of the interview showed that it is in German that she feels more closely connected to her past before her *aliya* (immigration of a Jew to Israel). This past rarely plays a part in the family dialogues with her children,[14] to whom she speaks Hebrew. Instead, that part of her past sometimes becomes the subject of conversations with her German-speaking friends in Israel.

During the first conversation, Mrs. Zweig told me her life story up to the time directly after the war. The second interview was used to continue her story. In the first conversation, a close relationship, characterized by trust, was created between Mrs. Zweig and me. In this way, Mrs. Zweig was able to speak about issues that had earlier been taboo. That I was a non-Jewish German conducting this interview undoubtedly played a role here. Sometimes it is easier for survivors to tell a German of experiences that were traumatic or that social dialogue makes taboo, as in a conversation of this kind they feel released to a small extent from their sense of having to try to protect the listener from the weight of these experiences.[15]

Mrs. Zweig related that in the camp, she slept with members of the SS and other inmates to earn food. Today she views this kind of "compulsory prostitution" as different from the acts of rape she suffered after the liberation, when she had no freedom of action. She interpreted the kind of prostitution she was forced into as an exchange: "And a human being who wants to survive, he simply sees it as a kind of business exchange . . . and they do not therefore feel themselves to be a whore."

Although her cultural sense of belonging was rarely mentioned in the first conversation—in which she related her multicultural socialization in detail and her different emigrations (from France to Prague and later to Germany)—she began the second conversation as follows:[16]

> On the one hand, I was born in France, so I feel very close to French culture, and all in all, I am, my whole being tends to be rather French. You've certainly noticed I talk with my hands and feet and am pretty lively. . . . On the other hand, I feel very much attracted toward German and Czech culture, you know, they really attract me . . . and also the languages, they also somehow attract me, and the fact that I grew up in Czechoslovakia meant I had a lot of contact with Germans; in school, too, we were taught German history and German poetry, and music too, a lot of German music. We had a lot of Czech music, too. I mean, I'd die for Smetana, etc., etc., but still, no matter how much I felt, eh, French, I've always felt that I really belong to the German and the Czech culture.

Up to this point, it may be seen that Mrs. Zweig feels part of three cultural nations due to her family history, as well as her own socialization. In terms of her life history, each of the three languages has a special meaning for her, each with its own problems. French links her to her parents and thus to the losses early in her life; Czech to her stepfather, whom she loved very much; German was a significant factor in her surviving the 3½ years' imprisonment in the concentration camp. After the *Shoah* (Holocaust), a sense of belonging to German culture is often problematic in terms of a survivor's self-perception. Yet because of Mrs. Zweig's traumatic experience with the Russians, which she found crueler than her compulsory prostitution in Theresienstadt, this is not a central theme for her. In the interview, she stated her point of view explicitly: "The Russians were even worse than the Germans." Mrs. Zweig then continued to elaborate on her sense of belonging:

> . . . and throughout everything, I knew, it was clear to me
> that I'm really a Jew.

Here Mrs. Zweig tried to bring together the three components that, in terms of her life history, she had no doubt experienced as connected until her persecution. However, she needed to attempt this synthesis because of the persecution and destruction by the Nazis. Only with her persecution, with her deportation to the concentration camp, and with the murder of her husband and stepfather was she irrevocably torn from her multicultural European orientation and seen as just Jewish. At another point in the interview, she said,

> My Christian friends *never*[17] made me feel, that I was differ-
> ent. Only afterward, then there was the Kristallnacht and so
> on and so forth and I was always warned from this and that
> and that. "Don't open your mouth, and don't talk too much,
> and nobody needs to know that you are a Jew." *Then* I felt,—
> I am different.

As the reconstruction of her life story shows, her Jewishness was self-evident to her until the time of her persecution, when, independent of her feeling of belonging, her persecution as a Jew illustrated to her in the cruelest way possible that she was regarded "only" as a Jew. However, the fact that her Jewishness could not be separated from the European cultural background means she repeatedly returns to the statement:

> Really, we have our own culture, our belief, our own tradi-
> tion. You can't even say it's just a Jewish culture, we were al-
> ways linked, to the European culture as a whole . . . so, if
> you like, we can consider ourselves European Jews.

In this way, Mrs. Zweig distanced herself from the Ethiopian Jews, as well as from the Jews who lived in Arab countries for generations. This was further exemplified in the following remarks:

> But I insist that I'm a Jew and, no matter what, I was always a Jew and will always remain one, because—you see, I came to this country and the first clash between European culture, the European way of living, the European background,, and this, this Oriental background and culture and way of life was then a huge shock for me.

On the one hand, in this section, Mrs. Zweig renounced her Jewishness—she did not come to Israel as a Jew but as a European—and, on the other hand, she simultaneously declared it: Mrs. Zweig experienced Israel as a European, because she decided on aliya as a Jew, that is, to emigrate to Israel and in this way complete her sense of belonging to the Jewish people. For Mrs. Zweig, the emigration to Israel was an experience in her life history in which, following her designation as a Jew by the Nazis and the traumatic years spent as a Jew in the concentration camp, her sense of belonging became a subject for her, too. Her own self-definition of a sense of belonging became relevant for her in her confrontation with an unknown culture. This is then seen in her life story: In the interview, she talked about her cultural identity only in the context of her emigration to Israel. This text structure shows that, for Mrs. Zweig, the question of which cultural circles she belonged to was of no biographical relevance during her childhood and youth. On the other hand, the reconstruction of this specific case shows on a general level how the need to interpret one's sense of belonging arises when experiences of being a stranger become a part of one's life history.

Later in the interview, she described her journey to Israel, her arrival in Haifa, the first time she ate falafel, and how she found everything very strange. She spoke of the difficult living conditions in the beginning, the scorpions, unknown diseases, and heat. What is interesting in this case is that she described her foreign experiences in most detail when referring to the strange food, the falafel. I associate this with a childhood memory of Mrs. Zweig's that for her symbolizes the experience of her difference from Christian children: Although her mother forbade her to eat nonkosher food, Mrs. Zweig loved eating her school friends' liver sausage sandwiches. When her mother found out, Mrs. Zweig was punished in a physically unforgettable manner: She had to wash her mouth out with soap. Today by eating pork in Israel, she is returning to her childhood preferences.

To sum up, Mrs. Zweig sees her emigration to Israel thus:

> I tell you, until I found my way around, it was awful, I can't understand it myself now,, why I left Europe and came to this country. But then I say to myself why not, you always wanted to be a Jew and you always wanted to live in a Jewish country, so you had to do it, had to swallow it as they say, . . . you've made your bed, now you have to lie in it,, and I lay in it and now it's worn out [laughing] that's life what're you meant to do?

Here it finally became clear that Mrs. Zweig's Jewish identity—let us formulate it in terms of action theory, her chosen course through life as a Jew—is drawn from her orientation toward a common country that constitutes part of her Jewish life and biography respectively. This orientation toward Judaism (which was declared each year on Seder evening within the family, which celebrated the holidays)[18] stayed with her after the Shoah, in contrast to her rejection of a life following Jewish law. This allows Mrs. Zweig to re-create a sense of continuity in a part of her life that was riddled with disturbances and losses from an early age onward. The re-creation of continuity is of special importance for the psychic stability of survivors whose former lifelines had been abruptly and irreversibly cut by the persecution (cf. Niederland, 1980, p. 229).

Mrs. Zweig lost everyone of significance to her in Europe, and her life in Prague was irrevocably destroyed after the Holocaust. She could return neither to marriage nor to a career. What remained was her sense of belonging to the Jewish people, which was not a religious affiliation but the idea of a common country and common history.

So does this now mean that somebody who has followed such a path through life considers him- or herself to be Jewish and/or that a sense of belonging to the Jewish people after the Shoah allows a sense of continuity to the past? Let us contrast this case study of Mrs. Zweig with the life story of a woman whose self-definition does not concentrate on Jewishness.

When I asked Amalia Teschner to tell me her life story, she began as follows:

> I belong, to the German-speaking island in, Slovakia.

Thus Mrs. Teschner (born in 1916), who speaks perfect German, did not introduce herself with "I come from" but with "I belong to." This sense of belonging—formulated in the present tense—shows that she belongs there, even though she no longer lives there. Thus, there are signs of creating continuity from this very first sentence in her autobiographical narration.

The island Mrs. Teschner referred to is an island where German is spoken, surrounded by another ethnic group with a different language within the same country. So is Mrs. Teschner a German or is she merely referring to the language? Let us see how she continued:

> My father was a teacher at the Jewish, Israeli primary school, which was a German school.

She introduced her father into the conversation by way of his profession. At this point, one hypothesis can already be formulated: The biographer was in this way explaining why the family lived on this German-language island. Mrs. Teschner continued,

> But my family really comes from Hungary.

Here we learn the family's actual nationality. As Mrs. Teschner explained later on, this part of Slovakia belonged to Austria-Hungary and was handed over to Czechoslovakia a year after the state was founded in 1918. Her parents originally came from an area that still belonged to Hungary after 1919. Their relatives continued to live there. Her father, however, decided to remain in Slovakia after the reorganization of the state. We have to remember that this decision would later have a decisive influence on the persecution of the family, because Hungarian Jews were protected from deportation to the extermination camps for a much longer period than Slovakian Jews. At this point, with this third piece of information about the family's

Hungarian origin, the family constellation begins to become apparent, a constellation that Mrs. Teschner still hands down today via her sense of belonging. In other words, the experience of discontinuity in the family history in terms of national affiliation is "healed" by maintaining a sense of ethnic belonging.

Thus, the concern here is a Jewish family from Hungary, which belonged to a minority both as Jews and Hungarians within the collective of Germans in Slovakia—a minority itself.[19] Mrs. Teschner continued,

> My *real* mother tongue, if our family has any such thing, is Hungarian. But we spoke German and I only learned German right until the end of school and did my school-leaving exam in German. I finished my schooling at a German grammar school in our little town. I then studied at the Slovakian university in Bratislava.

Thus, Mrs. Teschner's pre-university socialization was markedly German and/or was oriented toward German culture—not an uncommon situation for Jewish families. Her family may have come from Hungary, but her education and linguistic socialization were concentrated on German. Consequently, she still mainly speaks German with her brother and sister, who both emigrated to Israel as early as the 1930s, although they do repeatedly switch into Hungarian.

Yet Mrs. Teschner does not feel she now belongs to German cultural circles. Unlike Mrs. Zweig, she would never talk of an attraction to German culture. For Mrs. Teschner, who survived the Auschwitz extermination camp and lost her parents, parents-in-law, and husband immediately upon arrival there, her past predominant orientation toward German culture is a problem. This is one of the reasons why Mrs. Teschner so vehemently considers herself to be Hungarian these days. In order to distance herself from Germans, the Hungarian side, which was of family relevance prior to the persecution, gains in importance retrospectively. Although Mrs. Teschner never openly described herself as a Hungarian in the four interviews I carried out with her, for me, she was a Hungarian by the way she presented herself—especially during the private meetings after the interviews.

Thus, I did not doubt her answer when I once asked her about Jewish identity: "What would you say you felt yourself to be, an Israeli, Jew or what?" She replied without hesitation: "I'm Hungarian."

But why did she not describe herself as an Israeli or Jew? Even if we take into consideration the fact that Hungarian Jews in Slovakia during the period between the World Wars showed nationalistic Hungarian tendencies, as opposed to the Jews in Prague, Mrs. Teschner's self-definition as a Hungarian is still unexpected. In Slovakia, she was only socialized in a Hungarian background to a certain extent. Most of her friends were Slovaks or Germans. In contrast, all the family's relatives lived in Hungary. However, her affiliation with this very family constellation may have determined her early identification with the ethnic origins to which Mrs. Teschner still holds tight, even though she has led a life devoted to developing Israel ever since her emigration there in 1949. Although she very much misses the cultural and European part of Tel Aviv, she left Tel Aviv with her second husband, also a doctor, to move to the desert and build up a section of the hospital. Working in the Negev Desert means living as a European among mainly Oriental Jews and, furthermore, being responsible for the medical treatment of the Bedouins. Mrs. Teschner also attaches importance to her family being good Israelis. She is proud of the fact that her son and daughter continue to live in Israel despite the difficult living conditions and the constant threat of war and that they are committed to furthering the country in their careers.

So what is the biographical function of Mrs. Teschner's identification with Hungary? In contrast to her Jewishness and her German identity, the Hungarian side was not a problem in her life. As she never actually lived in Hungary, she did not experience Hungarian anti-Semitism. The Hungarian side is much more a part of her life due to her second marriage to a Jewish Hungarian, which provided her with a continuity to a destroyed past and/or re-created it after the war. Compared to Mrs. Zweig's experience, Mrs. Teschner's certainty of belonging was much more completely annihilated by her experiences in the extermination camp. For Mrs. Teschner, Auschwitz raised questions about belonging to mankind. For her, the question of humanity and the human race is far more threatening than the question of belonging to a certain collective. Mrs. Teschner still suffers from the dehumanization and deindividualization she experienced so profoundly at her arrival in Auschwitz. After her inmate number had been tattooed, she felt, "And in this moment one feels,,, actually you are no longer yourself,, you have no name,, and you go wherever you are sent to, and,,, any, any kind of, any,, future, if there will be a future." Thus, it was the tattooing of her number in Auschwitz which, as she said herself, "bored so deep into the soul" and not the cutting of her hair or other humiliating procedures. She continued, "I'm fed up with it, the whole time even now, the number, and no name."

Following her release, Amalia Teschner struggled against committing suicide. Only her medical studies and her employment as a doctor kept her alive. She spoke about a conversation with a friend that took place immediately after the liberation. The friend told her,

> "There are only two possibilities, either you draw a line,,,
> and what happened happened and you begin a new life or
> you hang yourself." And then I began to become active again
> and to take up my studies. I said to myself. I want to con-
> tinue to study . . . , because I want to prove to myself, that I
> can still manage something.

On the one hand, following the advice of her friend, Mrs. Teschner spoke about the line she should draw and the new life she should start; on the other hand, she expressed how she tried to connect to her past by resuming an earlier development in her biography. She completed her medical studies in Bratislava. Her profession is still central in her life today, and so her academic and professional careers are a dominant theme in her total life history. Her profession was part of her life that Mrs. Teschner could pick up again in 1945, giving her at least some feeling of continuity. She did not want to leave Czechoslovakia after 1945, although both she and her husband experienced difficulties in their clinic, being Jewish doctors. It was her second husband who pulled her out of her hopelessness and pushed for the emigration to Israel. Alongside her career, it was this marriage that kept her alive. She shares her Hungarian origins and language with her husband; thus, she can live out a part of her lost life in Israel. The couple speak Hungarian to each other, and many of their friends and acquaintances are Hungarians. Unlike Mrs. Zweig, Mrs. Teschner and her husband spoke their own native language to their children during the first years of their lives.

Summary

Both women were multiculturally socialized, both women have led a multicultural life until now, and, above all, both lead a consciously Israeli life. Even if they do not immediately define themselves as Israelis, they identify themselves with the country and are actively involved in its development. Neither of them belongs to those European Jews who, in their own minds, are still living in Europe in the good old days and who hardly speak any Hebrew. Their self-definition of their sense of belonging may be different, but not its function in their lives. In both cases, the definition of cultural affiliation helps them create a sense of continuity to their pasts prior to the persecution. They thus choose a self-definition that already lies within the horizon of possibilities of their families. This horizon of possibilities is always varied. The reason why Mrs. Zweig and Mrs. Teschner each chose one possibility and not the other is determined by their biographies and not unalterably imposed upon them during childhood.[20]

If we were to limit ourselves to the level of self-definition, we would learn very little about lived-through experiences. On the basis of self-definition, we would also probably be completely wrong in our prognoses about lived-through experiences. Without reconstructing the life story, the biographical relevance of this self-definition in people's current lives, as well as how it is composed in terms of the life history, would also remain unexplained. The question must be raised as to how we social scientists can deduce the meaning of a social act if we do not know the history of the individual leading up to it or the history of the social system. Social acts may only be understood and explained by analyzing the conditions prevailing at their conception, and this implies undertaking a biographical analysis.

Better than the analytical application of an identity concept more strongly oriented to the subjects' self-definitions within the framework of the here and now, a theoretical examination based on biography allows the reconstruction of the subject's actions and their effects on the present life. Identity is not based on belonging to a collective, but on belonging to the relevant biographical history, against the backdrop of the family history, embedded as it is in different collectives, in the social world, and in the active choice between different—if limited—possibilities. And this is exactly what we mean by biography.

Notes

1. The life stories narrated to the author in interviews are part of a study of Jews forced to emigrate and survivors of concentration camps. Compare Rosenthal, 1995c; Rosenthal, in press.

2. I prefer to use the term *biographer* instead of the term *autobiographer* in this context. In my opinion, the latter term does not lay adequate emphasis on the social construction of life stories.

3. In the German sociological discussion of identity, Krappmann's (1975) attempt to combine the identity concept of the symbolic interactionist tradition, traced primarily to Mead (1934), with Erikson's (1968) psychodynamic approach to identity, is one of those that would be relevant for a discussion in terms of biographical theory.

4. By life history, we mean the lived-through life; by life story, we mean the narrated life as related in conversation or written in the present time; compare Rosenthal, 1993, 1995a.

5. Compare the major theoretical contributions to the German biographical research of Fischer-Rosenthal, 1991; Kohli, 1986; Rosenthal, 1995a; Schütze, 1984.

6. On the procedure of hermeneutical case reconstruction, compare Rosenthal, 1993; Rosenthal & Bar-On, 1992.

7. This biographical construct, which is not at the biographer's conscious disposal, constitutes not only the selection of experiences out of memory. It also constitutes how the biographer perceives these experiences today.

8. On the influence of the Nazi past in three-generation families, compare Fischer-Rosenthal, 1995b, 57ff.; Rosenthal, 1995b.

9. The following discussion of the two case studies is result-oriented, that is, the process of interpretation cannot be reconstructed here. Therefore, we would like to make the reader aware of the fact that the analytical method applied here (Rosenthal, 1993, 1995a) implies that both the construction and the examination of hypotheses takes place in each concrete case. Essential principles in this method are reconstruction and sequentiality. The texts are not subsumed under specific categories but the meaning is analyzed in the context of the entire text. The sequential compilation of the text of the life story, as well as the chronology of the biographical experiences in the life history, plays an essential role.

10. All names have been changed.

11. Mrs. Zweig speaks about 20 men.

12. This information comes from an interview with Arieh's sister, who lives in the Czech Republic. In Arieh's interview with two Israeli researchers, Noga Gilad and Tamar Zilberman, he only hinted at his non-Jewish background. In the interview with the author, Mrs. Zweig, who has meanwhile been divorced from her husband, introduced him as a Jew.

13. The interviewees were asked to tell their life story according to the technique of the narrative interview (cf. Rosenthal, 1995a; Schütze, 1976). After the initial opening question, the ensuing story was not interrupted by further questions but was encouraged by means of nonverbal and paralinguistic expressions of interest and attention, such as a slight nod or "mhm." In the second part of the interview—the period of questioning—the interviewer initiated, with narrative questions, more elaborate narrations on topics and biographical events already mentioned, and blocked-out issues were addressed.

14. Interviews with Mrs. Zweig's daughter and her son were part of a research project on three-generation families supervised by the author (cf. Rosenthal, in press; Rosenthal & Völter, in press). Neither of them know much about their parents' past before the aliya.

15. In analyzing the interviews, I specifically reconstruct the effect of the interaction process. It is therefore possible to concentrate here on the structure of the life story and to present key aspects with a view to establishing findings.

16. The commas used in the transcript indicate short pauses. Multiple commas mean longer pauses.

17. Italics indicate stressed speech.

18. On this evening, the Haggada (the scripture on the exodus from Egypt) is read aloud during the ritual meal. At the end, all participants lift their glasses for the last time and wish each other: "Next year in Jerusalem."

19. About 10% of the population in Mrs. Teschner's hometown are Jews.

20. Whereas Mrs. Teschner, for example, leads a completely unreligious life, eating meat with cream, as Hungarians like to, her brother, who emigrated to Palestine before the Shoah, is strictly orthodox.

References

Breckner, R. (1994). "Ich war immer froh ein Entwurzelter zu sein:" Aspekte biographischer Migrationsforschung in Ost-West-Perspektive. In B. Balla & W. Geier (Eds.), *In einer Soziologie des Postkommunismus* (pp. 37-59). Hamburg: Lit.

Erikson, E. H. (1963). *Childhood and society*. New York: Norton.

Erikson, E. H. (1968). *Identity: Youth and crisis*. New York: Norton.

Fischer-Rosenthal, W. (1991). Biographische Methoden in der Soziologie. In U. Flick, E. v. Kardorff, H. Keupp, L. v. Rosenstiel, & St. Wolff (Eds.), *Handbuch Qualitative Sozialforschung* (2nd ed., pp. 253-256). München: Psychologie Verlags Union.

Fischer-Rosenthal, W. (1995a). The problem with identity: Biography as solution to some (post)-modernist dilemmas. *Comenius, 3,* 250-265.

Fischer-Rosenthal, W. (1995b). Schweigen—Rechtfertigen—Umschreiben: Biographische Arbeit im Umgang mit deutschen Vergangenheiten. In W. Fischer-

Rosenthal & P. Alheit (Eds.), *Biographien in Deutschland: Soziologische Rekonstruktionen gelebter Gesellschaftsgeschichte* (pp. 42-87). Opladen: Westdeutscher Verlag.

Glaser, B., & Strauss, A. (1967). *The discovery of grounded theory.* Chicago: Aldine.

Kohli, M. (1986). Biographical research in the German language area. In Z. Dulczewski (Ed.), *A commemorative book in honor of Florian Znaniecki on the centenary of his birth* (pp. 91-110). Poznan, Poland: Naukowe.

Krappmann, L. (1975). *Soziologische Dimensionen der Identität.* Stuttgart: Klett.

Laing, R. D. (1961). *The self and others.* London: Tavistock.

Lutz, H. (1995). The legacy of migration: Immigrant mothers and daughters and the process of intergenerational transmission. *Comenius, 3,* 304-317.

Mead, G. H. (1934). *Mind, self, and society.* Chicago: University of Chicago Press.

Niederland, W. G. (1980). *Folgen der Verfolgung: Das Überlebenden-Syndrom.* Frankfurt a.M.: Edition Suhrkamp.

Reinharz, J. (1986). Haschomer Hazair in Nazideutschland, 1933-1938 (in English). In A. Paucker (Ed.), *Die Juden im Nationalsozialistischen Deutschland* (pp. 317-351). Tübingen: Mohr.

Rosenthal, G. (1993). Reconstruction of life stories: Principles of selection in generating stories for narrative biographical interviews. In R. Josselson & A. Lieblich (Eds.), *The narrative study of lives* (Vol. 1, pp. 59-91). Newbury Park, CA: Sage.

Rosenthal, G. (1995a). *Erlebte und erzählte Lebensgeschichte: Gestalt und Struktur biographischer Selbstbeschreibungen.* Frankfurt a.M: Campus.

Rosenthal, G. (1995b). Familienbiographien: Nationalsozialismus und Antisemitismus im intergenerationellen Dialog. In I. u. a. Attia (Ed.), *Multikulturelle Gesellschaft und monukulturelle Psychologie? Antisemitismus und Rassismus in der psychosozialen Arbeit* (pp. 30-51). Tübingen: Dgvt-Verlag.

Rosenthal, G. (1995c). Überlebende der Shoah: Zerstörte Lebenszusammenhänge-Fragmentierte Lebenserzählungen. In W. Fischer-Rosenthal & P. Alheit (Eds.), *Biographien in Deutschland* (pp. 452-476). Opladen: Westdeutscher Verlag.

Rosenthal, G. (Ed.). (in press). *The Holocaust in three-generation families.* London: Cassell.

Rosenthal, G., & Bar-On, D. (1992). A biographical case study of a victimizer's daughter. *Journal of Narrative and Life History, 2*(2), 105-127.

Rosenthal, G., & Völter, B. (in press). Three generations within Jewish and non-Jewish German families after the unification of Germany. In Y. Danieli (Ed.), *Multigenerational legacies of trauma: An international handbook.* New York/London: Plenum.

Schütze, F. (1976). Zur Hervorlockung und Analyse von Erzählungen thematisch relevanter Geschichten im Rahmen soziologischer Feldforschung. In Arbeitsgruppe Bielefelder Soziologen (Ed.), *Kommunikative Sozialforschung* (pp. 159-260). München: Fink.

Schütze, F. (1984). Kognitive Figuren des autobiographischen Stegreiferzählens. In M. Kohli & G. Robert (Eds.), *Biographie und soziale Wirklichkeit* (pp. 78-117). Stuttgart: Metzler.

Stierlin, H. (1982). *Delegation und Familie.* Frankfurt a.M.: Suhrkamp.

Weinreich, P. (1989). Variations in ethnic identity: Identity structure analysis. In K. Liebkind (Ed.), *New identities in Europe* (pp. 41-75). Worcester: Billing & Sons.

❦ 3 ❦

Arbiters of Female Purity

Conversations With
Israeli Ritual Bath Attendants

Susan Starr Sered

When a woman has a discharge of blood which is her regular discharge from her body, she shall be in her impurity for seven days. (Leviticus 15:19)

Cross-culturally, women choose, are encouraged or forced, and encourage or force others to engage in diverse religious rituals (Falk & Gross, 1980). Although the study of women and religion has come a long way in the past few decades, social scientific approaches to women's rituals often remain caught up in reductionist explanations that treat women's ritual activity as a function of social, sexual, economic, or psychological oppression and frustration.[1] In this chapter, I move beyond unidimensional functionalist paradigms and offer an interpretive model of ritual composed of three tracks. Through an exploration of women's menstrual rites in contemporary Jerusalem, I argue that rituals and ritual roles are constituted and shaped by long-standing cultural themes and patterns, *and* by specific, historically discernable social forces, *and* by the individual personalities of the particular people who perform the rituals and fill the roles at any given time.

One of the greatest achievements of the most recent wave of feminist anthropology has been an insistence upon dismantling models in which women are treated as a homogenous class (most typically, oppressed) while men's roles and experiences are analyzed in terms of a variety of social and political forces (Moore, 1988, p. 11). Contemporary nuanced studies of women's experiences pay attention to the social locations of specific women: to class, age, ethnicity, education, sexual identity, marital and reproductive status, and so on (Leacock, 1986). This achievement has fruitfully coincided with another development in anthropology—an emphasis upon "the interpretive practices through which the realities of social settings are assembled . . . how participants articulate the stories they tell about themselves so as to construct biographies pertinent to the matter under consideration" (Gubrium & Holstein, 1995, pp. 46-47).

It is within this intellectual context—a context that moves beyond the illusory pursuit of "truth" and instead seeks the multifarious and always changing stories that pin down parts of human experience—that I endeavor to piece together an analysis of one of the most intriguing Jewish ritual sequences: *niddah* (sexual taboos around menstruation) and *t'vilah* (ritual immersion in a special bath at the end of the menstrual period). Niddah laws are first mentioned in Leviticus 15:19ff. in the framework of a lengthy discussion of numerous forms of ritual uncleanliness. Because most of these conditions were relevant only in relationship to the Temple cult in Jerusalem, after the destruction of the Temple in 70 C.E., the notion of impurity came to be associated almost solely with women's menstrual and childbirth blood. Jewish texts such as the *Talmud* and the *Shulhan Aruch* contain detailed exegesis of the biblical laws. Very briefly, couples are expected to refrain from sexual relations during the days of the woman's menstrual flow and for 7 "clean" days afterward, following which the woman meticulously washes herself and then immerses in a *mikvah* (ritual bath). The couple is then allowed to resume sexual relations. Actual observance of laws and rituals of niddah varies among Jews of different ethnic groups; for example, in Europe and the United States the mikvah is usually located in an inconspicuous building away from the main street so that women will be able to modestly enter the building without being seen, whereas in North Africa the mikvah was often located inside the public bath house and women were not expected to conceal their use of the mikvah. Nowadays secular Jews, for the most part, do not observe the laws and customs of mikvah and niddah.

In Israel the majority of *mikva'ot* (ritual bath, plural) are funded and supervised by municipal religious councils. The councils employ women *balaniot*—bath attendants who check women as they immerse in the mikvah to make sure that the entire body is submerged and that there is no dirt or other materials separating the woman's body from the water of the mikvah—as well as cleaning ladies, supervisors, and male rabbis who oversee the mikva'ot and who are called upon to make rulings in matters pertaining to Jewish law (*halacha*).

In this chapter, I introduce two women employed in positions of authority in Jerusalem's mikvah system. These women will serve as our guides to the niddah-mikvah ritual sequence. In contrast both to many American feminists, who argue that mikvah and niddah are immutably oppressive to all women (Lacks, 1980), and to many orthodox rabbis, who argue that mikvah and niddah are ennobling to women (Lamm, 1972), my own ethnographic approach treats rituals as interplays of textual (symbolic) traditions, historical processes, and the particular personalities of those involved in a ritual at a given time—no ritual is, by definition, immutably anything to everyone (cf. Buckley & Gottlieb, 1988, on menstrual rituals).

Introducing Rabbanit Stern[2]

The first time I met Rabbanit Stern (*rabbanit* means rabbi's wife), supervisor of most of Jerusalem's mikva'ot, she had little idea of why I wished to spend time with her. However, my credentials as a professor at an orthodox Jewish university, and my access to a car in which I could drive her around from mikvah to mikvah, served as good starting points for our relationship.

Rabbanit Stern is ultra-orthodox[3] and Ashkenazi (of eastern European origin; on religion and ethnicity in Israel, see Ayalon, Ben-Rafael, & Sharot, 1991; Sobel, 1991). She is in her late sixties or early seventies and lives with her rabbi husband in a small apartment in a suburb of Jerusalem. Her work with the mikva'ot takes her out of the house almost every evening and many days each week. Even when she is home, her phone rings constantly, yet her husband rarely interferes or complains, and he even takes phone messages for her.[4] Rabbanit Stern is a woman for whom niddah and mikvah have opened many doors—they are the cause of her having developed a high-status career in the public sphere. Mikvah work offers Rabbanit Stern opportunities to speak up and be heard, both by men and by women. Upon meeting Rabbanit Stern, I was struck by her elegant clothes and sophisticated makeup—both of which, to my eye, contrasted with the traditional turban-type hat that she wears to cover her hair in accordance with Jewish law. As we shall see shortly, this is a matter of principle for her—nice clothes and makeup demonstrate that mikvah is modern and high class (rather than *primitive*, a key word in her discourse).

At our first meeting, I told Rabbanit Stern that I am interested in parties held for brides at the mikvah. She agreed to help me, but "Before that," she said, "sit down and I will tell you how I began this work."

> My mother had been active in *taharat ha-mishpaha* [spreading information about the laws and rituals of niddah and mikvah; this phrase literally means "family purity"]. About 20 years ago, she told me that I am very sociable and should get involved. I was reluctant. At that time there were *madrichot* [counselors] who went to the mikva'ot and tried to teach the women about *hefsek* and 7 *n'kiyim* [*hefsek* means literally "break" or "stop" and refers to a woman meticulously inspecting herself to see that there is no more blood at the end of her period in order to begin counting 7 *n'kiyim*, 7 "clean" or bloodless days before immersing in the mikvah. Many North African and Asian Jewish women had not been accustomed to following these particular rules]. The counselors were usually accepted by the mikva'ot, but in [a certain

working class neighborhood in Jerusalem populated mostly by Jews who had formerly lived in North Africa], there was a mikvah with a very primitive bath attendant, and she had kicked out every counselor who had come. So my mother told me that I should go there.

At the time the National Committee for Family Purity [a voluntary, ultra-orthodox organization dedicated to raising money to build mikva'ot and to teaching women the laws of niddah and ritual immersion] was trying to do this. They would go to the mikva'ot and, with wisdom and psychology, try to talk to the women. But it depended upon the particular counselor; there were some who helped correct things and some ruined things. You need to know how to talk to the women. With some you need to say that the 7 clean days is like the baking powder in a recipe. That you can put in all the other ingredients, but if you don't have the baking powder you don't have a cake. With others, you explain the biological side [that sexual contact during or too soon after the period can cause cancer or deformed babies].

In that [working class] neighborhood, the bath attendant threw out the counselor, she called the police to get her out. A primitive bath attendant! On a very low level. There were bath attendants like that, on such a low level that they themselves didn't know what to do [about niddah and mikvah].

I decided that I would go out as a volunteer. I told that bath attendant in that neighborhood that I want to learn from her—that primitive bath attendant! I didn't tell her that I came to teach her, but that I came to learn from her. The Holy One Blessed Be He gave me these words to say; I didn't think of this in advance. And the bath attendant accepted me.

I would come every day and sit there and not do anything, just watch and tell her that I came to learn. A few times she asked me to supervise a woman immerse but I said, "No, I don't know how, I just came to learn from you." And so she got used to me, and once when I didn't come, they even called up to ask why not. By me, ethnic group doesn't make a difference. That bath attendant thought that an Ashkenazi had come to get on top of her [lehitlabesh aleha]. That the Ashkenazi is more intelligent. So at first I didn't speak to anyone there. But gradually I began to get involved there. . . .

I called the man in charge of the municipal Religious Council [the agency that funds religious services] to talk to him about the bad situation in the mikva'ot: dirt and bath attendants who don't know things. He said he didn't have anyone to send out into the field. He only had men. He didn't even know the bath attendants. Anyone who wanted to do it could do it. So he told me, "We are waiting for you." And Rabbi Aurbach told me I must do this. I told him, I told everyone, that I can't do it, that I have a house and children to take care of, that I am ignorant and don't know Hebrew [her first language is Yiddish]. But Rabbi Aurbach and then other rabbis, important rabbis, convinced me to do this.

Susan, do you know who the bath attendants were in those days? Old women, pathetic women, widows, those who couldn't even see well any more. Those were the bath attendants. And what mikva'ot! Terrible. I began to teach, to add more workers, and I made it into a profession. Today high-level women work with us, women with bachelor's degrees, from colleges, work with us. We couldn't just get rid of the older bath attendants, but gradually we added younger ones and gradually we have replaced the older ones at most of the mikva'ot. See this file, full of applicants for the bath attendant course. See, this one is so educated, so pretty.

Discourses of Hierarchy

Although Rabbanit Stern's discourse is a highly hierarchical one, with the partial exception of the account of her religious calling (see Discussion, which follows), she focuses upon issues other than gender. As we saw, throughout her discourse she sets up a series of oppositions based upon age, education, modernity, and ethnicity.

We learn from Rabbanit Stern that the bath attendant in the working class neighborhood was "primitive" and "on a very low level," like other attendants who "didn't know what to do [about niddah and mikvah]," whereas Stern herself and her associates "teach the women," and use "wisdom and psychology." The primitive bath attendant resorted to force, calling the police to throw out the counselor, whereas Rabbanit Stern and her associates "know how to talk" and use creative metaphors (like the baking powder) and cunning (like telling the primitive bath attendant that she had come to learn rather than to teach, which of course was what she had really come to do).

When Rabbanit Stern describes the previous bath attendants (old, pathetic, widows, half blind) and the new bath attendants (educated, high level, young, attractive), we see her binary scheme: knowledge-able, articulate, intelligent, attractive, young, scientific, and modern versus ignorant, inarticulate, dumb, old, unattractive, and primitive. Rabbanit Stern spoke repeatedly about aesthetics, both of the mikvah and of the bath attendants. When she and I went around visiting mikva'ot, she made a point of showing me how the bath attendants had added pictures or flowers to the mikvah decor, and of loudly praising the bath attendants for looking nice: for wearing pretty scarves, attractive makeup, and so on. The aesthetic discourse is part of the discourse of modernity: she wants her mikva'ot to be clean and modern and her bath attendants to look elegant and modern—not like the old-time mikva'ot and mikvah workers.

In Rabbanit Stern's discourse, I suspect, these traits are in fact tropes for ethnicity: knowledgeable and modern are equivalent to Ashkenazi—privileged and high-class; primitive and uneducated are equivalent to North African and Asian—weak and low-class.[5]

> *Mizrachi* [North African and Asian] women. They didn't know *tum'ah* and *tahara* [laws of impurity and purity]. They confused the secondary [*tafel*] with the primary [*'ikar*] and made the primary into the secondary and the secondary into the primary. There were women who would throw away the clothes they had worn before coming to the mikvah. They didn't know they could wash them; they would throw them away. There were women who didn't brush their teeth in the same sink as their husbands because of impurity. [These things are not required by Jewish law.]

According to Rabbanit Stern,

> Women in neighborhoods like [that one] are like babies.
> Their husbands won't let them come [to the mikvah] some-
> times, and it is a problem with husbands who break down
> during the 7 clean days [that is, demand sexual relations with
> their wives before it is permissible by Jewish law to
> immerse in the mikvah].

Rabbanit Stern and I discussed an issue that is the cause of almost
nightly arguments at Jerusalem's mikva'ot. According to Jewish law,
a bride must immerse in the mikvah before her wedding. In North
African Jewish communities, it was customary for the mother-in-law
and other women relatives to watch the bride immerse. From the point
of view of the mother-in-law, this was her opportunity to ensure that
her son would be marrying an anatomically normal, healthy, and
nonpregnant woman. Nowadays, brides often refuse to allow the
mother-in-law to watch the immersion, complaining that this is an
invasion of privacy. As I show in another paper (Sered, in press), in
dealing with the mother-in-law, the bride herself is usually somewhat
quiet and passive, except for crying. The more visible struggle tends
to be between the bath attendant, who ostensibly takes the side of the
bride (the attendant argues that according to Jewish law it is immodest
and unnecessary for the mother-in-law to watch), and the mother-in-
law, who tries to exercise her traditional rights to protect her husband's and son's lineage. In this dispute, the middle-aged or elderly
Ashkenazi bath attendant aligns herself with the bride (vis-à-vis the
mother-in-law) by emphasizing the mother-in-law's primitiveness (as
compared to the Israeli-born bride's and her own modernity).

> Once there was a woman with a birthmark, and she didn't
> want the mother-in-law coming in, and the mother-in-law
> and family insisted and began to carry on saying "What a
> deformed person she is." But I forbade them; I said that the
> law is that the bride must be [alone] with the Holy One
> Blessed Be He. They don't know the law anyway [so they
> believed me]. I said that it is written that the bride must
> have her mind on holiness.

Maisot [Yiddish word for "stories"] I made up. But they
don't know. They are so primitive with their drums [it is
customary for the bride's family and friends to celebrate her
immersion in the mikvah with singing, dancing, and drum-
ming]. They are like animals, some of them. I came out of
the room with the bride and went to talk to the family, and
they were all carrying on, and they laughed at me. And I
said, take your time to laugh at my [head-covering], but then
I will talk to you. So then they finally calmed down, and I
talked to them and they left the bride alone.

Rabbanit Stern enjoys talking about the dedication of her bath
attendants, how they even worked during the Gulf War. She explains
that this work must be done with *regesh* (feeling):
  "The acronym *ReGeSh* stands for wind [*ruah*], rain [*geshem*], snow
[*sheleg*]. That is how my bath attendants work." In contrast,

> Especially in the small villages [where she does not run the
> mikva'ot, which are used primarily by North African and
> Asian women], there are problems with bath attendants who
> are simple, the mikva'ot are dirty, and when women want to
> dip, the bath attendant says, "Come back tomorrow, I have a
> wedding today."

For Rabbanit Stern, it is important to demonstrate not only that
she and her bath attendants are dedicated, but also that they (and
especially she herself) are good managers and administrators. "I have
become known as the *balabusta* [housewife] of all the mikva'ot in
Israel, and there are 200 or so." Scrupulous accounting is made of the
money paid by women at the mikvah, Rabbanit Stern organizes study
sessions and parties for her bath attendants, and she makes a point of
describing the women who come to the mikvah as clients—implying
a professional, business-like relationship.
  Rabbanit Stern's hierarchical discourse sometimes seems to take
odd turns. For example, she often refers to the importance of psychology, yet emphasizes that "I learned at the university of the home, of
my mother and father," which, to Rabbanit Stern, is a better place to

learn than a university. In fact, Rabbanit Stern walks a fine line in such matters. Her discourse places herself and her associates on the "educated" side of the hierarchy, yet, in fact, she and her associates are far removed from mainstream Western educational institutions. No one in her community studies at a university; they do not take classes in psychology. In her community, girls attended Yiddish language schools in which little was learned beyond simple arithmetic, Bible stories, home economics, and selected aspects of Jewish law that are relevant to women. Education in the sense of modern high schools and universities is, for Rabbanit Stern, part of the impure outside world that, in most respects, stands in opposition to the holiness and traditional orientation of her ultra-orthodox world. Education in the sense of customary Jewish study is, in Rabbanit Stern's world, the domain of men, not of women. When she places herself in the category of the educated, she is, in a strange way, aligning herself with men and secular folk. This alignment is a problematic one, which, as I shall argue later on, she tries to resolve by telling her life story.

Introducing Shula

Shula is the head bath attendant at one of Jerusalem's busiest mikva'ot—a new mikvah in a neighborhood similar to the one about which Rabbanit Stern had spoken previously. Shula has been placed in her job by Rabbanit Stern, but she does in fact live in the community in which she works: She is not a member of Rabbanit Stern's ultra-orthodox Ashkenazi community. She is bustling, energetic, in her early forties, Moroccan (with a strong Moroccan accent), outspoken, assertive, and self-confident. Like Rabbanit Stern, she is very pious, covers her hair, and wears modest clothes. Besides working at the mikvah, she gives Judaica lessons to women in the neighborhood. Shula does not have a lot of time to sit and chat with visiting anthropologists. My conversations with her were held in bits and snatches as I followed behind her while she did her work in the mikvah.

Shula has put a great deal of thought and effort into decorating her mikvah. The walls are covered with pictures of rabbis and holy men and pictures portraying Jewish women's rituals (such as lighting candles at the start of the Sabbath). As women leave the mikvah building, she tells them to read a petitionary prayer (*tehina*) that she hung on the wall, although reading a petition is not part of the official mikvah ritual. This is in contrast to Rabbanit Stern, who tries to discourage superfluous rituals at the mikvah, such as drumming and singing for brides. Shula's petitionary prayer asks God to allow the ritual immersion to truly purify and to grant the ability to be a good wife and mother.

In Shula's discourse, the key word is *miracle*—she urges her women to pray for "wonders and miracles" and hangs up pictures and prayers that will help these miracles come about. Shula says,

> I tell the women to make personal requests from God [*bakashot*] while in the water. I have had women come and say that they wished for an apartment and then miraculously they bought one. One woman even wished for a bill of divorce [*get*] from her husband, and he miraculously gave her the divorce.

Shula's encouragement of personal prayer stands in contrast to Rabbanit Stern's dedication to teaching women to recite the standard blessing required by Jewish law, a blessing acknowledging that God commanded immersion in the mikvah.[6] Shula gives a great deal of personal attention to each woman, both in terms of the mikvah and dipping and in discussing personal problems. In contrast to Rabbanit Stern, who distances herself (the giver of a service) from her clients, Shula identifies herself with the women who come to mikvah, using the inclusive language of "we all": "These women come with heavy baggage, *we all have baggage* [italics added], but these women especially, and they need someone to talk to."

The population served by Shula is almost all of North African origin, and it is almost entirely secular—the women coming into the mikvah are young, wear pants, and do not cover their hair. Many presumably do not observe other aspects of Jewish law. Shula's discourse mentions ethnicity, but from a stance opposite to that of Rabbanit Stern.

> For the North African women, it [mikvah and niddah] is
> deeply rooted [*meshorash*]. They never really left it. Not
> like the Ashkenazim. . . . And my grandmother said that in
> Morocco women even did *b'dikot* [scrupulously checking
> themselves after the end of menstruation to make sure that
> no drops of blood remain—doing b'dikot would be a sign
> of pious women educated in Jewish law].

Like Rabbanit Stern, Shula denies having sought out a leadership
role. When I comment that she is very knowledgeable about Judaism
she replies, "I didn't study anywhere. All comes from the Holy One
Blessed Be He."

On the other hand, unlike Rabbanit Stern, who emphasizes that
she defers to male rabbis in all matters of Jewish law and that she has
several rabbis whom she consults on a regular basis, Shula describes
herself as more autonomous in matters of law. She was eager to show
me her mikvah, and she explained to me in great detail the laws
(*halachot*) regarding the construction of mikva'ot. In her discourse,
she expounded Jewish law in a way normally done by men and not by
women, ending with the statement that "this is the system of the Ari
[Rabbi Yitzhak Luria, 16th century kabbalist], and some rabbis rule
according to [*posek lefi*] the opinion of this Rabbi, and I rule according
to [*poseket lefi*] the opinion of that Rabbi."

Shula's use of language here is quite extraordinary for an orthodox
Jew: Only men—and only male rabbis—rule (*poskim*). In 15 years of
research among religious Jews in Jerusalem, I have never before heard
the feminine form of the verb *to rule*. Yet Shula does not blush or
stammer when she uses this language—it comes out of her mouth in
a most natural way. Later she explains,

> Sometimes women come and say "Rabbanit"—that is what
> some call me[7]—"I won't lie, I didn't do hefsek [cleansing rit-
> ual at the end of menstruation but before beginning to count
> the 7 clean days] and I didn't count the 7 clean days, but
> please don't turn me away, please let me dip." And I let them
> dip. We are all [protected] under the wings of the *Shekhina*
> [the female aspect of God in Jewish mystical thought].

Again, her language here is extraordinary. She has clear instructions from the Religious Council to tell women that they must do hefsek and count 7 clean days; she has been repeatedly taught to tell them that simply dipping at the end of the menstrual period is worthless and meaningless (like cake without baking powder). Yet, she takes it upon herself to allow the women to dip, justifying her decision in explicitly female language—language that bypasses the male rabbinical establishment, male constructed Jewish law, and even, in a sense, the male God. She explains that "we are all under the wings of the *Shekhina*," the female aspect of God.

In Shula's presentation of her work, she portrays herself as the advocate of neighborhood women in their dealings with God (allowing them to dip despite the omission of hefsek and the 7 clean days) and in their dealings with their husbands (cf. Wasserfall, 1990). "Some of the husbands make problems and don't want to wait 2 weeks [for the wife to immerse so as to resume sexual relations]. I have to help the woman."

Discussion

Throughout Shula's conversation, she clarifies that her reference group is women: that she is a woman just like the women who come to her mikvah, that she, like all women, has baggage, baggage often caused by problematic or violent husbands. Her authority comes from women who choose to call her Rabbanit even though she is not really a rabbanit. Rabbanit Stern, on the other hand, sees her reference group as men. She tries to convince the government agency to give more money to mikva'ot, she was told by male rabbis to take this job, she consults with rabbis over matters of Jewish law and chooses to enforce that law even when it conflicts with women's needs, and she is called Rabbanit because her husband is a rabbi. In Shula's discourse, gender is a highly relevant factor. She refers to women's problems with their husbands and to the female aspect of God (Shekhina). In Rabbanit Stern's discourse, other factors—most particularly ethnicity—override gender.

In an earlier paper (Sered, 1996), I argued that women religious leaders often use their life stories to reconcile culturally constructed notions of leadership with their own femaleness, when, in many if not most cultures, the very attributes that define leadership are perceived as male traits (e.g., strength, power, influence, and knowledge; cf. Collier, 1974). As Smith (1987) explains, women who tell their stories

> understand that a statement or a story will receive a different ideological interpretation if attributed to a man or to a woman. As a result, the [female] autobiographer . . . approaches her "fictive" reader as if "he" were the representative of the dominant order, the arbiter of the ideology of gender and its stories of selfhood. (p. 48)

In my first conversation with Rabbanit Stern, I had not asked her to tell me her life story, I had not asked her how she became involved in this work; I do not believe that I even emitted a subliminal message in this matter because, in fact, I had come to talk to her simply to enlist her aid in gaining admittance to a number of mikva'ot in Jerusalem in order to observe bride's parties. *She* volunteered her life story; *she* felt that there was something that I, a university professor, should hear in her story. The message that she wished to give me via her oral autobiography is a feminine one—she endeavored to situate herself correctly in terms of gender roles. In her story, she clarifies that she did not make a decision to be either a trailblazer or a top-level administrator. In fact, she wanted to stay home with her children and take care of her house. What caused her to embark on her mission of religious leadership? Her mother, a series of important [male] rabbis, and God (who put the right words into her mouth). The message in her story is that her own life path is one of continuity: She has continued her mother's work. It is not autonomous: She follows the instructions of the rabbis. And it is chosen for her by God: There is no issue of her own agency involved. Rabbanit Stern eagerly tells her life story, in part, to explain the all-but-unexplainable: why it is good for a woman to act like a man in a culture characterized by rigid gender roles, and to use her masculine prerogative to suppress the time-honored customs of other women. The fact that Rabbanit Stern has chosen to align herself with men demands an explanation: Her life story serves that purpose well.

When I first met Shula (after I had met Rabbanit Stern), I asked her to tell me how she came into this work. In contrast to Rabbanit Stern, Shula did not tell me her life story, even when I specifically asked. Instead, she talked about how she sees her role as a bath attendant. Whereas Rabbanit Stern seems to want to tell her story in order to clarify to the listener that her leadership is legitimate (blessed by God and Rabbi Aurbach) and that she is a good woman (concerned about her house and children), who also has the authority and skills of a man (good manager, educated, authoritative, scientific), Shula has no such need. Shula lets her work speak for itself. My sense is that Shula's power grows naturally from the female community in which she is situated—she does not need to tell her life story in order to give herself an aura of legitimacy. She does not treat me as an "arbiter of the ideology of gender" because for her, gender is clear-cut and unproblematic[8] She is her own arbiter.

In many ways, Shula turns Rabbanit Stern's discourse upside down. Whereas Rabbanit Stern sees men and the male way as superior (educated in Jewish law), Shula talks about the piety of women whose husbands are unable or unwilling to follow Jewish law and force their wives to have sexual relations too early. Whereas Rabbanit Stern sees law as God-given and ultimately more important than the needs of individuals, Shula puts the needs of her women before the letter of the law and argues for the legitimacy of this stance in the words of the mystical reference to the protection of the Shekhina. And finally, whereas Rabbanit Stern treats Ashkenazi as superior (knowledgeable, modern), Shula explains that North African women, unlike Ashkenazi women, are rooted (*meshorash*) in Jewish tradition; unlike many Ashkenazi women, North African women never abandoned the mikvah.

Both Rabbanit Stern and Shula present discourses in which power is a primary motif. Yet each refers to a different kind of power. Rabbanit Stern's power is what feminist writer Starhawk calls "power-over" whereas Shula's power is empowerment, what Starhawk (1987) calls "power-from-within."

> Power-over is linked to domination and control; power-from-within is linked to the mysteries that awaken our deepest abilities and potential. . . . Power-over . . . is the consciousness modeled on the God who stands outside the world, outside nature, who must be appeased, placated, feared, and above all, obeyed. . . . Power-over enables one individual or group to make the decisions that affect others, and to enforce control. . . . Power-from-within is akin to the sense of mastery we develop as young children with each new unfolding ability: the exhilaration of standing erect, of walking, of speaking the magic words that convey our needs and thoughts. But power-from-within is also akin to something deeper. It arises from our sense of connection, our bonding with other human beings, and with the environment. (pp. 9-19)

Significantly, the Shekhina, the aspect of God summoned by Shula in her discourse, is also understood in Jewish thought to be the immanent aspect of God. Whereas the male Holy One Blessed Be He stands outside the world, the female Shekhina remains in the world, accompanying the Jewish people in their exile, sharing their sorrows (Scholem, 1965). Shula has selected a divine image that is female and that represents the kind of power—power-from-within—that she herself represents in her community. Rabbanit Stern has selected a divine image that is male and that represents the kind of power—power-over—that she herself represents in the mikvah community.

The difference between power-over and power-from-within (or empowerment) has been illustrated in studies of female genital mutilation in Africa. These studies are relevant to our discussion here not only because, like niddah and mikvah, genital mutilation has a great deal to do with the ways in which patriarchy obtains control over women's bodies (Daly, 1978), but also because in both instances, a variety of social locations (such as class, age, and ethnicity) intersect and intertwine with gender as a ritual force. In a study of a West

African society, Bledsoe (1980) found that clitoridectomy, performed by old women upon young women, is part of the process by which old women gain control over young women. The model offered by Bledsoe is somewhat parallel to the model we saw in Rabbanit Stern's discourse: Contemporary mikvah has a lot to do with the Ashkenazi religious establishment gaining power over the bodies of North African and Asian women. In contrast, in a study of women's groups (secret societies) known as *Sande* in the same part of Africa, MacCormack (1979) found that, "Shared pain and risk of death from infection in initiation [clitoridectomy] help to bond initiates together into a cohesive group" able to defend itself, when necessary, against men (p. 32). In Sande, clitoridectomy teaches women and men that women are not sexual and reproductive animals, but rather that sexuality and reproduction are social constructs controlled by women. The model offered by MacCormack is parallel to the model we saw in Shula's discourse: Mikvah has a great deal to do with women gaining power over their own bodies and with women creating a space in which they can find empowerment through the sharing of their communal problems.

It is, of course, unnecessary and unhelpful to choose between Bledsoe's and MacCormack's models, just as it is unnecessary and unhelpful to choose between Rabbanit Stern's and Shula's models. Rabbanit Stern and Shula present competing discourses, both of which are true, both of which accurately represent portions of women's experience, both of which create women's ritual reality. And yet, this should not be taken to mean that the two discourses are equal: One (Rabbanit Stern's) has the official backing of the government and of Jewish textual tradition, one (Shula's) is backed up only by the force of her own personality and the loyalty of the women with whom she works.

The narratives offered by Rabbanit Stern and Shula deconstruct the illusion that rituals have "a meaning." We have seen that these two women understand and explain their ritual roles using very different rhetoric, imagery, and conceptions of power. I have argued that these differences reflect the distinctive social locations of the two specific women and the dissimilar cultural contexts in which their use of the ritual is embedded. Despite these differences, both women tell stories that prove their own particular approach to be legitimate.

Notes

1. See Sered, 1994, pp. 62ff., for a critique of this kind of approach.
2. All names have been changed.
3. In Israeli society, there are many shades of religious observance and identification. Ultra-orthodoxy includes those Jews who believe that all of Jewish law and custom is eternally true and who follow the guidance of particular rabbis in all aspects of life (both ritual and moral, and in questions such as where to live or whom to marry). Ultra-orthodox Jews generally see modern Israeli secular society as undesirable, polluted, and threatening. Most ultra-orthodox Jews are Ashkenazi, but there is a growing number of former North African and Asian ultra-orthodox Jews.
4. In this, she differs from other women religious leaders whom I have studied in Israel (Sered, 1996).
5. I use the word *class* here in a vague way that includes, but is not limited to, a sense that Ashkenazi Jews constitute the majority of well-off people in Israel. Rabbanit Stern's ultra-orthodox community, characterized by very large families, is typically much less well-off than other Ashkenazi Israelis.
6. Shula also teaches women to recite the formal blessing.
7. Shula's point here is that she is not really a rabbanit but that she lets the women use that title if they wish.
8. This does not imply that in her community gender roles lean toward egalitarianism; to the contrary, the families in her community are highly patriarchal—in many ways more patriarchal than Rabbanit Stern's Ashkenazi, ultra-orthodox community.

References

Ayalon, H., Ben-Rafael, E., & Sharot, S. (1991). Religious, ethnic, and class division in Israel: Convergent or cross-cutting? In Z. Sobel & B. Beit-Halahmi (Eds.), *Tradition, conflict, innovation: Jewishness and Judaism in contemporary Israel* (pp. 279-304). Albany: State University of New York Press.

Bledsoe, C. H. (1980). *Women and marriage in Kpelle society.* Stanford, CA: Stanford University Press.

Buckley, T., & Gottlieb, A. (Eds.). (1988). *Blood magic: The anthropology of menstruation.* Berkeley: University of California Press.

Collier, J. F. (1974). Women in politics. In M. Zimbalist Rosaldo & L. Lamphere (Eds.), *Women, culture, and society* (pp. 89-96). Stanford, CA: Stanford University Press.

Daly, M. (1978). *Gyn/ecology.* Boston: Beacon Press.

Falk, N., & Gross, R. (Eds.). (1980). *Unspoken worlds: Women's religious lives in non-Western cultures.* San Francisco: Harper & Row.

Gubrium, J. F., & Holstein, J. A. (1995). Biographical work and new ethnography. In R. Josselson & A. Lieblich (Eds.), *The Narrative Study of Lives* (Vol. 3, pp. 45-58). Thousand Oaks, CA: Sage.

Lacks, R. (1980). *Women and Judaism: Myth, history, and struggle.* New York: Doubleday.

Lamm, N. (1972). *Hedge of roses.* New York: Feldheim.

Leacock, E. (1986). Women, power, and authority. In L. Dube, E. Leacock, & S. Ardener (Eds.), *Visibility and power* (pp. 107-135). Oxford: Oxford University Press.

MacCormack, C. P. (1979). Sande: The public face of a secret society. In B. Jules-Rosette (Ed.), *The new religions of Africa* (pp. 27-37). Norwood, NJ: Ablex.

Moore, H. (1988). *Feminism and anthropology.* Minneapolis: University of Minnesota Press.

Scholem, G. (1965). *On the Kabbalah and its symbolism.* New York: Schocken.

Sered, S. S. (1994). *Priestess, mother, sacred sister: Religions dominated by women.* New York: Oxford University Press.

Sered, S. S. (1996). Conversations with Rabbanit Zohara. *Journal of the American Academy of Religion, 63,* 249-268.

Sered, S. S. (in press). Talking about mikveh parties, or discourses of gender, hierarchy, and social control. In R. Wasserfall (Ed.), *Niddah and mikvah in Jewish and Muslim cultures.*

Smith, S. (1987). *A poetics of women's autobiography.* Bloomington: Indiana University Press.

Sobel, Z. (1991). Conflict and communitas: The interplay of religion, ethnicity, and community in a Galilee village. In Z. Sobel & B. Beit-Halahmi (Eds.), *Tradition, conflict, innovation: Jewishness and Judaism in contemporary Israel* (pp. 25-46). Albany: State University of New York Press.

Starhawk. (1987). *Truth or dare.* New York: Harper & Row.

Wasserfall, R. (1990). Bargaining for gender identity: Love, sex, and money on an Israeli moshav. *Ethnology, 29*(4), 327-340.

❦ 4 ❦

Going Straight

Desistance From Crime and Life Narratives of Reform

Shadd Maruna

Charlie McGregor says, "My life is evidence that mental growth can take place anywhere. I lived in jail—one of the worst kinds of ghettos there is—but it didn't keep me from becoming an educated man" (p. 489).[1] A gang member and a drug dealer through his adolescence and young adulthood, McGregor detailed the failures, successes, and metamorphoses of his tumultuous life in his 1978 autobiography, *Up From the Walking Dead*. The following rough schematic of his book provides the gist of this history:

> McGregor was born in Harlem, to a single mother who beat him terribly because she thought he was less intelligent and less attractive than his lighter-skinned older brother. He became involved in gangs and drugs as a means of achieving a sense of power and self-respect amid a powerless ghetto existence. His young adulthood, however, was largely spent behind bars. Although he found a "family" of sorts in prison, he longed for female intimacy and material success. Each time he was released, however, he found that these goals were unattainable through legal means, so he returned to criminal behavior.

Finally, in prison for the last time, he was exposed to a social service organization called Reality House, run by former Harlem gang members like himself, but who had achieved respectability in mainstream society. After seeing the respectful way prison officials treated the counselors from the organization, McGregor agreed to go along to the group's meetings. He soon found that this "new family" was a far more peaceful and understanding group than his incarcerated peers. Upon his release from prison, he approached the agency to find a job, so he could be like one of the counselors he so admired. Although the process was anything but easy, several years later, Charlie McGregor became a licensed drug therapist, public speaker, and minor celebrity, who used his new position to help young people avoid making the mistakes he made.

McGregor's story is unique in many ways, but the transition away from delinquent behavior he describes is a surprisingly common social phenomenon. Colloquially labeled "going straight," this transition is referred to as *desistance from crime* in criminological literature. Little is known about this reform process except that it tends to take place for most delinquents in their late teens or early twenties (Farrington, 1986). In fact, Moffitt (1993) calls the "mysterious" relationship between age and crime "at once the most robust and least understood empirical observation in the field of criminology" (p. 675).

In one of the most thorough analyses of the topic, Rand (1987) suggests "the phenomenon of desistance has received no specific theoretical or empirical attention" (p. 134). Although this is overstated (see Greenberg, 1981, or Trasler, 1979), studies of desistance do tend to be difficult to locate and seem to exist in relative isolation from one another. In their 639-page definitive study of the causes of crime, for instance, Wilson and Herrnstein (1985) say that the linkage of age and crime "resists explanation" (p. 145). Shover (1985) writes, "Although it is conventional wisdom that most offenders eventually desist from criminal behavior, criminology textbooks have little or nothing to say about this process" (p. 15). Mulvey and LaRosa (1986) conclude, "In short, we know that many youth 'grow out' of delinquent activity, but we know very little about why" (p. 213).

In this exploratory study, I employ the methodology and insight of narrative psychology to try to better understand the psychological processes involved in the transition away from antisocial behavior. Following McAdams (1985, 1993), I content-analyze 20 published autobiographies, written by successfully reintegrated ex-convicts for similarities in theme, plot structure, and character—not simply the historical "facts" usually studied in sociological analysis (see Bennett, 1981). The goal of this project is to identify a type of subjective self-understanding expressed in narrative that seems to support desistance from crime.

Autobiography and Criminology: A Rationale

Criminology has had a long tradition of using life-history data, especially in the Chicago School of sociology during the first part of the century. Discussing life histories, such as *The Jack-Roller*, for instance, Shaw (1929) writes, "So far as we have been able to determine as yet, the best way to investigate the inner world of the person is through a study of himself through a life history" (p. 6). Scott and Lyman (1968) even argue that stories are intimately connected to behavior such as crime that is outside of socially approved boundaries: "Since it is with respect to deviant behavior that we call for accounts, the study of deviance and the study of accounts are intrinsically related, and a clarification of accounts will constitute a clarification of deviant phenomena" (p. 62; see also Hartung, 1965).

Nonetheless, the marriage of oral histories and criminology has been rocky, and the method has been all but abandoned by criminologists today (Thomas, 1983). Lewis and Maruna (1995) argue that this is largely because criminologists have traditionally viewed these documents as purely sociological rather than psychosocial data. Bennett (1981) writes that despite the numerous oral histories collected by criminologists over the last century, delinquent narratives have never been explicitly analyzed as explorations of "somatic, psychiatric, and psychological regions" of human identity (p. 236). He argues that the small amount of nonsociological commentary that was included in the life-story research in this time was merely "inserted to placate the psychologists who headed the institute for Juvenile Research" (p. 190). Finestone (1976) similarly points out, "Shaw made no attempt to pursue the implications of the Jack-Roller's idiosyncratic point of view for an understanding of his involvement in delinquent conduct" (p. 101).

Although life narratives provide valuable historical and social information for sociologists, McAdams (1985, 1993) also argues that narratives should be viewed as a psychosocial construction of a person's identity. According to this view, the modern adult defines him- or herself in society by fashioning an internalized and dynamic life story, or personal myth, that provides life with unity, purpose, and meaning. The construction and reconstruction of this internal narrative integrating one's perceived past, present, and anticipated future is itself the process of identity development in adulthood (McAdams, Diamond, de St. Aubin, & Mansfield, in press). According to Giddens (1991), in modern society, "a person's identity is not to be found in behavior, nor—important though this is—in the reactions of others, but in the capacity to keep a particular narrative going" (p. 54). I take this as my beginning point in analyzing the narratives of reformed ex-convicts.

Most often, these subjective interpretations of one's history are obtained through autobiographical interviewing or ethnographic research (Canter, 1994; Denzin, 1987, 1989; Katz, 1988; Toch, 1987). Verbal and written life histories are *not* identity myths themselves, but they "hold the outlines" of these internal narratives and can be hermeneutically mined for clues to individuals' self-understandings (McAdams, 1993). A large, untapped archive of this life-story data exists in public libraries, where "personal documents" (Allport, 1937) such as autobiographies have long been a staple. Discussing William James's (1902/1985) *The Varieties of Religious Experience*, Bakan (1996) argues that using published, and therefore public, autobiographic data also allows researchers to avoid the ethical problems of harming interview subjects by publishing sensitive information about their personal and inner lives. He writes, "I suspect that the library contains great narrative ore for much more psychological mining" (p. 6). The issue of privacy is of particular ethical concern when dealing with populations such as ex-offenders, so I exclusively employ published autobiographies in this study.

Still, the use of published data raises other important issues for psychological researchers. For instance, the data in this sample may be inappropriately shaped by literary demands. The content might reflect what is "publishable" under the pressures of the lucrative "true crime" publishing market rather than historical or personal truth. As Katz (1988), who also analyzes published accounts of offenders, writes, "It is reasonable to worry that the ubiquitous presence of . . . 'sensational' themes in life histories says more about the criteria of publishing than about robbers' lives in general" (p. 347).

Although this concern is real, the data are probably no more contaminated than oral histories collected by sociologists. Whenever people relate their life story, audience expectations will influence the tone or content. Sutherland (1932), for instance, suggests that the guidance of the social scientist during the interview process "is likely to result in some selection of material in a sense that the relative amounts of material on different topics are influenced by the interests and hypotheses of the investigator." Especially when dealing with the subject of deviant behavior, one is likely to hear a considerable amount of false rhetoric, regardless of the situation of the telling (Sykes & Matza, 1957). Still, although the "sustaining story" of reform may be an imaginatively distorted version of "reality," personality researchers argue that this fiction is meaningful (Adler, 1927). Rouse (1978) suggests our autobiographical tales are "much embellished but truthful even so, for truth is not simply what happened but how we felt about it when it was happening, and how we feel about it now" (cited in McAdams, 1994b, p. 721).

In this sense, committing one's life story to print may even make the work more personally meaningful. Josselson (1996) writes, "Written events gain a substantiality above that carried by memory or speech" (p. 60). Presumably, autobiographical authors are aware that many of the people close to them will be able to read the book (and verify its accuracy). Therefore, they probably have *more* incentive than the individual talking to a researcher in a laboratory setting to be honest and consistent in their self-exploration. At the least, published autobiographies more directly reflect what individuals want significant others to know about them than do anonymous interviews.

Finally, published autobiographies also represent *public* stories as well as *private* stories. American literature, media, and cinema have a long-standing obsession with stories of crime and criminals, from Al Capone to the Crips and Bloods. The number of criminal offenders portrayed on prime-time television on any given night is wildly out of proportion to the number of offenders in "real life," for instance. All of these public stories directly or indirectly influence voters and lawmakers in their opinions of key crime policies from "three strikes" legislation to the death penalty (see Leps, 1992). Positive stories of the ex-con who "makes good" and turns his life around, from Hugo's (1862/1963) *Les Miserables* to *The Autobiography of Malcolm X* (1965) magnify the notion of the unlimited potential and plasticity of the human being. Negative public stories of the incorrigible ex-offender, such as George Bush's Willie Horton commercials, on the other hand, support the competing notion of "once a criminal, always a criminal."

Public stories about criminality also affect young people who are in the process of finding their own identities. Adolescents' stories will reflect the influence of the countless public stories the young person has been exposed to, from television programs to religious parables. The stories in this sample, therefore, not only reflect public mythology, but because the stories themselves are published, they too become mythological artifacts (Denzin, 1989). The story of "going straight" is a staple in Western fiction that serves a culturally relevant function. Like the story of the child of poverty who becomes president, the story of the ex-offender who becomes a community leader serves as a testament to human plasticity and the potential for adaptation and change (Brown, 1988). Understanding the key elements of these reform stories may be helpful in understanding desistance from crime.

The Desistance Literature

One of the first social scientists to address the question of reform was Adolphe Quetelet (1833). Like other students of criminal behavior in this period, Quetelet takes a biological approach to delinquency.

He argues that the penchant for crime "seems to develop by reason of the intensity of man's physical vitality and passions." Criminality peaks when physical development has "almost been completed," then "diminishes still later due to the enfeeblement of physical vitality and the passions" (cited in Brown & Miller, 1988, p. 13). Glueck and Glueck (1940) develop this into their theory of *maturational reform*. They argue that criminality naturally declines after the age of 25. With the "sheer passage of time," juvenile delinquents "grow out" of this transitory phase and change their life goals. Glueck and Glueck find that "aging is the only factor which emerges as significant in the reformative process" (p. 105). Specifically, young adults "burn out" physiologically and can no longer maintain the type of energy and aggressiveness needed in delinquency.

Although Glueck and Glueck (1940) explicitly urged future researchers to "dissect maturation into its components" (p. 270), Shover (1985) corrctly asserts that criminology's "explanatory efforts have not progressed appreciably beyond (the Gluecks') work" (p. 77). Maturational reform continues to be one of the most influential theories of desistance in criminology. For instance, Wilson and Herrnstein (1985) argue that none of the possible correlates of age, such as employment, peers or family circumstances, explain crime as well as the variable of age itself. "That is to say, an older person is likely to have a lower propensity for crime than a younger person, even after they have been matched in demographic variables," they argue (p. 145). Similarly, Gottfredson and Hirschi (1990) write, "We are left with the conclusion that (desistance) is due to the inexorable aging of the organism" rather than any social variables (p. 141).

According to each theory, age "causes" desistance. Yet, as Sutton (1994) suggests, "To say that age influences everything is to say nothing" (p. 228). Could anyone imagine, after all, social scientists saying the same thing about crime itself: "Criminal behavior peaks at age 17; therefore, crime is caused by turning 17." Developmental psychologists are increasingly beginning to view biological age as an ambiguous and irrelevant variable, with little meaning except that which is socially attached to it (Neugarten & Neugarten, 1986; Rutter, 1989). Criminologists need to "unpack" the meaning of age, according to Sampson and Laub (1992). After all, a simple notion like burning out, as Matza (1964) writes, "merely reiterates the occurrence of maturational reform—it hardly explains it" (p. 24; see also Wooton, 1959). If we accept the seriousness of antisocial behavior, as nearly all criminology texts insist we should, then "going straight" must be an immense change, worthy of problematizing beyond a label such as maturation.

Elsewhere (Maruna, 1995a), I have argued that the most important reason that desistance has remained an unexplained process is criminology's reliance on measures of dispositional traits to understand the "delinquent personality." McAdams (1994a) would call this the "psychology of the stranger," or precisely the types of attributes one knows about the person one knows relatively little about. Although traits are critically important for understanding behavior, they do not constitute the "whole person" (Murray, 1938). Moreover, personality traits, which by definition are largely stable over time, cannot explain how an individual is able to radically change his or her behavior (Matza, 1964; Moffitt, 1993). To understand desistance, research is needed that goes beyond the level of dispositional traits and explores personal identities and stories.

Methodology

I randomly selected 25 autobiographical accounts from Briscoe's (1982) *Bibliography of American Autobiography*. Briscoe's useful volume, one of the only comprehensive indexes of published autobiographical material, categorizes published life histories based on the occupations and achievements of the authors. The index includes a listing of books by artists, architects, and academics, as well as books concerning travel, teaching, or psychology, for instance. I randomly selected 25 titles from the categories *criminals*, *prisoners*, *crime*, and *prison*, and I ordered the books through an interlibrary loan system. After reviewing these 25 works, 5 were discarded, because the narrators did not seem to experience significant changes in their behavior or outlooks toward crime by the end of the autobiographies.

The 20 autobiographies in the final sample range from 120 to 490 pages in length, and all but two meet Allport's (1937) criteria for comprehensive autobiographies (see Table 4.1 for a list that includes publication information). The writing ranges from literary to passably literate, and most of the books were published by small, reasonably accessible houses, rather than major presses. A few of the narrators, in fact, did not write their story at all, but rather provided an oral history for a ghost writer to compose (which may be problematic to some narrative analysts).

Other criminological studies have taken advantage of the rich data provided in several of these published life stories (Jolin, 1985; Katz, 1988; Shover, 1985), but there has been no previous attempt, to my knowledge, to systematically study a random sampling of these personal documents. Although I use random selection of cases from the Briscoe bibliography, in no sense is this a random or representative sample of ex-offenders. There may be a strong selection bias based on the fact that these were the "types" of ex-offenders who were willing to and capable of authoring or co-authoring an autobiography.

Nonetheless, the basic demographics of the sample match up fairly well with large-scale research on offenders: The narrators in this sample are overwhelmingly poor, urban, and male. According to their stories, all of the individuals would have at one point met the *Diagnostic and Statistical Manual of Mental Disorders (DSM-IV;* American Psychiatric Association, 1994) criteria for people with *antisocial personality disorder*, and all could be described as "career criminals" (Blumstein & Cohen, 1987). They are not individuals who, in a fit of passion or adventure, broke the law once or twice or even a half dozen times. All 20 individuals were solid members of the "underground economy" and admit to regularly engaging in illegal behavior.

To a certain degree, the authors vary in the types of crimes in which they had previously engaged. Yet, Gottfredson and Hirschi (1995) argue,

> With trivial exceptions, research has failed to discover specialists in particular types of crime. As a consequence, theories and programs that identify offenders as robbers, auto thieves, or drug users and see each type as being the product of distinct causal forces must be wrong. (p. 31)

TABLE 4.1 Autobiographical Sample

Author	Date of Publication	Title	Publisher
Atkins, Susan	1977	*Child of Satan, Child of God*	New York: Logos International
Baker, Albie	1973	*Stolen Sweets*	New York: E. P. Dutton
Braly, Malcolm	1976	*False Starts*	Boston: Little, Brown
Brown, Jack, as told to Allen Groff	1971	*Monkey Off My Back*	Grand Rapids, MI: Zondervan
Coss, Richard	1977	*Wanted*	San Diego: Beta Books
Duke, Harry	1977	*Neutral Territory*	Philadelphia: Dorrance
Erwin, John	1978	*The Man Who Keeps Going to Jail*	Elgin, IL: Cook
Geraway, William	1976	*There's $50,000 on My Head*	Hicksville, NY: Exposition Press
Howard, Mattie	1963	*Pathway of Mattie Howard: To and From Prison*	New York: Pageant Press
Howland, Larry	1979	*Going Straight*	Irvine, CA: Harvest House
Hyatt, Henry	1949	*Alias Jimmy Valentine Himself, By Himself*	Philadelphia: Dorrance
Karpis, Alvin	1971	*The Alvin Karpis Story*	New York: Cloward, McCann and Geoghegan
King, Harry	1972	*Box Man: A Professional Thief's Journey*	New York: Harper & Row
Krist, Gary	1972	*Life, the Man who Kidnapped Barbara Mackle*	New York: Olympia Press
McGregor, Charles	1978	*Up From the Walking Dead: The Charles McGregor Story*	Garden City, NY: Doubleday
Morris, Ed	1974	*Born to Lose*	New York: Mason & Lipscombe
Murphy, Frank	1968	*The Frank Murphy Story: His Years in Florida Prisons, His Rehabilitation, and His Conquest of Alcohol*	New York: Dodd, Mead
Rogers, Kenneth Paul	1974	*For One Sweet Grape*	Chicago: Playboy Press.
Torok, Lou	1974	*Straight Talk From Prison*	New York: Human Sciences Press.
Vaus, James	1974	*The Devil Loves a Shining Mark*	Waco, TX: Word Books.

Like Kaplan (1980), they suggest that drug use, theft, assault, and other delinquent behaviors are products of a common underlying tendency. I also make the assumption that the desistance processes from these disparate behaviors could be considered together. My procedure for analyzing these autobiographies resembled a grounded theory approach, although my structured readings of the texts were guided by McAdams's (1985, 1993) conceptual framework for understanding narratives. In particular, I began to chart similarities and differences in three of the key features McAdams and his students have identified in life stories: *nuclear episodes, imagoes,* and *themes.*

Nuclear episodes include high points, low points, beginnings, endings, and transformational episodes or turning points in the narrative. These are frequently long passages or passages flagged as major climaxes that are used to develop characters in an autobiography. Through these scenes, readers gain an understanding of the narrator's motivations and personal identity. These nuclear episodes, according to McAdams (1993), "are windows into the organization of human desire" (p. 297).

Imagoes are the personified idealizations of possible selves each of us use to understand and guide our behavior. Over a lifetime, a person may assume many different imagoes chosen from among the popular archetypes of culture. People might see themselves as being the good soldier, the clown, the drunk, or the loyal companion at various points in time. These character (or caricature) types are important aspects of a person's self-concept.

Finally, life-story themes are recurrent goal-oriented sequences that main characters pursue in narratives. According to McAdams (1994b) and theorists such as Bakan, the major themes of Western narratives can be understood in terms of levels of agency (or power) and communion (or intimacy). Bakan (1966) describes agency and communion as the "two fundamental modalities in the existence of living forms" (pp. 14-15). He defines agency as the "existence of the organism as an individual" manifesting itself in self-protection, self-expansion, and the mastery of the environment. Under this category, McAdams and his colleagues include themes of self-mastery, status attainment, achievement, responsibility, and empowerment (McAdams,

Hoffman, Mansfield, & Day, 1996). Communion, which includes themes of love, friendship, dialogue, care, help, and community, can be defined as "the participation of the individual in some larger organism of which the individual is a part" (Bakan, p. 15). I used this modality to guide and structure my analysis of the thematic patterns across my sample.

Although each story was unique in many ways, I tried to identify what Bertaux (1981) calls a "saturation" of various episodes, imagoes, and themes across the 20 cases. Bertaux (1981) describes saturation as the attainment of a representative sampling of data reflecting the major sociological and/or psychological structures and processes inherent in a given phenomenon. An investigator of life narratives reaches a saturation point in the research when he or she begins to discern the same or highly similar patterns from one case to the next. The stories contain numerous differences, as well, of course, but with such a small sample size, few meaningful patterns or interpretations could be drawn from this diversity. Strong cross-case similarities, on the other hand, might lead to important hypotheses to be further explored in future research. Finally, all of the case studies in this sample are available in public libraries, so this study can be replicated for alternative findings and interpretations.

Findings

Charlie McGregor's story is unique in many ways, but it also has much in common with the other cases I analyzed. Together, the narratives in this sample reveal a definite pattern, a generic or prototypical story of reform. In this section, I will describe these common themes and character types as they relate to the different narrative phases or "chapters" in the life stories: childhood, adolescence, young adulthood, and later adulthood.

Like any narrative, reform stories need to be coherent and believable, to make internal sense. Although no one story perfectly fits the prototypical reform story model outlined in this chapter, the stories in this sample largely follow this common, Western narrative structure (see Figure 4.1).

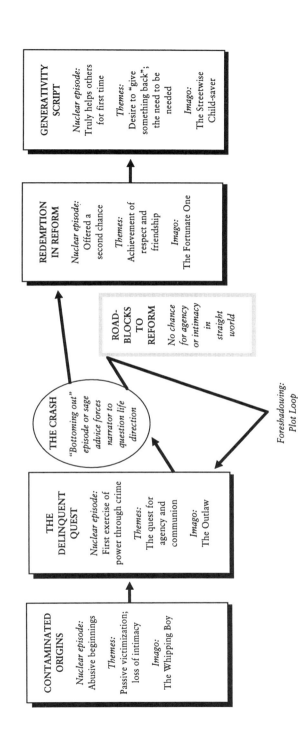

Figure 4.1. The Prototypical Reform Narrative

CONTAMINATED ORIGINS

Nuclear episode:
Abusive beginnings

Themes:
Passive victimization;
loss of intimacy

Imago:
The Whipping Boy

THE DELINQUENT QUEST

Nuclear episode:
First exercise of power through crime

Themes:
The quest for agency and communion

Imago:
The Outlaw

THE CRASH
"Bottoming out" episode or sage advice forces narrator to question life direction

ROAD-BLOCKS TO REFORM
No chance for agency or intimacy in straight world

Foreshadowing:
Plot Loop

REDEMPTION IN REFORM

Nuclear episode:
Offered a second chance

Themes:
Achievement of respect and friendship

Imago:
The Fortunate One

GENERATIVITY SCRIPT

Nuclear episode:
Truly helps others for first time

Themes:
Desire to "give something back"; the need to be needed

Imago:
The Streetwise Child-saver

The plot begins with a long period of passive victimization in childhood. This leads to an ill-fated search for agency and communion in delinquent subcultures. At several points during this criminal involvement, all of the narratives contain breaks or nuclear episodes where the narrators are faced with the tragic discrepancy between their morals and their behavior. This "moment of clarity" is often preceded by a tragic episode or sage advice from a trusted friend. As a result, the narrators decide to desist from criminal behavior or at least seriously question the direction of their life to that point. Nonetheless, the narrators frequently experience structural or psychological "roadblocks" that prevent them from going straight. Usually they are confronted with a lack of opportunity for achieving respectability and intimacy outside of a criminal subculture, and therefore they drift back into criminal behavior. This "plot loop" can be seen as a type of foreshadowing for a major life change to come later in the narrative.

At some point in all of the autobiographies, the narrators report experiencing a "final" transformative experience—often endowed with supernatural importance—when all previous behaviors are called into question. Following this experience, the narrators also find noncriminal opportunities for agency and communion that help them sustain a "new," reformed identity. This "redemption" is usually credited to the enormous generosity of others (frequently a higher power) who are willing to reach out to the narrators and give them a chance to succeed. Following this experience, the narrators develop a generative plan for their life in order to "give something back" and help their contemporaries who were not as lucky. The narrators also seek to atone for their past crimes and explicitly "advertise" a new, prosocial identity to secure others' trust and to help prevent others from making the same mistakes they did as a youth.

Contaminated Origins

Probably the least surprising finding of this study is that almost every former offender's identity myth begins with a tragic childhood. In his discussion of various "ontologies of the self," Hankiss (1981) calls this a "self-absolutory" narrative strategy, in which a negative present follows linearly from a negative past. Goffman (1961) similarly discusses the "sad tales" told by people in institutions, and Sykes and Matza (1957) say that "denial of responsibility" is a primary "neutralization" used to rationalize and justify behavior now considered reprehensible. None of this is to suggest that the personal tragedies described by the ex-offenders are untrue—undoubtedly, individuals in prison have experienced far higher rates of childhood poverty, abuse, and neglect than other segments of the population. Instead, these stories illustrate how this "cumulative disadvantage" (Sampson & Laub, 1994) or "multiple deprivation" (Currie, 1993) is internalized and understood by offenders in later life.

The level of tragedy described in this sample ranges from the irritating restrictions of Vaus's early life ("We weren't allowed to go to dances or movies," p. 30) to Morris's horrific tales of abuse ("The more I hollered the more she beat me. Then she said that a rotten Jewboy like me should not be allowed to play with other children on Christmas Day . . . [and] I was put down in the cellar," p. 9). Yet, almost every author describes the events in a way that seems like she or he was uniquely unfortunate and essentially alone in the world as a child. Hyatt's story, for instance, brims with bitterness. He writes,

> It must be pleasant for most people to think back upon their childhood days. What is your first recollection? Probably some supremely happy moment—your first doll or roller skates. . . . But my earliest recollection is one of horror and unhappiness. (p. 73)

Likewise, Torok says of his life, "If anybody could be said to have been 'born to lose,' I am that person. . . . I spent all of my childhood in orphanages and boarding schools without love, without affection, without close personal friendships" (p. 20).

Each description of early childhood is saturated with passages that reflected what McAdams et al. (1996) call *contamination*, where an episode or life passage that seems to begin with promise turns suddenly bad. Braly provides the clearest example of such a story. He writes, "I

was born with a silver spoon in my mouth—or at least one of sturdy
nickel plate—but at age five . . . it was abruptly snatched and probably
my mouth was torn" (p. 4). Others were separated from their families
because of death or poverty, leaving them orphaned and alone. King,
for instance, says his mother gave him up for adoption because she
could not afford to care for him. "I was no problem child at the time,
but my mother had to do something with me since there were four
children in the house" (p. 5).

The Search for Agency and Communion Through Crime

Following almost linearly from these accounts of contamination
in childhood, the narrators describe involvement in delinquent behavior as an adolescent or young adult as a way to gain a sense of agency
and communion. Early deprivation, the authors contend, left each of
them with a reduced stake in conformity. Criminal behavior and deviant subcultures, moreover, provide a rather easily obtainable avenue
for "success," as well as a new "family." Erikson (1959) suggests that
teenagers may "vindictively" choose a "negative" identity or identification in order to regain "some mastery in a situation in which the
available positive identity elements cancel each other out" (p. 142).
This is the phenomenon of preferring being someone "bad" to being
"not-quite-somebody" or suffering the in-between stage of adolescence (p. 143; see also Moffitt, 1993).

Usually, the stories in this sample imply that the traumas the
narrators experienced as young persons directly *caused* delinquent
behavior in adolescence. For instance, Hyatt describes getting involved with crime as an effort to "get even with society" for what it
had done to him (p. 185). Coss begins his childhood story by saying,
"From early childhood I was destined to live a rough life. . . . There
was never much love in our home. . . . The only sure way I knew to
get attention was to make trouble" (p. 18).

Most of the narrators describe achieving a sincere sense of power
and control through youthful delinquency. Coss, for instance, brags
that his gang "literally ruled the neighborhood" (p. 25) and that

"every time I served another sentence, I came out more of a hero in my neighborhood" (p. 26). Similarly, Baker writes, "To the rest of my family, I was 'the successful one,' as if I were a lawyer, doctor, or accountant—only I was a burglar" (p. 7). Duke, who lost both parents to a gunman, writes, "I wanted to join the gang in the worst way. . . . I wanted to be like Nick and Jesse and get the respect that they got wherever they went" (p. 4).

Braly describes his first times shoplifting with his small rural gang as "an exercise of real power over the remote adult world" and an attempt to "transcend my common life" (pp. 11, 12). He says, "Stealing cast me in my first successful role" (p. 12). McGregor says he found that he could overcome the torments and cruelty of his childhood through violence:

> While on the stoop wielding the .22, I felt powerful. It was the first time I gave hell to someone else, even though I had been catching some kind of hell from the very day I was born at Harlem Hospital. (p. 2)

Finally, Vaus describes his desire for "the power to make people respect me, the money to pay them off . . . [and] the strength of making someone do what I wanted him to do" (p. 16).

According to the narrators, part of the process of "prisonization" or the acceptance of deviant values inside correctional institutions, involves learning this need for power. Braly says,

> What one learns to want in a "crime school" [prison] is the respect of one's peers. This is the danger. The naive will be drawn into competing for status in a system of values that honors and glorifies antisocial behavior. (p. 52)

Similarly, describing learning to fight inside Hart Island Penitentiary, Baker writes,

> From that point on, nobody fucked with me again. It was the animal sense of wariness and respect for one who would fight back savagely. They all said I was a good kid. This

> recognition was my downfall in a way. If I hadn't fought
> back, if I'd submitted to the threats and become somebody's
> punk, I'd never have gone back [to prison]. Instead I had
> gained respect and self-assurance. I had lost my fear of
> them—the guards and the other prisoners. I had learned
> new tricks and become one of them. (p. 21)

This search for agency is supported by the creation of romantic "outlaw imagoes." Former offender Warren Rhodes writes that his past delinquency was directly related to his efforts to fulfill the role of a mythical "bad dude." Shorr (1977) similarly describes the way in which a drug addict used a Humphrey Bogart fantasy to maintain his self-destructive behavior. These character or caricature types are what McAdams (1993) refers to as imagoes.

In this sample of ex-offenders, these imagoes tended toward romantic outlaws and heroic vigilantes. Braly says he saw himself as a blend of Robin Hood and Jesse James (p. 122) and later says he told himself that "I was a hunter and this was the elemental" (p. 210). McGregor says his "favorite jailhouse fantasy" involved an idealized image of himself as the prince of the Harlem underworld. "Regardless of all the dudes around me, I am the finest. I am so clean, junkies stop shooting up and whores stop flatbacking to remark, 'That is the sharpest nigger we ever seen' " (p. 369). Each narrative expressed an awareness of what a "bad" individual should be like, and these imagoes are often borrowed from literature and history. Describing fellow offenders, for instance, Rogers writes, "I wouldn't say that these screaming human beings aren't attempting to appear as the stereotyped con. Nor would I say that a few would not give up much . . . to attain the 'con' image" (p. 92).

Many of the narratives also suggest that the desire for communion is a key motivating force for involvement in criminal behavior. Torok writes,

> This hunger for acceptance and for deep, personal, and inti-
> mate love has followed me every day of my life. I suspect it
> has been the principal reason for the "acting out" of my re-

pressed aggressions throughout my life, leading me into so
many difficult and trying extra-legal activities. (p. 20)

Frequently criminal subgroups can at least temporarily provide a sort
of familial communion, symbolized in ritual and dress, for those who
have experienced little of it in their lifetimes. King writes, "In those
days, thieves were very clannish, very close, and would help one
another" (p. 7). Braly says that he perceived the delinquent gang as a
team of outlaw bandits who were "fiercely loyal to each other, their
relatives, their immediate friends, and only disloyal to that larger and
more abstract society" (p. 122).

Even in prison, frequently, the characters describe more communion and agency than they say they experienced in their home lives.
At Sing Sing, McGregor says, "I got a certain kind of respect from the
hacks and inmates because I was a veteran jailer." In fact, he admits,
"It's a terrible thing to say, but my brother inmates greeted me with
more love and enthusiasm than my mother and sister had when I returned home from prison. . . . Prison was more like home than home"
(p. 153). Geraway writes,

> A sampling of adult offenders in any institution will turn up
> case after case of men who, upon release from prison, not
> only committed other offenses, but committed them in a stu-
> pid and careless fashion, virtually pleading with someone to
> catch them. Because to them, prison is a womb, a subcultural
> environment where all decisions are made for them, where
> their needs are fulfilled by the state and, most of all, *where
> they are somebody* [italics added], where they are recognized
> by their peer group as being someone of importance. (p. 35)

The Crash: Crime Doesn't Pay

At some point in every story, however, there is a severe breakdown
between the fantasy of the gangster clan and the reality of the person's
life. In his "topography of transformational metanoia," Loder (1981)
calls this a "rupture" in the person's understanding of the world (see

also Miller & C'deBaca, 1994), and it is similar to Durkheim's (1972) notion of the individual becoming "divided against himself" (p. 92). In this process, structurally motivated behaviors come into conflict with cultural or personal values (Groves & Sampson, 1986; see also Matza, 1964), and individuals are forced to question the direction of their lives.

All the reform stories in this sample contain numerous points at which the narrators say they reached this point. Frequently, these moments of clarity were preceded by a betrayal by fellow offenders, allegedly bonded by what Geraway decides is a "mythical" brotherhood. Howard, for instance, learned that "a gang will tolerate you as long as it is convenient, but when they are through with you, they are through" (p. 241).

For others, the turning point incident involved words of wisdom from a trusted source. While at a prison revival meeting, for instance, Coss says, "For the first time in my life, I took a long hard look at my past. All I saw was hatred and bitterness and heartache and sorrow. . . . Suddenly the sight was unbearable to me" (p. 73). Howland says he had the same experience after reading a passage in the Bible. Murphy claims to have seen the light at an Alcoholics Anonymous session, whereas an older couple befriended Erwin and allowed him into their lives. In all of these instances, outside figures in the narrators' lives merely "reminded" them of what they already believed in or thought they believed in. This reminder made the narrators see for the first time how their behavior contradicted their ideals.

For some narrators, the jolt of some "bottoming out" experience (Denzin, 1987)—like the death of a son (Brown), a drug overdose and 4-month hospital stay (Atkins), the murder of a lover (Howard), or a confrontation with one's victim (Krist)—is necessary to shine light on the contradiction between their lives and their desires. Duke, for instance, describes a traumatic car chase where he was nearly shot. After that, he says,

> I would wake up wondering how and why I ever got mixed up in this business in the first place, and how I could get the hell out of it. I would have gladly given up my jars of money . . . to get out of the rackets. (p. 83)

Roadblocks to Reform

It is important that such moments of clarity are *not* always followed by decisive life changes in the stories in this sample. Early in his autobiography, Vaus writes, "That was the first time I'd seen anyone shot and killed. The incident jarred me enough so that I reflected about life, death, and God, but that was only a momentary reflection" (p. 25). As with smoking, moreover, a person apparently can "give up" crime many times before actually going straight. Earls, Cairns, and Mercy (1993) suggest, "Initiating change is but the first step. The second step involves maintaining the change. . . . [And] the skills required for initiating behavior change are usually different from those required for maintaining it" (p. 291).

Geraway writes,

> The decision to draw away from crime and criminals and the prison society was easy to come to; it was logical. Abiding by it, though, would turn out to be the most difficult thing I had ever done, and it would be a process that would last eight years. (p. 24)

Erwin says, "I tried to change. I honestly tried, but it seemed as though years of fighting the world from behind a wall of emotional armor was too much" (p. 64). Brown, too, writes,

> Then, all but overcome with loneliness and nostalgia for my family, I would return for awhile, telling [my wife] I was sorry . . . and declaring, and meaning it, that I was going to do better. I would try, but my efforts were always short-lived. (p. 33)

These plot loops—where narrators know they should have changed their behavior, but instead returned to old ways—often take the form of "foreshadowing" in the autobiographies. Braly, for instance, writes,

> Still I recall a moment late one night in the back alleys of
> Sacramento . . . and the same quiet voice, which had for-
> merly urged me to join the Navy, whispered: If you keep this
> up you'll find yourself in San Quentin. I realized a moment
> of despair because I knew I had just told myself the obvious
> truth. Perhaps the mad have similar moments of such clarity,
> when the hard truth of their life is briefly apparent, and then
> they, as I did, drown again in fantasy. (p. 65)

Almost 150 pages later in the story, Braly is lying in a bed in San
Quentin, and he recalls this brief interruption of his earlier life
(p. 211). Similarly, after watching one of his best friends die in gang
violence, Duke remembers an older gang member telling him to "take
a tip from an old timer and get the hell out of here as fast and as
far as you can" (p. 23). Although he vividly recounted the incident,
Duke became something of an old-timer himself before heeding this
warning.

Frequently, recidivism is blamed on structural forces outside of the
individual's control. The narrators insist that they "knew better," but
something outside of their control kept pushing them back into
criminal behavior. The most common roadblock to reform involves
those who want to go straight but cannot achieve the type of agency
and communion they became used to in delinquent subcultures. For
instance, after serving 3½ years in a Salem prison for his work with
a narcotics syndicate, King got married and tried to change his life for
good. "I tried to settle down there but it was awfully hard. I was having an awful time of it. Consequently, I got myself in bad debts. The
baby came and . . . I was so far in debt it was pathetic." Within half a
page, King is back in Seattle breaking into a drugstore. Torok summa-
rizes the problems ex-convicts face upon release. "With fifty dollars
in his pocket, he must find a place to live, pay for his food, and try to
keep himself solvent until he gets a job. . . . It is simply unrealistic"
(pp. 23-24).

Many narrators complain that they would not settle for the low-
wage, dead-end jobs for which they were qualified. Brown writes,
"The prospect of some menial laborer's work didn't choke me up very
much. The [jobs] I might be able to get excited about were out of my

class because of my lack of formal preparation" (p. 107). After spending 8 years behind bars, Murphy writes, "I was on my own now and it was up to me to prove to everyone that I was capable of living a decent, normal life. But I would first have to find a job" (p. 135). Two pages later, he writes, " 'Good, hell,' I said. 'I'm just a cook in a hospital and the pay is lousy, but I can't do any better because I don't have any references' " (p. 137), and he returned to criminal behavior.

Several narrators say they used to adhere to an ethos that tightly links money and respectability. Braly, for instance, writes,

> When the Cynic warned me not to try to play catch up, he was aware I would find myself far behind my contemporaries, my doubles, who had spent the last 6 years learning and earning. There was no easy way back, and it could be said I had never been there. The life I saw reflected from the advertising everywhere around me was a life I could see no way to obtain. I wanted things. I wanted clothes, a car, a hi fi, I wanted my share of that river of products Americans had begun to produce. We judged each other by these things.
> (p. 207)

Likewise, after his release from prison, McGregor says, "I recited a whole list of resolutions. . . . I promise to get married and raise a family. I promise to get a square job and stay out of trouble. Promises I had made a million times before" (p. 94). By the next page, however, McGregor says,

> [Then] the street dude in me . . . perked up and laid some heavy shit on me, "Nigger, if you squaring up, you better find yourself some rich broad to lay up with, 'cause you ain't gonna make it by your lonesome. That job the parole officer has lined up for you only pays chump change. How you gonna get sharp with no money to spend? . . . Without money, you're nobody." (p. 95)

Finally, the narrators frequently say they were shunned and stigmatized by the community to which they tried to return. Howard, for instance, says that she would not have returned to the gang if only she had been "trusted enough to have been given honest work, and if friendly hearts had opened up to help and encourage" her (p. 224). As in all plot loops, the narrator returns to "old ways" only to "crash" again later.

The Quantum Change

Eventually, these plot loops are broken, and the reform narrative moves linearly to a new stage of development. The nuclear episodes that "cause" this change appear to be largely the same as earlier internal conflicts and crises that led only to stunted efforts to reform. In fact, the events that led to this change in the story—usually going to jail or church—are not uncommon events throughout the narratives. Nonetheless, "something about" this one incident makes the experience subjectively different, according to the narrators.

The transformational nuclear episodes in the sample resemble what Miller and C'deBaca (1994) refer to as a *quantum change*, where whole sets of attitudes can supposedly be called into question, leading to complete reversals in behavior. William James (1902/1985) also discusses these sudden and profound changes, which he regards as qualitatively different from ordinary and gradual personality change. Rather than describing their desistance from crime as a gradual process, most of the narratives in this sample impart considerable significance to the moment of "the change." Vaus and Coss, for instance, both cite the exact time and place of their "conversions." Others magnify the importance of the crisis that led to their decision compared to the events that sparked past, aborted efforts to go straight.

The impetus for the change, like other events in the person's life, is almost always attributed to forces outside of the narrator's locus of control. In almost every narrative, the transformational experience was something that happened to the narrator, rather than something the narrator brought upon him- or herself. Bill Wilson, the cofounder of Alcoholics Anonymous, describes the turning point away from his alcoholism as being catapulted into a new spiritual realm (Miller & C'deBaca, 1994). Likewise, Coss writes, "At that very moment, the

Holy Spirit penetrated my hard shell of bitterness and melted my pride" (p. 73).

Following their change experience, offenders seem to recast their lives as being "planned" or orchestrated by a higher power for a certain purpose. Geraway writes, "All of the times I have lived when I should have died were not accidental; they were part of a design that God has set aside for me as one of his children" (p. 280). Vaus similarly says, "One of my first lessons was to be grateful, to know I wasn't the one in control" (p. 58). By pushing the responsibility for reform onto some power other than the self, the narratives maintain a sense of consistency and believability. Early criminal involvement, after all, is almost always characterized as the result of structural and environmental forces beyond the narrators' control, as well. Several other empirical studies have supported Sykes and Matza's (1957) hypothesis that offenders tend to appeal to an external locus of control when explaining their own behavior (Schonbach, 1990). A similar story seems to be told about reform.

After frequent attempts and failures to change their behavior on their own, many narrators may lose confidence in their own ability to control their own destinies. Explaining reform by pointing to outside influences might therefore be the only internally credible narrative strategy. Moreover, making reform a religious experience endows the process with larger-than-life importance. A story such as, "I am a changed person because I decided I wanted to change," may not be nearly as convincing as a story that suggests, "God has turned me into a new person." Again, this may only be an artifact of this sample; explicitly religious recovery stories may be the most marketable types of recovery stories. Yet, if this is so, it may also indicate what types of quantum changes Western audiences find the most believable.

Redemption: Agency and Communion in Reform

The critical difference between a true turning point episode and an earlier foreshadowing episode, however, is not to be found within the experience itself. Rather, it seems to be more connected to the perceived possibilities for identity change in the life circumstances and situations narrators face following the turning point episode. In other words, even though the narrators "see the light" during an alleyway shootout some Friday night, they might ignore the sign if they do not perceive any structural opportunities to achieve the sort of agency and communion they could obtain through criminal behavior.

One of the key elements of all the successful reform stories was the existence of intimate or valued connections *outside* of criminal subcultures and prison society. These individuals provide both a means of emotional support and an incentive to stay out of prison. In this sample, these friendships are frequently made through reform institutions and religious organizations. McGregor says that his therapy group became "the family I never had" (p. 473). Likewise, in regard to the religious organization he joined after going straight, Howland states, "I had found companionship and human beings I could trust."

Moreover, almost all of the narrators describe finding (or being handed) an opportunity to achieve power and respect outside of a criminal subculture. A criminal lifestyle can be both exciting and empowering (Katz, 1988). Many ex-offenders suggest that they seek similar fulfillment from their straight life. Hyatt says professional criminals are "as unhappy in other vocations as Michelangelo would have been digging ditches." He says "at heart he always has a love of the excitement and adventure of the game" (p. 221). Seeking power, prestige, and adventure, for instance, Baker volunteered for the infantry during wartime following his release from prison. "I was determined to get into the most dangerous part of the armed forces, the paratroopers." Moreover, King speaks eloquently about the need for ex-convicts to find a way to get their "self-respect" back. "He'll go straight a heck of a lot quicker if he knows that he's going to a job he understands . . . and a job that he likes" (p. 120). Those who reform, and stay reformed, seem to find ways to achieve self-respect and find adventure in contexts other than crime.

Because most ex-convicts have limited resources, few job skills, and few connections in the straight world, this empowerment is often achieved by using their status as reformed ex-convicts. Many find that social work is the only field for which their talents are well-suited. "I knew the language. I felt I understood the men, and they understood me," Erwin writes (p. 95). Like several of the other authors, Vaus capitalizes on his prison experiences to become a successful evangelist.

> The daily invitations for me to speak at churches, clubs, schools, and independent organizations became a frame for our future. Interest snowballed. Requests for me to talk about my conversion trickled in at first, then . . . turned into my new full-time job. (p. 59)

Narrators find a *new* way to achieve considerable agency and prestige and avoid the dangers of a criminal lifestyle.

These transformations from victim, to delinquent, to prisoner, to respected community reformer seem far-fetched, yet they flow almost naturally from these narratives as they are told. The idea of "hitting rock bottom," then rebounding "straight to the top," is a common element in Western fiction and mythology (Denzin, 1989). McAdams et al. (in press) call this the theme of *redemption*, where good consequences seem to result almost directly from negative circumstances. Erwin, for instance, writes, "I know now at least that my own pushed-around childhood has contributed directly to my work as a chaplain" (p. 43). The narrators have discovered a way to find "something positive" to build on from their otherwise negative pasts. They have found a way to change their behavior and still maintain a consistent internal narrative.

Generativity Scripts

Finally, almost all of the narrators emphasize the desire to "give something back" to others who may not have been as fortunate as they were. Just as earlier in their autobiographies, narrators justified criminal involvement by appealing to childhood victimization, the authors explain this new transition as a sort of "thank you" to the world for giving them a second chance to succeed. Howland writes, "God had touched me with a 'power from on high' and . . . He was going to expect me to put that power to use" (p. 101). Frequently, the recipient of this care is young people who are in situations similar to those the narrator experienced as a youth. Coss says, "Because of my past life and conversion, I have a special burden in my heart for prison inmates" (p. 118). Murphy writes,

> I was confident my own life was ruined beyond repair, but I found I could derive a certain vicarious satisfaction by becoming concerned with the future of the younger inmates—kids who had gotten into trouble once or twice, but who still had a useful life ahead of them if they could be straightened out in time. (p. 268)

Finally, Torok says, "I feel now that I can suffer personally the tragedies of other human beings, having myself touched bottom" (p. 50).

McAdams (1993) refers to this theme as a *generativity script*, whereby individuals begin to develop plans for what they hope to do in the future to leave a symbolic gift for subsequent generations. This "legacy of the self" can involve a desire for "symbolic immortality" and/or a "need to be needed" (McAdams, Hart, & Maruna, forthcoming; Stewart, Franz, & Layton, 1988). McGregor, for instance, writes, "It's taken me twenty-seven years of jailin' to learn that *I am needed* to do more than fill a shitbowl in some damn institution" (p. 368). Brown writes,

> Daily I look into the upturned, eager faces of youth filled with potential. . . . I also know that one bald-headed old ex-con is not going to convert the world, but I humbly thank God that it is the kind of world where one man *can make a big contribution—that I can be a part of molding plastic, young life.* (p. 146)

Connected to this development of generative motives is the notion of becoming a completely "new person." For most of the stories in this study, going straight is an "all or nothing" proposition, a complete shift in identity. McGregor writes,

> The pain of change is enormous. It must be similar to what a woman feels like when the seed of life is sprouting inside of her. When I became pregnant with new life, the new me took root in my belly and sucked up everything that was nutritious inside of me. . . . I went into labor and gave birth to him so my pain would be over. (p. 394)

Like Saul in the Bible, many of the narrators are even called by a different name following their conversion, as if to solidify the magnitude of the identity change. McGregor, for instance, asked his friends to stop calling him by his gang nickname, Peewee, and to refer to him by his given name. Similarly, Erwin says, "Someone . . . long ago had tagged me 'Little John.' Now they gave me a new name, 'John the Baptist' " (p. 85).

The old life, although integrated into each person's understanding of him or herself, is widely viewed as an altogether different world, never to be entered again. Coss writes, "My sins were not only forgiven, they were forgotten. As far as the east is from the west, that far has God removed our transgressions from us" (p. 123). Braly concludes his autobiography by saying, "That happened eight years ago. . . . It seems long ago, in another lifetime" (p. 375).

As if to guarantee that there is "no going back this time," many of the ex-offenders in this sample loudly advertise their new generative identity. Like the boy who cried wolf, people can only announce being "reborn" so many times in life, before those around them become a little skeptical. It is possible that the more widely and emphatically people announce their new identity, the more incentive they will have to maintain that new version of themselves. This advertising of the new identity takes several different forms in the sample. Vaus and McGregor discuss their desire to tell their reform stories to local journalists. The public ceremony of an adult baptism symbolized and helped maintain a reborn identity for Howard, Erwin, and several others in the sample. Finally, several narrators suggest that the very act of constructing an autobiography is, in a strong sense, a public securing of one's new "self."

This advertising also plays a generative role in the narrators' lives. Many authors suggest that they are publishing their autobiographies to leave a lesson for younger generations, so they do not have to repeat the mistakes the narrators made. McGregor concludes his autobiography by saying, "I hope that some of the young people who read this book will learn from what they read about me" (p. 486). Torok says, "My burning hope for the remainder of my life will be to share my criminal and prison experiences with young people everywhere in the hope that they can get some insights into their own feelings" (p. 27).

Conclusions

In his 1925 dissertation, *Autobiographical Documents and Personality*, Ernest Kreuger suggests that the construction of one's own autobiography should be seen as an important behavior—an activity to be studied in and of itself (cited in Bennett, 1981, p. 185). In this sample it seems that autobiography construction itself may be an important element of sustaining significant behavioral reform. At least, the findings of this study are consistent with the idea that the development of a coherent story that can integrate past faults into a generative script for the future may contribute to the process of desistance from crime. The reform story outlined in this chapter appears to be one effective version of this narrative.

Like Alcoholics Anonymous members, all of the narrators in the sample have come to terms with their past. They openly acknowledge their past mistakes and claim to view their lives from a new vantage point. These reevaluations of the past often involve cognitive reappraisals of past identities as well. For instance, Braly says that he *was* (in past tense) "a liar, a sneak, a braggart, a show-off, and a thief" and that he "was unable to grasp or calculate consequences" (p. 4). Geraway writes, "For my own part, I had been as much a part of the sickness as the others" (p. 23).

According to Brewin (1982), self-blame can be both positive and negative. If a person dwells upon a more or less permanent fault ("I'm just stupid"), then self-blame is maladaptive. Yet, taking responsibility for past behavior ("I did a very stupid thing") may be adaptive. Most of the ex-offenders in this sample suggest instead, "I used to do stupid

things," but now "I have been changed." Specifically, the narrators
view their past criminal behavior as a reaction to powerlessness and a
lack of opportunities, and they similarly credit their reformed identities to external empowerment and outside opportunities for success.

These findings may have practical implications for offender reintegration and rehabilitation policy (see Maruna, 1995b). Moreover,
this saturation of themes in reform stories provides evidence in
support of a new understanding of the desistance process beyond
simple maturational reform or burning out. Although turning 30 was
an important event for Charlie McGregor, for instance, his desistance
from crime probably had more to do with the development of a new
identity and self-understanding than it did with his biological age.
Additional narrative research should seek to further develop this
understanding of the reform narrative and reformed identity.

Note

1. The 20 published autobiographies, written by successfully reintegrated ex-
convicts, that are the subject of this chapter's analysis are listed in Table 4.1 and not
included with the more traditional references. For economy, citations include only the
author's name and page numbers for any quotations. The years of publication are available, along with other information, in Table 4.1.

References

Adler, A. (1927). *The practice and theory of individual psychology*. New York: Harcourt
& Brace.
Allport, G. W. (1937). *Personality: A psychological interpretation*. New York: Holt,
Rinehart & Winston.
American Psychiatric Association. (1994). *Diagnostic and statistical manual of mental
disorders* (4th ed.). Washington, DC: Author.
Bakan, D. (1966). *The duality of human existence: Isolation and communion in Western
man*. Boston: Beacon.
Bakan, D. (1996). Some reflections about narrative research and hurt and harm. In
R. Josselson (Ed.), *The narrative study of lives* (Vol. 4, pp. 3-8). Thousand Oaks,
CA: Sage.
Bennett, J. (1981). *Oral history and delinquency*. Chicago: University of Chicago Press.
Bertaux, D. (Ed.). (1981). *Biography and society: The life-history approach in the social
sciences*. Beverly Hills, CA: Sage.
Blumstein, A., & Cohen, J. (1987). Characterizing criminal careers. *Science, 237*,
985-991.

Brewin, C. (1982). Adaptive aspects of self-blame in coping with accidental injury. In C. Brewin & C. Antaki (Eds.), *Attributions and psychological change*. London: Academic Press.

Briscoe, M. L. (1982). *A bibliography of American autobiography, 1945-1980*. Madison: University of Wisconsin Press.

Brown, W., & Miller, T. M. (1988). Following up previously adjudicated delinquents: A method. In R. L. Jenkins & W. K. Brown (Eds.), *The abandonment of delinquent behavior: Promoting the turnaround*. New York: Praeger.

Brown, W. K. (1988). The post-intervention experience: A self-report examination of deviancy devolution. In R. L. Jenkins & W. K. Brown (Eds.), *The abandonment of delinquent behavior: Promoting the turnaround*. New York: Praeger.

Canter, D. (1994). *Criminal shadows*. London: Harper Collins.

Currie, E. (1993). Shifting the balance: On social action and the future of criminological research. *Journal of Research in Crime and Delinquency, 30*(4), 426-444.

Denzin, N. (1987). *The recovering alcoholic*. Newbury Park, CA: Sage.

Denzin, N. (1989). *Interpretive biography*. Newbury Park, CA: Sage.

Durkheim, E. (1972). *Selected writings* (A. Giddens, ed.). New York: Cambridge University Press.

Earls, F., Cairns, R. B., & Mercy, J. A. (1993). The control of violence and the prevention of nonviolence in adolescents. In *Promoting the health of adolescents: New directions for the 21st century*. New York: Oxford University Press.

Erikson, E. (1959). *Identity and the life cycle*. New York: Norton.

Farrington, D. F. (1986). Age and crime. In N. Morris & M. Tonry (Eds.), *Crime and justice* (Vol. 7, pp. 189-250). Chicago: University of Chicago Press.

Finestone, H. (1976). *Victims of change: Juvenile delinquents in American society*. Westport, CT: Greenwood Press.

Giddens, A. (1991). *Modernity and self-identity: Self and society in the late modern age*. Stanford, CA: Stanford University Press.

Glueck, S., & Glueck, E. (1940). *Juvenile delinquents grown up*. New York: Commonwealth Fund.

Goffman, E. (1961). *Asylums*. Garden City, NY: Anchor Books.

Gottfredson, M., & Hirschi, T. (1990). *A general theory of crime*. Stanford, CA: Stanford University Press.

Gottfredson, M., & Hirschi, T. (1995). National crime control policies. *Society, 32*(2), 30-36.

Greenberg, D. F. (1981). Delinquency and the age structure of society. In D. F. Greenberg (Ed.), *Crime and capitalism: Readings in Marxist criminology*. Palo Alto, CA: Mayfield.

Groves, W. B., & Sampson, R. J. (1986). Critical theory and criminology. *Social Problems, 33*(6), S58-S80.

Hankiss, A. (1981). On the mythological rearranging of one's life history. In D. Bertaux (Ed.), *Biography and society: The life-history approach in the social sciences*. Beverly Hills, CA: Sage.

Hartung, F. E. (1965). A vocabulary of motives for law violations. In F. E. Hartung (Ed.), *Crime, law, and society*. Detroit: Wayne State University.

Hugo, V. (1963). *Les miserables*. Paris: Garnier Freres. (Original work published 1862)

James, W. (1985). *The varieties of religious experience: A study in human nature.* Cambridge, MA: Harvard University Press. (Original work published 1902)

Jolin, A. (1985). *Growing old and going straight: Examining the role of age in criminal career termination.* Unpublished dissertation, Portland State University, Department of Urban Studies.

Josselson, R. (1996). On writing other people's lives: Self-analytic reflections of a narrative researcher. In R. Josselson (Ed.), *The narrative study of lives* (pp. 60-71). Newbury Park, CA: Sage.

Kaplan, H. B. (1980). *Deviant behavior in defense of self.* New York: Academic Press.

Katz, J. (1988). *Seductions of crime: The moral and sensual attractions of doing evil.* New York: Basic Books.

Leps, M.-C. (1992). *Apprehending the criminal: The production of deviance in 19th-century discourse.* Durham, NC: Duke University Press.

Lewis, D. A., & Maruna, S. A. (1995, October). *Putting the person in policy analysis.* Paper presented at the Association for Public Policy Analysis and Management conference, Washington, DC.

Loder, J. E. (1981). *The transforming moment: Understanding convictional experiences.* New York: Harper & Row.

Maruna, S. (1995a, November). *Criminology, desistance, and the psychology of the stranger.* Paper presented at the American Society of Criminology Conference, Boston, MA.

Maruna, S. (1995b). *New directions in offender reintegration policy.* Unpublished paper, available upon request from the author.

Matza, D. (1964). *Delinquency and drift.* New York: John Wiley.

McAdams, D. P. (1985). *Power, intimacy, and the life story: Personological inquiries into identity.* New York: Guilford.

McAdams, D. P. (1993). *The stories we live by: Personal myths and the making of the self.* New York: Willam Morrow.

McAdams, D. P. (1994a). Can personality change? Levels of stability and growth in personality across the life span. In T. F. Heatherton & J. L. Weinberger (Eds.), *Can personality change?* Washington, DC: American Psychological Association.

McAdams, D. P. (1994b). *The person: An introduction to personality psychology.* Fort Worth, TX: Harcourt Brace & Company.

McAdams, D. P., Diamond, A., de St. Aubin, E., & Mansfield, E. (in press). Stories of commitment: The psychosocial construction of generative lives. *Journal of Personality and Social Psychology.*

McAdams, D. P., Hart, H., & Maruna, S. (forthcoming). The anatomy of generativity. In D. P. McAdams & E. de St. Aubin (Eds.), *Generativity and adult development: Psychosocial perspectives on caring for and contributing to the next generation* Washington, DC: American Psychological Association.

McAdams, D. P., Hoffman, B. J., Mansfield, E. D., & Day, R. (1996). Themes of agency and communion in significant autobiographical scenes. *Journal of Personality, 64,* 339-377.

Miller, W. R., & C'deBaca, J. (1994). Quantum change: Toward a psychology of transformation. In T. F. Heatherton & J. L. Weinberger (Eds .), *Can personality change?* Washington, DC: American Psychological Association.

Moffitt, T. E. (1993). Adolescence-limited and life-course-persistent antisocial behavior: A developmental taxonomy. *Psychological Review, 100*(4), 674-701.

Mulvey, E. P., & LaRosa, J. F. (1986). Delinquency cessation and adolescent development: Primary data. *American Journal of Orthopsychiatry, 56*(2), 212-224.

Murray, H. (1938). *Explorations in personality.* New York: Oxford University Press.

Neugarten, B. L., & Neugarten, D. A. (1986). Changing meanings of age in the aging society. In A. Pifer & L. Bronte (Eds.), *Our aging society.* New York: Norton.

Quetelet, A. (1833). *Recherches sur le penchant au crime aux differents ages.* Belgium: Hayez.

Rand, A. (1987). Transitional life events and desistance from delinquency and crime. In M. Wolfgang, T. Thornberry, & R. Figlio (Eds.), *From boy to man: From delinquency to crime.* Chicago: University of Chicago Press.

Rouse, J. (1978). *The completed gesture: Myth, character, and education.* New Jersey: Skyline Books.

Rutter, M. (1989). Age as an ambiguous variable in developmental research: Some epidemiological considerations from developmental psychopathology. *International Journal of Behavioral Development, 12,* 1-134.

Sampson, R. J., & Laub, J. (1992). Crime and deviance in the life course. *Annual Review of Sociology, 18,* 63-84.

Sampson, R. J., & Laub, J. (1994). A life-course theory of cumulative disadvantage and the stability of delinquency. In T. P. Thornberry (Ed.), *Developmental theories of crime and delinquency: Advances in criminological theory* (Vol. 6). New Brunswick, NJ: Transaction.

Schonbach, P. (1990). *Account episodes: The management or escalation of conflict.* Cambridge: Cambridge University Press.

Scott, M. B., & Lyman, S. M. (1968). Accounts. *American Sociological Review, 33*(1), 46-61.

Shaw, C. (1929). *Delinquency areas.* Chicago: University of Chicago Press.

Shorr, J. (1977). *To see the movie in your head.* New York: Popular Library.

Shover, N. (1985). *Aging criminals.* Beverly Hills, CA: Sage.

Stewart, A. J., Franz, C., & Layton, L. (1988). The changing self: Using personal documents to study lives. *Journal of Personality, 56,* 41-74.

Sutherland, E. (1932). Review of *The Natural History of a Delinquent Career. American Journal of Sociology, 38,* 136.

Sutton, J. R. (1994). Children in the therapeutic state: Lessons for the sociology of deviance and social control. In G. S. Bridges & M. A. Myers (Eds.), *Inequality, crime, and social control.* Boulder, CO: Westview.

Sykes, G. M., & Matza, D. (1957). Techniques of neutralization: A theory of delinquency. *American Sociological Review, 22,* 664-673.

Thomas, J. (1983). Book reviews. *American Journal of Sociology, 89*(3), 770-772.

Thomas, W. I., & Thomas, D. S. (1928). *The child in America: Behavior problems and programs.* New York: Knopf.

Toch, H. (1987). Supplementing the positivist approach. In M. Gottfredson & T. Hirschi (Eds.), *Positive criminology.* Newbury Park, CA: Sage.

Trasler, G. (1979). Delinquency, recidivism, and desistance. *British Journal of Criminology, 19,* 314-322.

Wilson, J. Q., & Herrnstein, R. J. (1985). *Crime and human nature.* New York: Touchstone Books.

Wooton, B. (1959). *Social science and social pathology.* London: George Allen and Unwin.

X, Malcolm, with the assistance of Haley, A. (1965). *The autobiography of Malcolm X.* New York: Grove.

❧ 5 ❧

Soldiers' Narratives of Selective Moral Resistance

A Separate Position of the Connected Self?

Ruth Linn

The heart has its reasons, which reason does not know.

—Blaise Pascal

𝒯o fight for one's own democratic state is one of the most serious moral obligations that citizenship is said to entail: "A man has enormous debts to his native land and to his polity;" he receives from both of them not only "physical security but also moral identity" (Walzer, 1970, p. 112). Yet, "the [occasional] need to kill is surely the most awful of the burdens" (p. 121). In some cases, this need may clash with the individual's conscience. Yet only a few may dare to translate their decision to resist into a (deliberately) public, individualistic, and detached position of moral disobedience to the law of war (Cohen, 1971). The primary aim of such resistance is to describe (to oneself and to others) what is wrong in a way that suggests a remedy (Walzer, 1988). The moral resister, says Cohen (1971) "is motivated not merely

by the desire to achieve some social good but [also by] the intense wish
to eliminate some serious social evil" (p. 12).[1] The protester does what
he does in the honest belief that he is (morally) right, even though
disobedience against the law is illegal. Yet,

> a man's belief about the moral character of his own act is
> surely not the only court before which that act may be
> judged. But a reflective conscience is one court, and a very
> important one. Doing what one honestly thinks one is obli-
> gated to do is not a sufficient condition of a morally honor-
> able act, but is a necessary condition of such moral honor.
> (Cohen, 1971, p. 21)

This chapter aims to try and understand this narrative of declared
honesty in the service of resistance.

Moral resistance in the form of disobedience can be shown in two
very different and distinct ways. The first is evinced by the *absolutist*,
who objects not only to war but also to serving in the armed forces
under any circumstances. The second is evinced by the *selective
refuser*, who is willing to serve in the armed forces and advocates
qualified use of power. Yet, he claims the right to judge his obligation
to take part in each military conflict and each mission. This form of
lawbreaking is recognized as a nonviolent public declaration of the
individual's moral conviction (Rawls, 1971).

This rather unpredictable form of selective moral resistance is
likely to evoke a legitimate suspicion in the resisters' immediate social
circle and society at large: What right do these resisters have to claim
moral superiority? How loyal are these critics of the society in which
they want to go on living if they are willing to let others sacrifice their
lives for them? Is it possible that they are simply cowards hiding behind
moral principles? How sincere is their moral struggle?

Selective moral resistance, known as a *cry of conscience* (Cohen,
1971), is a form of separation from the community through "moral
selfishness," which is sometimes "the only resort of the principled but
lonely man" (Walzer, 1968, p. 14). It is not detached from moral
narrative: The resister has to (and actually wants to) present and

defend his "moral selfishness" (Walzer, 1970), and explain why he is not only disobeying the law but also forcing other people around him to carry the burden of his conscience (Linn & Gilligan, 1990). The public, even though hostile, is eager and willing to hear his explanation (Walzer, 1988). Even if isolated, this action is wrong primarily because every citizen has more than a legal obligation to obey the law. This wrongness is salient particularly in a democracy, where citizens have the right to participate in making the laws of their own community.

The selective refuser is obliged to explain to the hostile public why and how he came to the decision to assume an unconventional and deviant moral position of resistance at a most critical time for the community (i.e., wartime). Moreover, because selective disobedience may incur legal punishment, financial losses, and some form of personal humiliation (sometimes all three), it is in the refuser's interest to explain to the public the social evil that he is acting against, and why he could not resort to less extreme measures. Moreover, because it is not an accidental act, and because the refuser is aware of the consequences of his act for himself and others, he is prepared to carry the burden of proof and tell his story to whomever wishes to hear it. The subject is well-prepared to elaborate on those other moral components in the situation that forced him to refuse.

A full understanding of selective moral resistance in the form of disobedience requires an appreciation of the narrative of the refuser. Such an appreciation of narrative is still missing in the literature. In order to judge the moral resister, we must go beyond the analysis of the objectively performed act and inquire into the subjective and hence murky sphere of his character and aims. Above all, we must try and understand the paradox of moral connection that seems to constitute the very nature of resistance in a form of moral separation from the community. This paradox lies in our assumption that moral resistance is primarily "a way of relating to other people" (Walzer, 1988, p. x). If this is so, how might one relate oneself to other people when placing oneself, deliberately and publicly, *outside* the community and its critical physical and moral efforts in the very hard days of war? How do we detect this paradox in the narrative of the resister, of which we know very little?

The present chapter is a pioneering attempt to portray the narrative of moral resistance, based on a series of studies of Israeli moral resisters during the Lebanese war (1982-1985) and the Intifada (1987-1994). These resisters are only males (because female soldiers are not sent to the battlefield, nor are they required to do long-term reserve service following their discharge from their obligatory service from ages 18 to 20).[2] In each of these two recent morally controversial military conflicts, more than 165 reserve soldiers disobeyed the command to join their units for their assigned mission. They argued that service in the these specific conflict zones would contradict their moral convictions. Because Israel has no legal status for selective refusers, these reservists later underwent court-martial for offenses of discipline (refusing the command to join their unit in its assigned mission) and were sentenced to 14 to 35 days in military prison; some were imprisoned more than once when refusing additional drafts. Following the war in Lebanon, the press was quick to declare that soldiers' individual moral resistance was a new phenomenon in Israeli society. The refusing soldiers were named *sarvanim* (refusers). This epithet emphasizes that the refusers were not fulfilling their obligation without any reference to the possible moral concerns they might have held. In spite of the growing public controversy over each conflict, the sarvanim were condemned almost unanimously as leftists, delinquents, and law breakers and were seen as undermining democracy.

Studies based on open-ended interviews after their release from prison, with 36 soldiers who resisted duty in the Lebanese War and 48 soldiers who refused duty during the Intifada, revealed that the average resister was a college graduate in his thirties, married, and a father (Linn, 1996). The data suggest that Israeli moral resisters were selective: They had participated in previous military missions and selectively refused to serve a particular tour of reserve duty in the war zone, usually after having performed one such tour in the area. In most cases, the selective refuser admitted that he was the only refuser in his specific unit to refuse. Moreover, in spite of their individualistic detachment from the unit, most refusers sought to return to their own core unit on release from prison and to remain part of the group (Linn, 1989, 1996).

Trained as a Kohlbergian interviewer, I originally intended to score, rank, and evaluate the resisters' claims for moral maturity, consistency, and integrity (Linn, 1996). Yet many of the responses given to me in the Kohlbergian semistructured interviews were in narrative form (Mishler, 1986). Large sections of this narrative were not scorable: I could hear many voices (Mair, 1988), moral emotions (Solomon, 1991), and the voice of care as well as the voice of justice (Linn & Gilligan, 1990).

It was not only the hostile reaction of the Israeli public that made my research on the refusers a scientific and personal challenge. Given the soldiers' anxiety in face of a collapse of values (May, 1979), the narrative itself became a "place of battle" (Mair, 1988). Listening to the stories was once again a reminder that "man does not simply 'stand outside' in his subjectivity, like a critic in the theatre, and look at the necessity and decide what he is thinking of it" (May, 1969, p. 261); he seems to try and find his way into the shared story of his time without which he will (physically or spiritually) die (Mair, 1988).

Because moral resistance entails a new way of presentation in public (Goffman, 1959), each of the refusers was eager to present his new moral identity in a narrative form: "One's self-identity is the story one tells one's self of who one is" (Laing, 1969, p. 93). Yet, due to the hostile atmosphere, access to these stories was not simple, and many of the interviewees were sure I was a secret service investigator using the academic research as a cover-up. Paradoxically, the most convincing argument on my part was presentation of myself as belonging to the other side of the dilemma—being married to a reservist who served in the war zone in spite of his moral dilemmas—as well as my desire to get familiar with other types of soldiers and moral resolutions. Unlike many psychological researchers, I did not have to hide the exact nature of my study, my interest in moral dilemmas. On the contrary, this line of research was quite appealing to many of the resisters, who were actually looking for the opportunity to present a renewed model of their moral self.

With the exception of one interviewee who criticized me for not joining the resistance movement and for spending my life in the academic sphere, all the men thanked me for giving them the opportunity to narrate their resistance story. By telling their story, they seemed to gain some form of moral harmony: "It was like a visit with a psychiatrist," said one, whereas another declared that "only after telling you my story do I know why I did it and who I am."

Using Kohlberg's (1984) theory and methodology provided me with some partial clues regarding the refusers' claim for moral maturity. The refusers succeeded in maintaining their moral thinking across situations. This success stood in contradiction to Kohlberg's theory, which suggests that only a few highly moral thinkers (those who achieve the highest form of moral judgment) may be able to manifest some form of moral consistency because they are not susceptible to situational and personal influence on their action.

Yet, "wrong acts," says Cohen (1971), "are often done by good men, and that man is governed, genuinely and deeply, by the demands of his conscience is one factor (but not the only one) that we properly weigh in judging his goodness" (p. 212). Altogether, the position of moral resistance also demanded an understanding of the resisters' credibility as they were individually willing to "pay" and suffer for their deviant (yet just) decision.

Four concerns—conscience, individualism, credibility, and distance— seem to play a central role in the difficult and complicated way in which resistance is decided upon. These are also some of the major concerns of the public who come to judge the resister. As has been noted by Melzer (1975), "the task of clarifying the concept of 'acting conscientiously' is itself very difficult, let alone the task of judging conscientiousness in particular cases—questions to which God alone can know the answer" (p. 174).

Conscience

Conscience is at the heart of moral resistance because it is the incentive as well as the stated reason of the individual resister for performing this deviant act.

The resister's claim of moral maturity and superiority (Linn, 1989) is viewed by leading moral philosophers (Rawls, 1971) and psychologists (Kohlberg, 1984) as a narrative of moral separateness. The separate moral narrator is viewed as a privileged person who has the cognitive competence to take "a point of view distanced from the controversy" (Habermas, 1990, p. 162); he is capable of holding a "decentered understanding of the world in which he lives" (Habermas, 1990, p. 138). He arrives at this disconnected position as a result of reflective equilibrium—his vacillation between his moral judgments and moral principles. This individual has probably realized that war objectives or conduct do not follow moral constraints, and therefore he gives "voice to conscientious and deeply held convictions" (Rawls, 1971, p. 128). Because he is willing to accept the consequences of his actions, he is regarded as a loyal citizen.

Although not claiming to be above the law, the moral resister claims to have the right to disobey in the very special and perhaps agonizing circumstances surrounding a specific war. Thus, he should be able to explain why his action is not contempt for the law, self-ishness, taking the law into his own hands, undermining respect for the law, self-defeating, unjustifiable when lawful channels remain open, or a subversion of the democratic process (Cohen, 1971).

This view of the moral resister as a narrative of moral separateness (Kohlberg, 1984; Rawls, 1971) is relatively uncomplicated. The separate moral resister is an individual who decides to voice his criticism and objection from a stance where the parties who deliberate the position are rational and mutually disinterested and the decision is made without the decider knowing his future in the distribution of mutual talents and abilities.

We propose, however, to view the very same narrative of moral separateness as a narrative of moral connectedness (Linn & Gilligan, 1990; Walzer, 1988). From this perspective, the selective refuser is seen as being tied to the rest of the world not only by principles, but also by moral emotions, moral language, and moral action. He is not only morally committed to principles but also, and primarily, to other men "from whom or with whom the principles have been learned and by whom they are enforced" (Walzer, 1970, p. 5). This commitment emerges from the conviction and understanding that if injustice is done in the resister's name, "or it is done to my people, I must speak out against it. Now criticism follows from connection" (Walzer, 1988, p. 23).

Within this framework of moral connectedness, no one can view the selective resister as simply deciding to detach himself from the controversy (Habermas, 1990, p. 162). The resister is a person who understands that not to participate in a given war might be seen as minimizing one's own danger at the expense of others. Walzer (1977) explains,

> There is a rough solidarity of men facing a common enemy and enduring a common discipline. . . . To disobey is to breach that elemental accord, to claim a moral separateness (or moral superiority), to challenge one's fellows, is perhaps even to intensify the dangers they face. (pp. 315-316)

The following Lebanon refuser exemplifies the view of moral resistance as a narrative of moral connectedness when he explains the following:

> I am close to 40 years old and I have taken part in all the wars in Israel since I was 18 years old. . . . I could easily be transferred to a unit where I could serve in an office and not on the battlefield. . . . I am not going to do so since I feel that it would be an escape to close my eyes and say to myself I'm OK. I got out. . . . This is wrong because in this way I solve my problem and let my friends in the unit do the work. I want to return to my unit upon release from prison since if I continue to serve and remain part of the unit, I buy myself the right to criticize and the right to shout. (Linn, 1989, p. 132)

Individualism

The path toward disobedience is a lonely one. As has been noted by Fromm (1981), "in order to disobey, one must have the courage to be alone" (p. 21). The lonely courage to say no seems to match the resister's Socratic logic, as explained by Arendt (1972):

> These are the rules of conscience, and they are—like those
> Thoreau announced in his essay—entirely negative. They do
> not say what to do; they say what not to do. They do not
> spell out certain principles for taking action; they lay down
> the boundaries no act should transgress. They say: Don't do
> wrong, for then you will have to live together with a wrong-
> doer. (p. 63)

This logic is echoed in the narrative of this refuser: "My decision
to refuse was primarily the decision not to be part of that which is
being done. . . . [Maybe] it is easier not to do wrong than to do right"
(Linn, 1989, p. 50).

The data suggest that individualistic courage seems to have various
origins: Some resisters were new in the unit; others felt ideologically
detached; some were always rebellious in their decision-making process. Some did not know they had this individualistic courage, as this
refuser explains:

> We were facing the Syrians, and I said to myself, "I do not
> know what I am doing here," and I planned that if there was
> a sudden attack, I would crawl out of the side of my tank
> and not take part in the fighting . . . but then I knew that
> if it happened, I would not have the determination to do
> so. . . . The social pressure in war is sometimes irresistible.
> . . . The decision to refuse was my second hard decision.
> The first was my divorce. . . . They were two recent and
> close decisions, and they gave me the feeling that I had the
> inner strength to do what I felt was right . . . even if the rest
> of the world did not share my ideas. (Linn, 1989, p. 57).

Individualistic courage is needed not only for the performance of
the action of disobedience but also to face the public and present one's
own narrative. The resister knows that at some point he may have to
stand alone and defend his personal integrity against his fellow
citizens. "But this is hard to do, and we should not pretend that it is
[morally] easy. Nor ought we make it easy" (Walzer, 1970, p. 130).

It is important that the narrator must be able to convince the
audience that his action is well-considered, that it is reflective thought

about a means and an end; that as a moral decision maker, he has not been socially influenced; and that his actions are not part of a planned rebellion and group pressure but a result of a morally painful individual decision. Paradoxically, even from the connected perspective, the more individualistic the narrative, the less it entails a threat to society.

We will argue that the apparent individualistic and separate form of moral resistance needs to be seen as a moral position from which the resister dares to tell a narrative of moral connection, as has been explained by Walzer (1970): "Socrates is bound because he chose to act like a citizen in a world where citizenship was morally significant" (p. 98). This is well-exemplified in the reasoning of this Intifada resister, who explains,

> I refused to wear the army uniform and therefore I disobeyed. There are many undemocratic actions done by our soldiers in the territories. They are done by private citizens who wear this uniform. If I wear the uniform, it means that I have come to terms with what they are doing, since all that is being done there is being done in my name as long as I remain silent and obey army orders.

Credibility

The resister's argument concerning justice does not guarantee that these principles are honestly held or believed, particularly when his own life is at stake as in a war situation. These principles might be used as an excuse for not doing one's own duty, as a cover for fear, or even for revolutionary goals. These principles may place extra risk, and greater likelihood of casualties, on those who are left in the unit and obliged to carry out the burden of the refuser's conscience. As noted by Cohen (1971), "If in obeying his conscience another man is obliged to do what he believes—in good conscience—to be morally wrong, the genuineness of that conflict must give us a pause" (p. 212). Thus, the justice narrative of the resister calls for examination of its credibility.

Credibility refers to the weight given to admissible testimony. This characteristic is a crucial factor in any decision making regarding a witness's entitlement to belief (Feeney, 1987). It is thus a crucial dimension in the attempt to evaluate the claims and actions of selective conscientious objectors, particularly if we believe that "the principle of respect for persons does not require respect for the insincere conscience" (Childress, 1982, p. 215).

The validation of a deliberate choice to refuse is not only the responsibility of the objector but also the duty of the community/ audience. No psychological researchers seem to address this question in spite of its relevance to the assessment of the resister's intentions regarding the lawbreaking involved. The only psychological insight into this enterprise is found in Walzer's (1977) writings, even though they are geared primarily to the sphere of political philosophy. Walzer suggests that a combatant's credibility be determined in line with the following three questions: How did the refuser reach his decision? How did he honestly confront his obligations? How seriously did he weigh the alternative course of action and consider the consequences for others as well as for himself?

Although they were the only soldiers in their unit to refuse, most of the Israeli selective refusers asked to return to their unit upon their release from prison (Linn, 1989, 1996). This move is another indication that refusal is a sign of attachment rather than separation. Obviously, it is a sign of credibility, as the refuser shows that he is not evading his military obligations, which continue (in Israel) for at least two decades of his life.

The narrative of the credible moral resister is primarily moral— namely, concern for one's own principles—rather than political (Cohen, 1971). An example is given by this Intifada refuser:

> There was no specific reason for [my] refusal—I just felt I should not be able to do it [reserve service in the occupied territories]. . . . To disperse demonstrations of kids and women. . . . Where on the last occasion I had been forced . . . and . . . an old person had been killed. . . . If I decided not to refuse but to fight within the system, there would be two options: not to disperse the demonstrations . . . or to do the job but avoid thinking about it in conscientious terms . . . then I would not be frustrated and be able to do my job. I felt that if I had been a private soldier I would not have re-

fused. . . . A private can always volunteer to guard the back yard or stay in the kitchen, and he can afford not to know the end result of his action in the field. I think that there is a limit to my ability to contribute morally while I am in the field. . . . My refusal is very much a hesitant one.

The political narrative is primarily addressed to the whole community, and structurally it focuses on the act itself (such as disobedience) and emphasizes its effectiveness. This Intifada refuser explains,

I intentionally published my refusal story in the press . . . and therefore I felt much better during this time [prison term, R.L.]. one of the reasons I became politically active in *Yesh Gvul* [the refusers' protest movement] was to help others overcome their hesitations regarding the prison term . . . not to vanish while they are there . . . not to be forgotten . . . my refusal was originally a moral one but I try to make it a political issue for Yesh Gvul.

The narrative takes the form of a moral personal story when the narrator focuses on his personal regard of principles and values that he accepts as governing his conduct. The moral narrative also has political import even though the focus is on the actor rather than on the act, and even though the act itself was not intentionally performed in public.

Within a democratic society, the political narrative elicits more danger and suspicion than the moral narrative. The political narrator carries the message that one who does not refuse is immoral and that all moral people should follow this path. Concerning the moral narrator, as long as he argues that he cannot commit an immoral act, it is sufficient that the audience is convinced of the genuineness of his claims (Gabison, 1986).

Distance

The selective refuser knows that the task of explaining his moral selfishness is not an easy one (Walzer, 1968), and therefore he often chooses to position himself at a critical distance: "a close place to stay in order to be heard by the audience but not too close a position, otherwise he will be engulfed by the audience" (Walzer, 1988, p. 10). This distance does not imply separation because how "would we care about justice if we did not care about people?" (Solomon, 1991, p. 420).

According to Walzer (1988), different critics position themselves differently in relation to their audience; they adopt different linguistic strategies, and they make different claims to authority.

I argue that this linguistic moral and physical distance is very often an identification with the particular that gives the narrator the courage to tell his story: "Disappointment is not enough," says Walzer (1988),

> nor does a disinterested desire for the well-being of human-
> ity seem a sufficient motive. A moral tie of the agents or the
> victims of brutality and indifference is more likely to serve.
> We feel responsible for, we identify with particular men and
> women. (p. 23)

Distance from the audience is an essential part of the resister's criticism. This distanced position is not only physical but moral and intellectual (Walzer, 1988). Moreover, it might even be imaginative, as this Intifada resister says:

> I am the third generation after the Holocaust, but in terms
> of feelings, I feel as though I am the first or second genera-
> tion. It makes me angry that my people, my nation, is put in
> a position where these considerations must be raised.

Sooner or later, the selective refuser knows that the public de-mands the right to hear the resister's story and judge its morality. The greater the sophistication of the narrative, the greater the distance between the resister and his audience. I argue that the resister's narrative, even if voiced from a distance and followed by an action of blunt detachment, is nevertheless a struggle for connectedness, an attempt not to discharge oneself in face of moral conflict with the community. This argument might be regarded by moral psychologists as a problematic one, given the complex relationships between moral judgment and action (Kohlberg, 1984). That is to say, whereas the individual portrays his action of detachment as a form of connection, this verbal form of justification does not necessarily reflect any form of cognitive consistency nor moral integrity (Blasi, 1983). I would argue, however, that this mode of justification might suggest some form of moral sensitivity—meaning, an understanding of the impact of one's action upon other acting individuals in the community, or what I have termed *moral communication* (Linn & Breslerman, 1995), voicing one's own moral concerns (whether justice or care or both) without threatening the moral integrity of the other, the audience. Whereas thoughts about resistance, let alone the construction of the action, are extremely lonely ones, I would like to argue that the resister functions against an existing community: whether it is an imaginary audience of the ideal moral community in which he would wish to live, a concrete and immediate audience to whom he wants to provide justification for his action, or the larger audience to whom he is obliged to do so. I therefore further argue that in the action of resistance, as primarily suggested to the audience via narrative, the moral actor finds himself oscillating between the crucial need for social affiliation, on one hand, and a temporary detachment in times of moral crisis—a move that he desperately needs for the sake of re-connection to the community. An Intifada resister explains,

> I see refusal as my way of not emigrating. In this way, I feel that I am here and whatever I can do to stop the occupation of the Territories I do. This is my involvement with this country. . . . I have an American passport and could leave at any time. . . . My decision, however, is to stay here . . . and resist.

Another refusing Intifada soldier said,

> There are moments when I tell myself that I will emigrate from this country, but on reflection I realize that I have not emigrated. It seems as if there are still more ordeals than I am capable of facing up to.

Both these resisters are trying to relate themselves to the world by moral language, moral action, and moral commitment, and not only to the sphere of moral principles (Walzer, 1988). It is this particular commitment that brought them close to the social injustice and the eventual criticism.

The narrative of the moral resister, then, is not an attempt to match reality to some abstract idea (Kohlberg, 1984; Rawls, 1971). It is rather a story used with the rhetorical language of justice. It seems to be a struggle from within to come to terms with the way the world is and to persuade both ourselves and others to attack this particular injustice and adopt a specific course of action. As noted by Solomon (1991), "our sense of justice is our persuasion to do what we can" (p. 19). Thus, the narrative of the moral resister is more of a narrative of moral emotion than a narrative of moral cognition.

Although it may well be interpreted that the resister is cutting his social and emotional ties to the community, I would argue that the narrative of moral resistance is a narrative of moral emotions and connection (Solomon, 1991), not only one of moral cognition and detachment (Kohlberg, 1984). I would further argue that the narrative of the selective moral resister is a "claim for a particular personal identity," not necessarily a story of "general cultural values" (Mishler, 1986, p.104). In addition, I contend that the apparent individualistic form of moral selfishness and separateness from one's fellows marks a struggle for moral belonging. I maintain that a study of the narrative of the detached moral resister may expand our knowledge of the psychology of moral connectedness. As noted by Walzer (1988), a "complaint is one of the elementary forms of self-assertion, and the response to the complaint is one of the elementary forms of mutual recognition" (p. 3). The resister questions the moral foundations of the military mission. He is sent on this mission by his community. Thus, any questioning regarding the mission, and any moral position assumed, inevitably shows up the moral norms of the people in the community involved. In the words of one resister,

> The army authorities love the absolute resisters—they leave the system and the authorities owe them no response. We,

the selective refusers, are wrecking their easy life—we question the nature of our mission, not because we want to evade it but because we want to understand it. If they do not have an answer for us, this implies that they do not have a moral explanation for their job: What are they doing behind these tables? Under what moral flag do they send others to die?

In various morally ambiguous situations, the moral resister would not ask himself primarily what the moral principles being violated here are (Kohlberg, 1984) but "what is the right way to feel?" This Lebanon refuser said,

> In the case of refusal, you first feel that you have no option but to act in a certain way. It is a very strong feeling and you cannot stay calm unless you do it. Only then does one's moral thought become clear. (Linn, 1989, p. 126)

Following Solomon (1991), I suggest that the moral principles presented in the resister's narrative are primarily a way of participating in the world, a way of being with other people—even if the moral resister is a lonely decision maker. He tells a narrative that is not constructed in a lonely manner but in regard to other people's moral narrative (Walzer, 1988). According to Solomon (1991), we should not search for Socratic insights in the principles of the resister's justice but for his way of promoting some basic emotions among them; a sense of being personally cheated or neglected. "The locus of justice," says Solomon (1991), "is neither the isolated individual nor the fixed and rigid community, but the complex confluence of interrelated and mutually dependent individuals who move in and out of various relationships and communities" (p. 99). Like many other narratives, the narrative of moral resistance "includes a multitude of discourses" and cannot be reduced "to a single voice" (Josselson, 1995, p. 35). It is constructed upon the resister's past discourse as a member of his family and of a given society, a product of its moral education (Walzer, 1983), his present moral distress, and his vision of the ideal moral future where he sees his ideal moral self. In the words of one Intifada resister, " These people are dear to me, and refusing means separating myself from them. . . . I felt that I was removing myself from the womb of Israeli society." Another resister further explained the connected nature of resistance:

> I think that the decision to exclude yourself from the main-stream is very serious . . . you have to be in deep distress to refuse . . . and for those who experience this distress, refusal is inevitable . . . you must realize that the only difference between people involved in the conflict is the depth of the distress, its level of authenticity, and their spiritual independence.

Conclusion

The narrative of the moral resister is constructed by man for himself, as well as for other men; it is only the other men and the resister's connection to them that help him to discover and validate his own inner power to unfold himself (Linn, 1991, 1996). The narrative of moral resistance is thus a narrative of an individual who feels that he must reach outside himself in order to be himself (Moscovici, 1985). It is a narrative of an individual who has experienced a collapse of moral values around him (May, 1979), at the time when the entire system remains silent as if it were not threatened by this collapse. By temporarily leaving the system in search of moral values, the selective moral resister is able to tell himself, without any interruption, his ideal moral narrative. Once equipped with this narrative, he finds the minimal courage needed to face the hostile audience, who are still obsessed with his departure from the community, puzzled about his courage to come back, but far from troubled or intrigued by the violated norms and moral values—which triggered the resister's need to find in himself the individualistic courage to detach himself publicly and deliberately. This process of reaching out and becoming one's own self is a process for and out of moral connection. Without this connection, there is no narrative of separation.

Notes

1. This chapter deals exclusively with male reservists in the Israeli army, and therefore masculine pronouns are used in referring to resisters.

2. In Israel, 18-year-old males and females are obliged to serve in the Israel Defense Forces, males for 3 years and females for 2 years. Only males, following their discharge at age 21, are also required to perform 1 month of reserve service every year until age 45. In times of security crisis, this service may increase in length and pressure.

References

Arendt, H. (1972). *Crisis in the republic.* New York: Harcourt Brace.

Blasi, A. (1983). Moral cognition and moral action: A theoretical perspective. *Developmental Review, 3,* 178-210.

Childress, J. F. (1982). *Moral responsibility in conflict: Essays on nonviolence, war, and conscience.* Baton Rouge: Louisiana State University Press.

Cohen, C. (1971). *Civil disobedience—Conscience, tactics, and the law.* New York: Columbia University Press.

Feeney, T. J. (1987). Expert psychological testimony on credibility issues. *Military Law Review, 115,* 121-177.

Fromm, E. (1981). *On disobedience and other essays.* New York: Harper & Row.

Gabison, R. (1986, April 7). The crime of the blue-white collar. *Politics,* pp. 28-30.

Goffman, E. (1959). *The presentation of self in everyday life.* New York: Doubleday.

Habermas, J. (1990). *Moral consciousness and communicative action.* Cambridge: MIT Press.

Josselson, R. (1995). Imagining the real: Empathy, narrative, and the dialogic self. In R. Josselson & A. Lieblich (Eds.), *Interpreting experience: The narrative study of lives* (pp. 27-44). Thousand Oaks, CA: Sage.

Kohlberg, L. (1984). *The psychology of moral development.* San Francisco: Harper & Row.

Laing, R. D. (1969). *Self and others.* Baltimore: Penguin.

Linn, R. (1989). *Not shooting and not crying: A psychological inquiry into moral disobedience.* Westport, CT: Greenwood.

Linn, R. (1991). Holocaust metaphors and symbols in the moral dilemmas of contemporary Israeli soldiers. *Metaphor and Symbolic Activity, 6*(2), 61-86.

Linn, R. (1996). *Conscience at war: The Israeli soldier as a moral critic.* Albany: State University of New York Press.

Linn, R., & Breslerman, S. (1995). Women in conflict: On the moral knowledge of daughters-in-law and mothers-in-law. *Journal of Moral Education, 25*(3), 291-307.

Linn, R., & Gilligan, C. (1990). One action, two moral orientations: The tension between justice and care voices in Israeli selective conscientious objectors. *New Ideas in Psychology, 8*(2), 189-203.

Mair, M. (1988). Psychology storytelling. *International Journal of Personal Construct Psychology, 1*, 125-137.

May, R. (1969). *Love and will.* New York: Norton.

May, R. (1979). *Psychology and the human dilemma.* New York: Norton.

Melzer, Y. (1975). *Concepts of just war.* Holland: Sijhoff.

Mishler, E. G. (1986). *Research interviewing: Context and narrative.* Cambridge: Harvard University Press.

Moscovici S. (1985). Innovation and minority influence. In S. Moscovici, G. Mugny, & V. Avermaet (Eds.), *Perspectives on minority influence.* Cambridge: Cambridge University Press.

Rawls, J. (1971). A theory of civil disobedience. In P. Harris (Ed.), *Civil disobedience.* Lanham, MD: University Press of America.

Solomon, R. C. (1991). *A passion for justice: Emotions and the origins of the social contract.* New York: Addison-Wesley.

Walzer, M. (1968, January-February). Civil disobedience and resistance. *Dissent*, pp. 13-15.

Walzer, M. (1970). *Obligations: Essays on disobedience, war, and citizenship.* Cambridge: Harvard University Press.

Walzer, M. (1977). *Just and unjust wars.* New York: Basic Books.

Walzer, M. (1983). *Spheres of justice: A defense of pluralism and equality.* New York: Basic Books.

Walzer, M. (1988). *The company of critics.* New York: Basic Books.

❦ 6 ❦

Loneliness in Cultural Context

A Look at the Life-History Narratives of Older Southeast Asian Refugee Women

Jane A. Bennett
Daniel F. Detzner

Since the end of World War II, the number of refugees has continued to swell from more than 2.5 million in 1970 to an estimated 20 million worldwide (Marsella, Borneman, Ekblad, & Orley, 1994). Lost in the magnitude of the numbers are the voices of those whose lives have been uprooted. Their stories reveal the courage of the human spirit and the meaning of homelessness.

During the past two decades alone, more than 1.7 million Southeast Asian refugees have been permanently resettled in the United States, Canada, Australia, France, and China. In the United States, California, Texas, Washington, and Minnesota have become home to a majority of these refugees, most of whom arrived after 1980

AUTHORS' NOTE: Funding for the larger study on Southeast Asian Families with Elders (SAFE) was supported by the Agricultural Experiment Station (MN No. 52668). We are grateful to Harold D. Grotevant and Paul C. Rosenblatt for their suggestions and thoughtful reading of an earlier draft of this chapter.

(Schwartz & Schlader, 1995). The group includes people from diverse cultures: Vietnamese and ethnic Chinese "boat people"; Khmer survivors of the Pol Pot regime in Cambodia; lowland/ethnic Lao and hill tribe Hmong people (exclusively rural farmers who farmed in the mountains of Laos). These refugees came with a more traumatic history and fewer human resources than previous U.S. immigrants. Many were involved in farming and production occupations and had lower levels of education and literacy than earlier migrants (Rumbaut, 1989).

The conditions of their flight parallel those of other refugees. Most left their homelands on short notice with few possessions, seeking safety and refuge from the ravaging effects of war, torture, and starvation. Families were fragmented and scattered with little time to say good-bye. Many ran for months, hiding in thick jungle forests and scavenging for food. Others traveled by boat or handmade bamboo rafts to the Mekong, swimming across the river to Thailand. For some the physical journey took months; for others, it involved multiple relocations extending over many years. Those who survived the journey faced tremendous upheaval and disorganization in their lives.

Having lived most of their lives in a cultural context radically different from the host society, older refugees are among the most vulnerable to difficulties in the resettlement process. Their life experiences, values, religious beliefs, and language are largely unknown to people in the United States. Although smaller in numbers,[1] older refugees have suffered more extensive losses and have fewer opportunities for replacing them than younger refugees. Yet as the oldest living members of their families, their role in the family is important in the acculturation and adjustment of future generations.

Identifying the Research Questions

This investigation emerged from the life-history narratives of 20 refugee women elders, collected as part of a larger study on the family lives of Southeast Asian refugees living in a midwestern urban area (Detzner, 1992a). Reading their narratives left us with a feeling of tremendous sadness at the enormity of loss they suffered. For these refugee elders, forced relocation and resettlement meant losing everything that was once familiar. Central was the loss of being able to use their native language to reach others in their new world. They described this condition of isolation as being "deaf and dumb" in the social world that was supposed to become their "home."

The terrible aching loneliness they expressed emerged as a prominent theme in their stories, as told to Western researchers. Reflecting on the loneliness in their lives, we became aware of the privilege and irony of our position in relationship to theirs. We were able to read the translated narratives of their lives in our native tongue. Paradoxically, the privilege of language and culture that allowed us to feel included in their lives through the stories they told was simultaneously a source of disconnection and discontinuity for them. The dominant language, which afforded us an opportunity to learn about them, contributed to their own feelings of not really belonging anywhere. Our position made it possible to talk about the tragic events of their lives and to convey our knowledge of Southeast Asian culture to others. None of these things were as possible for them. They were trying to find their way in an alien environment, where others understood little about their lives or the extensive change required of them to survive in America.

Although loneliness must be a normative experience for refugees, its meaning in their lives is little known. The experiences of older refugees in general and women in particular have been overlooked, their voices nearly inaudible. The purpose of this chapter is twofold: to honor the perspectives of these refugee women and to demonstrate the importance of culture and cultural discontinuity in understanding the nature of loneliness in everyday life.

Before discussing the sample and research methods used, we look at loneliness and how it has been conceptualized in Western psychology. Then we briefly describe the organizing principles of family and community life in Southeast Asia before migration. Finally, we discuss the nature of loneliness in these older women's lives as it is found within the changing meaning of old age, in the conditions of the home environment, and as a consequence of family separation and the reorganization of family roles throughout the migration and resettlement process.

Loneliness as an Acculturation
Factor for Older Refugees

Widespread loneliness and isolation are problems for refugee elders in the United States (Gozdziak, 1988; Yee, 1992). Differences in the acculturation experiences of older refugees and their children have resulted in intergenerational tension and conflict, leaving old people more isolated from family and society (Detzner, 1992b). As younger family members become more rapidly socialized in the ways of the majority culture and as the importance of traditional cultural values diminishes in their new "home," older family members experience increasing isolation (Chung & Kagawa-Singer, 1993).

Acculturation is more difficult for those who are older (Rumbaut, 1989) and for people whose cultural and linguistic traditions are least similar to those of their new national home (Brettell & Simon, 1986). Those with less education and fewer economic resources are at the greatest risk for adjustment difficulties following resettlement (Rumbaut, 1989). Older refugees are likely to experience problems associated with acculturation and aging concurrently (Seelbach & Die, 1988). Their adjustment requires the reconciliation of enormous losses and construction of a new identity at a time in life when continuity is necessary for "healthy" aging (Atchley, 1989).

Stress and mental health problems are predictable consequences for those whose lives have included such enormous loss and trauma (Chung & Kagawa-Singer, 1993; Mollica, Wyshak, & Lavelle, 1987). Women and older people are among those at greatest risk of psychological distress—depression, anxiety, and post-traumatic stress (Chung & Kagawa-Singer, 1993). Refugee loneliness has been linked to problems with depression and psychological adjustment (Kleinman & Good, 1985; Nicassio & Pate, 1984) and associated with the most serious obstacles to resettlement—separation from family members, painful memories of war and resettlement, homesickness, and communication with home country (Nicassio & Pate, 1984). Good, Good, and Moradi (1985) found themes of loneliness prominent in the accounts of depressed Iranian immigrants.

Loneliness Defined in the Literature

Loneliness is a shared condition of humanity, a presence that ebbs and flows across the life course in accord with the unique circumstances of our existence. Its meaning differs across the life course, varying with interpersonal events and sociohistorical and cultural contexts. In Western culture, old age is commonly depicted as lonely, its increased prevalence attributed to role loss, the diminishing size of social networks, and less frequent social interactions (Peplau & Perlman, 1982).

Peplau and Perlman (1982) have identified three characteristics commonly included in definitions of loneliness developed by Western social scientists. First, loneliness is a subjective experience and one that cannot be based on observation of features in one's social world. Second, the experience of loneliness is unpleasant and often distressing. Third, loneliness is characterized by a deficit or absence in a person's relationships with the social world. It is commonly experienced when the individual's need or desire for social relatedness doesn't match the actual quality or quantity of contact (Perlman, 1988).

Three theoretical perspectives inform contemporary discussions of loneliness. Social needs approaches developed by Weiss (1987) emphasize the affective experience of loneliness and the satisfaction of individual needs through social relationships with others. Weiss distinguishes between emotional and social loneliness. Emotional loneliness is a subjective experience caused by the absence or loss of an attachment figure. Social loneliness, sometimes characterized by feelings of boredom or alienation, refers to the absence of a recognized social role in an accepting community.

Refining and building on earlier theoretical ideas, Mikulincer and Segal (1990) propose a two-dimensional model of loneliness representing people's beliefs about what causes loneliness on one continuum (self vs. social world) and their attitude toward loneliness on another (struggle/conflict vs. acceptance/adaptation). Using a multidimensional analysis of verbal self-reports, they differentiate four types of loneliness feelings. The first, *social estrangement*, parallels Weiss's social loneliness and is associated with being in a new place or situation without close ties. A *paranoid* type of loneliness is, like Weiss's emotional loneliness, linked to the loss or absence of intimate ties. It is further distinguished by the tendency to direct angry or negative feelings toward the social world. Also linked to a lack of intimate ties, a *depressive* type of loneliness combines depressive feelings, boredom, and yearning for the loved person. It is distinguished from the paranoid type in that negative feelings are primarily directed toward the self instead of the social world. The fourth type of loneliness involves feelings that tend to be *self-focused* and "may reflect intrapsychic identity conflicts" (p. 224).

Cognitive perspectives on loneliness, such as those favored by Peplau and Perlman (1982), emphasize the individual's perception and evaluation of social relationships. These evaluations are made by comparing present circumstances with those expected. Past relationship experiences become one reference point for self-evaluation.

In general, social psychologists have paid little attention to the influence of culture on the subjective experience of loneliness. Contemporary scholars are beginning to acknowledge its salience in shaping expectations for social interaction (Johnson & Mullins, 1987; Jylha & Jokela, 1990) and as a context for the development of values. In their work, Jylha and Jokela (1990) found the variability in loneliness among old people in six regions of Europe best explained by both the different values of the cultures and the life situation of the individual.

Psychological perspectives on loneliness are predicated on a Western view of the self. In Western societies, or other similarly individualistic cultures, the self is conceptualized apart from others as a solid, coherent, autonomous entity: self-as-separate. The self consists of a unique and stable internal core of attributes that differentiate it from others (Markus & Kitayama, 1991).

Asian constructions of the self are more relational. The self is fluid and interdependent, its structure changing according to the social context or situation within which it seeks connection (Markus &

Kitayama, 1991). This interdependent self internalized by Southeast Asian refugee elders over the life course shapes expectations for social interaction and individual-community relationships. Unlike the independent self fashioned in the West, the self of Asian cultures exists only within a relational context of important others. The relational structure is supported by the external environment and by the traditions and values of the culture.

Family Kinship in Southeast Asian Culture

The family or clan group is central to the organization of life among Southeast Asian cultures. Among these cultures, "family" ideology is significantly different from Western notions. In the Asian family context, one's individuality is subordinate to the collective or group identity maintained by the culture (Marsella, 1985). The self seeks connection with others and the experience of "self-in-relation-to-other" is the focus of individual experience (Markus & Kitayama, 1991).

In this context, Asian women view themselves according to their place in the family—as daughter, mother, sister, and wife (Hsu, 1985). A woman's fortunes and accomplishments are connected with those of the group, and meeting their needs and goals is requisite for satisfying her own (Markus & Kitayama, 1991). Positive feelings about the self are derived from occupying an appropriate place within the web of family relationships and from fulfilling one's obligations to others, accommodating the needs and goals of the family as a whole.

Family relationships are hierarchical and organized according to age and gender. Relationships between generations are characterized by reciprocity and exchange according to one's position in the group. The patriarchal structure of kinship patterns among Vietnamese, Lao, and Hmong grant the most authority and decision-making power to the eldest or highest-ranking male member of the family or clan. In most cases, women are expected to live with their husband's family after marriage and care for his parents until their death. Despite variation between groups, the family is an institution of central social importance.

Recognition of the diversity between and within cultural groups is a prerequisite for understanding older Southeast Asian refugees' experience of life in the United States. In general, Vietnamese refugees had more exposure to Western beliefs and more opportunities for formal education than the Khmer, Lao, or Hmong. Before 1970 the majority of Cambodians were rice farmers. Their fields were the site of American bombings that preceded the Cambodian holocaust of 1975 to 1979, when half of the population was killed or starved to death during Pol Pot's reign of terror. Laotian culture was also primarily agrarian and organized around the royal family. However, clear distinctions were made between the ethnic Lao of the lowlands and the hill tribe Hmong, who were dependent on farming the mountainous countryside of the north for their survival. The practice of Buddhism was more predominant among the Vietnamese and Khmer than among the Hmong, for whom animism and ancestor worship were central to village life.

Older women play an important part in the economic and psychological adaptation of refugee families following migration. They provide the unpaid labor of child care, prepare and cook food for family members, and maintain the family household, maximizing opportunities for others to participate in paid labor (Rumbaut, 1989). They contribute to the well-being of families by maintaining cultural traditions and religious practices, providing a sense of connection and continuity to the homeland, and ensuring the transmission of cultural values to future generations.

The purpose of this chapter is to explore the nature of loneliness in the lives of older Southeast Asian refugee women. What is revealed about the nature of loneliness in their life-history narratives? How do the conditions of everyday life influence their experience of loneliness? How do they cope with feelings of loneliness? Do contemporary Western theories of loneliness reflect the realities of their lives?

Methodology

Life-history methods are compatible with the assumptions of symbolic interaction theory, which have informed many qualitative methodologies (Rosenblatt & Fischer, 1993). These approaches share an interest in the subjective meanings that people give to the events and social relationships that constitute their lives (Cohler, 1982; LaRossa & Reitzes, 1993; Widdershoven, 1993). Several scholars have suggested using phenomenological and descriptive approaches to expand our understanding of the meaning of loneliness for different people in different circumstances (Stokes, 1987; Weiss, 1987). Wiseman (1995) uses phenomenological methods and objective measures to study continuity and change in the narratives of trait-lonely young adults. Investigations of subjective phenomena such as loneliness are well-suited to these methods because participants are encouraged to talk in their own words about salient events and experiences and to describe feelings and thoughts they have about them. Narrative accounts allow for the emergence of the participants' meaning as it is constructed in the present in relation to past realities and with some view of the future in mind.

Data Collection

The data in this investigation were collected by the second author as part of a larger study on the family lives of 40 Southeast Asian refugee elders in a large midwestern city (Detzner, 1992a). The larger project includes the life histories of five men and five women in each of four ethnic groups: Cambodian, Hmong, Laotian, and Vietnamese. This study uses only the life histories of the 20 women elders.

Three semistructured interviews were conducted in the home of each participant by a female graduate student and a native-speaking female interpreter. The first focused on family structure and memories of childhood. During the second interview, participants were asked about the transition to marriage and important family and life events during the middle years. The trauma and impact of wars on family life, stories of their flight and escape, of family separations and reunions, and of life in refugee and work camps were central in these accounts. The final and third interview focused on relocation to the United States and present realities of the elder's life.

The interview schedule was developed in English, translated by an interpreter into each of the four languages of the participants, and translated back to English by a second native-speaking interpreter, ensuring as much consistency of meaning across cultural groups as possible. Each interview was about 2 hours in length.

The retrospective nature of the interviews enabled women to describe the events and memories that were most salient and meaning-ful for them. Given the extent of trauma they had already survived, the positive tone of the interviews allowed them to engage at a level and pace that felt comfortable. Subjective realities could be revealed by these women elders on their own terms—when and as much or as little as they wished.

The Sample

Participants were nominated by staff referrals from community organizations serving Southeast Asian refugees. Staff members were instructed to suggest elders who might welcome an opportunity to talk about their lives and for whom the process of recalling their histories would not be traumatic. A purposive sample was selected from those nominated to ensure demographic representation of Southeast Asian refugee elders living in the area. Because of their affiliation with community organizations, it is likely that the women in this sample were healthier and had better social relationships than refugees who lack these connections (Seabloom, 1991).

The physical appearance of the women in the sample was much older than their chronological age might suggest, a reflection of their difficult and labored lives. They were between 41 and 83 years of age at the time of the interview. The average age was 66. A few women approximated their ages for immigration purposes, and several found it difficult to convert them to the Western calendar.

As a group, they had lived in the United States for an average of 7 years. The Hmong women most recently arrived ($X = 4.2$ years), followed by Laotian women ($X = 7$ years), Vietnamese women ($X = 8$ years), and Cambodian women ($X = 9.6$ years). Although two Vietnamese and two Cambodian women were among the first wave of refugee immigrants to arrive, most resettled after 1980. All of the Vietnamese women reported some formal educational experiences. The majority of the sample, however, had no formal education or schooling. Most of the Hmong women practiced the traditional Hmong religion—a belief system that includes animism and ancestor worship. Nearly all of those in the other groups were Buddhist.

With one exception, all were married at some point in life. At the time of the interviews, 12 were widowed and 7 were married. Nearly all had children (six to seven was average), and most experienced the death of two or more children to sickness, starvation, or war. One woman in the sample lost six of seven children during the Pol Pot murders. Many left children and grandchildren behind in Southeast Asia. Some had children who resettled in Canada or France.

With the exception of the never-married woman, all lived with other family members: 5 lived with spouses, 16 in households with children and in-laws, 8 had grandchildren in the household, and 3 lived with grandchildren or other relatives. Because of the extensive separation and reorganization of families that occurred during the process of flight and resettlement, this data on household composition should be considered approximate.

Although a few women lived in their own homes, a majority lived in public housing apartments located in poor, unsafe, ethnically mixed, urban neighborhoods. Most living quarters were stark and often in poor repair. The main living area was minimally furnished with two or three chairs and a small table—often just enough seating for the elder, the interviewer, and the interpreter. Most contained a Buddhist altar with photos of deceased ancestors prominently displayed. For some women, the interviewer was the first American to visit their homes. All of the women in the initial sample continued their participation in the study after the first interview, and many welcomed the interviewers' return and the opportunity to have Americans witness and record their stories for future generations.

Data Analysis

The experiences or life events that participants call *lonely* or that refer to the experience of *loneliness* are central in this exploration. It is the women's perception of loneliness that we are interested in, and their life stories elicited in interviews provide the context for this investigation. No specific questions about loneliness were asked in any of the interviews. The semistructured life-history approach allowed participants to talk about loneliness on their own terms and if they wanted to do so.

The process of data analysis began with several careful readings of each narrative.[2] The words *lonely* or *loneliness* appear in the English translation of the narratives 23 times. In order to focus on the phenomenon of loneliness without imposing a formal definition, each account was delimited using the full text of the woman's response to the question that generated the words lonely or loneliness.

Each account was read and re-read in the context of the overall life narrative and coded for general themes. Of particular interest were the placement of the word lonely in the narrative, the context of its use, its relation to other experiences, and references to other subjective realities. The results are elaborated in the findings section below.

Detailed notes about the experience of loneliness for each woman were made using each account as a starting point and moving from them into the entire narrative and corresponding case study. In this way coding and analysis was an iterative process throughout. Because the response to the question, What do you do on a typical day? generated information relevant to the experience of loneliness, it was also included in the analysis. During the interviews, narrators were asked about their "thoughts of the past." Because past expectations are theoretically relevant to understanding loneliness, these responses were also included.

As notes and codes were completed for all cases in a cultural group, patterns unique to the group as a whole were identified. The process of reading and coding the data across the narratives continued, and broad themes encompassing smaller analytic categories were identified.

Narrative Mention of Loneliness

The words lonely or loneliness appeared in the English transcriptions of 11 life-history narratives translated from audiotaped interviews conducted in the narrator's native language (Hmong, Lao, Vietnamese, or Khmer). A total of 23 accounts were generated. Of the women, 3 Cambodians, 2 Hmong, 1 Lao, and 5 Vietnamese mentioned loneliness, and these accounts were evenly distributed across the three interviews. Although no one directly said, "I am lonely," the women described loneliness as something they had personally experienced or as a universal experience of elders in their ethnic group. Nine (9) women in the sample did not use the words lonely or loneliness to talk about their lives.

Variations in the social worlds of each ethnic group are reflected in language, making it difficult to find terms or concepts of loneliness that are equivalent across cultures (Dunnigan, McNall, & Mortimer, 1993; Kleinman & Good, 1985). Some emotions are expressed more freely by members of one cultural group than others. Generally speaking, in Southeast Asian cultures, it is usually considered inappropriate to show one's feelings directly, especially to an outsider.

Social conditions and cultural values also shape the internal experience and nature of emotions (Lofland, 1985; Rosenblatt, 1988). Even if people share common ideas about what loneliness is, their willingness to acknowledge the experience may be different (Perlman & Joshi, 1987). Some people may be less aware of lonely feelings or how to label them. People may also use different words to describe comparable experiences. Lonely feelings may be so pervasively experienced that they are overlooked in conversation or accepted as part of how things are for that person in the world. So, for a variety of cultural, social, and individual reasons, loneliness might not be mentioned in an interview.

Findings

Many women talked about feeling lonely in the narratives when recalling a past event or activity. These events typically involved developmental transitions or those necessitated by forced relocation and resettlement. Whether loneliness was connected to moving into their husbands' household after marriage or experiences of flight, it involved disruptions in relationships with family members and friends. Moving away from parents, celebrating holiday gatherings with relatives, leaving the country without relatives, and recalling the death of loved ones evoked mentions of loneliness.

Loneliness was also mentioned in relation to the presence or absence of opportunities for social exchanges: being alone at home, loss of familiar work roles, elder groups, and friendship interactions. Some participants linked lonely feelings to the uncertainty of relationships in the future. Two women anticipated the loneliness they might experience in the future if their sons left home for continued education. The experience of loneliness was connected to past relationships, present social interactions, and future relationship expectations.

Characteristics of Loneliness

References to past experiences of loneliness were often associated with other feelings and emotions. Being sad and lonely or depressed and lonely were the most frequent combinations. Other subjective feelings that occurred in relation to lonely were: homesick, unhappy, heartbroken, guilty, and helpless. When the women talked about loneliness in the present, it was described as a condition common among older refugees and as something other relatives and family members understood about their experience. In these narratives, the phenomenon of loneliness connected powerfully with other subjective realities and emotions.

Certain behaviors are concomitant with feeling lonely. Crying and doing nothing are its most frequent manifestations. Somatic complaints are also prominent. Participants describe feeling dizzy and having headaches, aching knees and backs, and general feelings of sickness when they think of the past. Somatization related to the trauma experienced by Southeast Asian refugees has been well-documented (Mollica et al., 1987). Sleeplessness is nearly universal among these women elders. For many, bedtime is a difficult and lonely time.

Xee, a 66-year-old Hmong woman, describes the tension inherent in reconciling past memories with current realities,

> When you go to sleep but can't fall asleep and you think about it [the past], and you keep rolling from side to side. And you think constantly about the past and missing your people because you have come to this country. You think

very far to the tip of your toes. Then you think of different places. Doing this is like a rope that is being pulled back and forth. Then you think and think until you fall asleep.

The life-history narratives reveal the temporal nature of loneliness in these women's lives. Some lonely experiences are related to the past—to missing one's homeland and way of life. Others locate loneliness in the isolation of the present, where depending on the context, it is more or less salient than other emotions—fear, grief, or anger, for example. Loneliness is embedded in the everyday circumstances of life in an unfamiliar culture. The women anticipate future feelings of loneliness related to changing role arrangements and family relationships.

Changing Meaning of Old Age

Traditionally, in Southeast Asian cultures, the period of life most respected and revered is old age. Wisdom accumulates with age and the circumstances witnessed through many years of living (Gozdziak, 1988). Younger generations are expected to defer to the greater wisdom and authority of an elder who "saw the sun rise first" (Smith-Hefner, 1993). Elders are the "teachers and keepers" of cultural wisdom providing a sense of continuity, support, and connection to the values and traditions of the culture for subsequent generations. These role expectations, well-established by previous generations, are supported and reinforced by Buddhist and Confucian practices (Kalab, 1990).

The traditional meaning of old age among Southeast Asian refugees is contained in the organization of family and community relationships. For the elder, depending on one's children for care in old age is a reflection of the success and honor of one's life. Having fulfilled their moral obligations of caring for their children, elders are assured of receiving their children's care, devotion, and respect in old age (Seabloom, 1991). This interdependent view of aging is contrasted with American views, which prize self-reliance and the ability to maintain one's independence as long as possible.

For these refugee women, attainment of the privileges long associated with old age is more uncertain than ever. Threatened by a weakening generational hierarchy and a loss of certainty of place in the family, these women acknowledge that the likelihood that traditional expectations will be fulfilled is increasingly dim (Weinstein-Shr & Henkin, 1991).

The nature of role arrangements themselves is a source of separation and loneliness. The conditions of their dependence are isolating and frustrating. Although performing household responsibilities and providing child care enables fulfillment of family obligations, opportunities for interaction with children and engagement with the broader culture are increasingly constricted. Xee, who lives with her husband and three of her nine children, says,

> My son and daughter-in-law go to work at 5 a.m. and return home at 12 a.m. every day. You wait for them because you want to talk with them, but when they return, you are very sleepy and the next morning you wake up to cook for them, and they go to work. On the weekend, they are home, but you talk about loneliness and you think to yourself that if this life here is like this, then I want to return to Thailand.

Many Southeast Asian women find American household arrangements and role expectations bewildering. They conflict with expectations of reciprocity and filial piety that have long been the guiding principles of traditional family life (Seabloom, 1991). Ker, a Hmong woman with two college-age children, expresses her confusion.

> What I don't understand is why do the girls over here go off to live on their own after they turn 18. I would be afraid if I was to live alone. What if I get sick and there is no one there, what do I do? I would want someone to take care of me if I was sick. If I lived with my family, they would help me with everything when I am sick.

In the rapidly changing context of their lives, imagining the future is difficult. The belief that they will grow older secure in the company of family members and relatives is fading. The uncertainty of not knowing how children will reconcile the demands of the new culture with traditional cultural values is a source of tremendous anxiety for older refugees. Relinquishing the remaining authority and control that was once theirs means putting the future in the hands of their children, many of whom are rapidly assimilating the values of the new culture.

Bopha, a Cambodian woman who with her young son escaped the 1975 invasion of the Khmer Rouge, subsequently learned that the children she left behind were murdered by Pol Pot. Arriving in the United States without any family support, she and her son were exploited by the first two families assigned to assist them. Despite confidence in her son's loyalty to her through the hardship they have shared together, she is uncertain about their future relationship.

> I want to stay alive because I want to see my son finish school and get a good job, so I can live with him. My son can take care of me. I don't have to depend on strangers anymore. For now, I know my son is going to take care of me, but in the future when he has his own family, he might change.

Women elders with married children are no more certain about the future than those whose children are not yet married. Most are careful not to interfere with their children's lives, afraid of hindering their success or jeopardizing future care. They hope current contributions will engender feelings of obligation and loyalty from children so that when care is needed, it will be reciprocated.

> I help around the house. I help to take care of my great-grandchildren. I try to help as much as possible since she takes me to the doctor when I'm sick. I don't have a husband or sons to take care of me, so I have to depend on my grandchildren.

While government assistance offers elders some financial independence from children, it contributes to the disruption of generational ties and loyalties. Anh, an 83-year-old Vietnamese widow, reveals bitter disappointment about the failure of reciprocity between generations:

> I raised my children until they grew up, but they don't take care of me back. In Vietnam, the children usually have to take care of their parents. But now in the United States, the elders get money from the U.S. government, they receive medical care, so there is no need for the elders to depend on their children.

Although all of the women elders note changes in generational relationships and filial obligations, Vietnamese women more explicitly acknowledge the influence of Western values.

Loneliness is revealed in the changing role expectations that govern relationships. With the realization that the revered generational position of elders in Southeast Asian families is changing comes increasing recognition that the position and status they have worked a lifetime to attain is being lost. Growing awareness of the diminished status of old people in America, despair over the declining demonstrations of respect shown to elders, and feelings of uncertainty about the future coalesce among the oldest generation of refugees. These experienced and anticipated role losses are an important part of the loneliness experienced by older women.

Alone With Nothing to Do

Many live each day confined to the family household where cleaning, preparing food, and caring for children and grandchildren are central activities. Although their domestic labor contributes to the well-being of the family, adherence to family obligations keeps them isolated from the culture at large. Smaller households also diminish opportunities for social interaction. Multigenerational households were traditionally idealized (particularly in Cambodian, Hmong, and Laotian cultures), but only 25% of the women live in households with three or more generations. Nearly half live with children or grandchildren that require care.

Women elders, most of whom expected to live their lives surrounded by kin, are increasingly isolated and alone. Loneliness seems to be a label for the sharp contrast of the past with present conditions. For many women, the absence of meaningful work contributes to their loneliness. When asked to describe a typical day, these refugee women elders frequently responded, "I don't know what to do" or "I do nothing" or "There is no work to do."

Hard work is a pervasive theme in the narratives of the Hmong women and a cultural virtue. Working hard was essential for survival and a valued quality in selecting a mate. Hard-working women contributed to the farm *and* cared well for the husband's parents. Today their lives are the antithesis of what came before. As Ker says,

> I don't really know what to do. I just do anything that comes to mind. On Thursday, I usually go with Bee to play (an elder group). When I get back I cook for my son. If, sometimes I am not too dizzy I do *paj ntaub*.[3]

Sometimes other elders invite her to join them in their activities. Occasionally, she gets together with cousins, but mostly she continues, "I don't know what to do. I don't have a car to go and do my laundry, I just wash it by hand downstairs. Sometimes I sew my son's pants also. Sometimes I make threads of useless clothes."

The lack of meaningful activity in daily life contrasts with the years preceding resettlement and the constant demands of moving, hiding, and searching for food required to ensure their family's survival. Boredom itself may be unfamiliar and a reminder of one's helplessness and inability to contribute to the family's well-being as they used to. The extent of disparity between the past and present may heighten present feelings of emptiness.

For many older Southeast Asian women, the combination of being at home alone and the feeling of having nothing to do are conditions for feeling lonely. Many associate being alone with thoughts of the past. Roeth, a 63-year-old Cambodian business woman, enjoys helping her son with his business and conversing with the Khmer-speaking customers.

> Usually when I'm alone, I think about my past a lot and I
> can't talk about it. But if I come here to help my son in the
> store, I forget about it because I'm constantly working and
> talking all the time.

Lien, a 62-year-old Vietnamese widow and teacher for more than 30
years, describes overwhelming feelings of sadness and helplessness
when she thinks about the past.

> Yes, I think about my past very often when I have nothing to
> do at home. I think of my students. . . . After the Commu-
> nists took over Vietnam, some of my students went to reedu-
> cation camp in Hanoi. I don't know if they're still alive or
> dead. . . . Sometimes I think about my friends. I wonder how
> they're doing in Vietnam right now. I want to help my
> friends, but I have so many friends, I'm unable to help all of
> them. I feel very sad when I'm thinking about my past. I feel
> very sad.

Two different patterns emerge in the narratives related to thinking
about the past.

Some women commented, "Thinking of the past makes me unhappy." Most of those who mentioned traumatic and horrendous
experiences in their narratives are included in this group. For these
women (the Cambodian women and most of the Hmong women),
thoughts of the past are accompanied by unpleasant or intrusive
memories, feelings of sadness, helplessness, and loneliness.

Others tend to "think of the past when I am unhappy." Their
recollections are also associated with feelings of loneliness. Although
the content of the memories they recalled are sometimes sad, the
process of remembering seems to offer comfort. For these women,
thoughts of the past are validating and seem less overwhelming than
those of the women in the first group. Most often their thoughts
include fond memories of the past now tinged with sadness.

These memories may have confirmed the existence of something
in the past now lost in the present, enabling the person to recognize

and grieve its absence. Often these accounts reveal a longing to bring something known but left behind in the past into the present—the satisfaction of a work accomplishment, the ability to provide for one's family, or traditional role arrangements. Anh, the 83-year-old Vietnamese woman, longs for the certainty of her place in the family constellation and the reciprocity that once characterized family relationships.

> Yes, I think about my parents; I remember when I lived with them, I had a happy life; they loved me. But now I don't have a husband, I don't have anybody to love me. My sons have grown up, gotten married, and established their own families. For me, I'm old, when I'm sick, there is nobody there to take care of me.

These memories and reminders of the past are part of the experience of loneliness. Jylha and Jokela (1990) suggest that loneliness follows from the awareness that a community of people exists elsewhere when an image of the community is retained in one's memory. In their view, it is not simply the awareness of the community's existence that makes loneliness painful, but rather its absence when an image of it remains actively present in the person's mind. Feelings of loneliness then seem to reflect the relationship between the individual and the community.

For these women, reminders of loss are scattered throughout everyday life (Rosenblatt, 1983). For many, nearly everything in the present is discontinuous with life as it was once lived. The condition of discontinuity may also increase the search for memories of the past as the elder seeks to establish the continuity of the self (Atchley, 1989). Pleasant memories of the past support one's sense of self, and in the face of extreme disorientation, these are exactly the memories needed. Traumatic experiences make retrieval of affirming memories difficult (Gonsalves, Torres, Fischman, Ross, & Vargas, 1993). For many of these women, the inability to retrieve soothing memories may magnify existing feelings of loneliness.

Family Separation: "Lonely With No Relatives"

Loneliness is connected to an awareness of the presence or absence of family members among Southeast Asian women elders. Sometimes lonely feelings are stimulated by memories of the circumstances surrounding deaths of family members. Pleasant thoughts or memories of a particular person evoke intense feelings of loneliness. This loneliness is similar to the concept of emotional loneliness described by Weiss (1987) as the absence or loss of an important attachment.

Others talk about the process of separation and having to leave relatives behind. Hmong and Cambodian accounts reveal more traumatic experiences of separation and horrifying deaths of family members. The narrative accounts suggest that past bereavements are powerfully influential in the experience of loneliness.

Six of Bopha's seven children were killed during the Pol Pot terrors. Four siblings died from starvation. Following the invasion of the Khmer Rouge in 1975, she and her 7-year-old son boarded a ship headed for an unknown destination. She recalls how she felt leaving the refugee camp in the Philippines for America.

> I was worried because I did not speak English, and I was old with my son who was very young. I only knew French a little, so whatever it was going to be, I would try to speak as much as I could. I felt sorry for my son. We were very lonely with no relatives. I was afraid that if something was wrong with me and I died, my son's life would have no future.

Throughout her narrative, Bopha connects her subjective experience of loneliness with the absence of the family members and relatives that constituted her world. Describing her initial impressions of life in the United States, she says,

> I was impressed by their modernization. They used machines to do almost everything. But I was not happy because my children were not with me. Those who have their families around them, they are happy here. Whatever problems they have they're still happy because they are here together with their families.

The condition of being in the United States without family or relatives, or living in geographically distant locations from relatives brings feelings of loneliness for many women elders. Holidays, trips to the grocery store where other mothers have children in tow, and family mealtimes serve as reminders of the losses of both children and culture. The pangs of loneliness and cascading emotions one might experience eating a meal alone or without the savor of familiar food are easily imaginable.

Feelings of loneliness sometimes influence family interactions, increasing intergenerational tension and conflict according to gendered and generational perspectives of the family toward its goals. Like other women in the sample, Bopha asked her only son not to move away from home to continue his education. Although she worries he might resent her request, she hopes to avoid the pain of loneliness and the reminder of all that has already been lost.

Limited financial resources for transportation or telephone calls to family members, even those who live a few hours away, make maintaining important connections difficult. Many women feel guilty about not having enough money to sponsor relatives left behind. Their strong desire, but lack of opportunity to effect changes in current or past situations, is typical of the helplessness that sometimes relates to feeling lonely.

Experiencing Daily Life in America

The conditions of daily life in America shape the experience of loneliness for these older Southeast Asian women. Limited opportunities in everyday life for meaningful interaction with the larger society, neighborhood communities, or other family members are central to the quality of loneliness they experience. Two participants describe the situation of not living among others of one's ethnic group as part of the cultural context of loneliness. Conditions of poverty limit opportunities for participating in community events and for connecting with family members who live in more distant locations.

The frustrations of not being able to speak English and lack of familiarity with the practices of daily life in the new culture keep them isolated and amplify feelings of discontinuity from all that was previously known. Not knowing the English language inhibits agency. It makes dependence on children and grandchildren for translation and interpretation normative and self-reliance difficult.

Housing conditions are unfamiliar and isolating. Formerly accustomed to large multigenerational households with greater proximity and access to kin and neighbors, these women find that housing arrangements illustrate the differences between American cultural values and their own collectivist values.

> Over here, I don't like how we live in our house and keep a closed door where you can't visit each other. You have relatives living all around your neighborhood, but you can't visit each other, and it makes you very sad that you are dumb and you don't know their language.

These conditions of daily life are contrasted with life in rural villages, where farming required the cooperation of everyone in the community and daily interaction with siblings, relatives, and friends who lived nearby.

Helplessness frequently accompanies feelings of loneliness that emerge from the isolating conditions of daily life in America. Women elders express frustration at not being able to meet their own needs for connection and social support. Although some want to drive, they can't; they can't talk to people, and many find it difficult to "go anywhere." They feel isolated and cut off from the new culture. The conversations Ker describes with other women in her neighborhood depict a collective powerlessness in their isolation from society. When asked what they talk about, she says,

> We talk about how we want to go and play, but there is no road to take us there. We can't go, and how we live everyday looking at the door and go out of the door and look around and then after awhile, come back home.

Fewer opportunities for engaging in the culture constrict the development of new meanings and interests.

Coping With Loneliness

These older refugee women have endured and survived circumstances unimaginable to most people. The fact of their survival is testimony to incredible courage, resilience, and determination. How do they cope with loneliness? What strategies seemed to alleviate or help in managing the pain of loneliness in their lives?

Keeping Busy

Many women describe "keeping busy" as something to divert their attention from unwanted feelings of loneliness. Finding engaging activities at home provides distraction from past recollections that invite lonely feelings. Staying busy keeps at bay the ache of missing people and connections. As Xee said,

> If you are home alone and working, then you don't remember the past. If you are in the house alone without anything to do, then when you look outside, then you say to yourself, why do I miss my life in the past so much?

While keeping busy is helpful in avoiding unwanted feelings, it is also a useful strategy for redefining daily life in the present. Activities offer a focus for living and thinking in the present. Washing, sewing or mending, and embroidering pillowcases are among the activities the women are involved in at home. Vietnamese women mention reading Vietnamese books and newspapers to stay connected with their culture and watching videos and television to practice English-language skills.

Having People to Talk to—Friends and Family

Social relationships with contemporaries are important to these women, and same-sex friendships provide pleasure and enjoyment. Although no one said having friends makes them less lonely, they did say that having friends makes them happy. Some social contact with friends, no matter how limited, is preferred to isolation. And although important, interactions with "new" friends are secondary to relationships with "sisters and old friends."

Given the sample, it is not surprising that social and religious organizations are important in developing new friendships. What's more surprising is that for many elders these are the *only* opportunities they have to talk with other refugee elders. Temple activities and weekly social gatherings provide the context for getting together with friends and offer opportunities for conversation and company. The women admonish each other to try hard to adapt, they learn new things together and from each other, they exchange stories about children and grandchildren, and they meet people with whom they share new experiences. Getting together with others provides an escape from loneliness.

Many women talk about the changed context of friendship interactions. Whereas once they might have visited each other at home, now they rarely do so. They are more likely to call friends on the telephone or gather at the temple. The importance of receiving phone calls from friends or family members is frequently mentioned. They call friends for comfort during sad times and to share memories about the past. They talk about the taste of fruits, the smell of freshly harvested rice, the contours of the land, and the celebration of holidays. They exchange memories that are pleasant and affirming as well as those that are bitter and sad. Interactions with friends offer relief from the burden of intense feelings and help contain feelings of bitterness and loss.

Managing feelings effectively in the context of relationships is another aspect of coping with loneliness. Knowing what not to talk about is important in avoiding nightmares and death terrors and in managing sleep disturbances. Those who select different strategies to use with friends benefit more from their interactions. They are able to talk about the past and the present, a little or a lot, and to choose when one might be more helpful than the other. Some use strategies to forget painful events, to "shut your brain off" and gain control over their thoughts. Bopha articulates the implicit rule of communication she and her cousin follow. "We never talk about Cambodia or our dead relatives and families. We only talk about our relatives who are alive, even that we still don't talk much about our bitter past."

Contributing to Family and Community

Many women express a strong desire to help others and demonstrate tremendous devotion to their families and communities. Most enact their commitments in ways that provide a sense of purpose and usefulness. The greatest of these is a commitment to care for children with whom they endured hardships and shared many losses. In addition to raising their biological children, they care for foster children, cousins, and other relatives. They organize bake sales and fund-raising campaigns for temple buildings. They take classes and participate in mutual assistance programs to more effectively address the needs of their peers. Bopha, the Cambodian widow whose six children were killed during Pol Pot, found telling her story beneficial to others. Although she cries privately at home alone, when talking with others, she says, "I don't even have a drop of tear." Telling her story in settings where she limits her emotional expression seems to provide her with control and distance from the tangle of grief and loneliness. Despite enormous losses suffered, or perhaps because of them, these women express a strong desire to help others, to do good deeds, and to demonstrate devotion to their communities.

Discussion

The purpose of this study is to understand the phenomenon of loneliness in the lives of Southeast Asian women elders. Although it is not a specific focus in the original investigation, our interest in loneliness emerged from the narratives. This investigation is limited by what is revealed in the interviews, how the women label their experience, and the interview context.

Under any circumstances, variation in the nature and meaning of subjective experience makes cross-cultural translation exceedingly difficult. Because we are cultural outsiders and have never been refugees, we offer a conservative interpretation of the data. Although our experience is undoubtedly different from theirs, we have tried to remain "true" to their experience of loneliness as revealed in the context of the life-history narratives.

Loneliness is not a topic that has previously been studied in relation to the lives of refugee families, and their subjective experiences are little known. In fact, one can comfortably read the literature and feel as detached from their life circumstances as they do from their U.S. neighbors. This quality of cultural disconnection is an important part of the experience of loneliness among these women elders.

Do Western Theories Fit?

The narratives of these Southeast Asian women confirm the subjective and distressing nature of loneliness common to Western definitions (Peplau & Perlman, 1982). For these women, loneliness is sometimes connected to somatic complaints, associated with other feelings, and related to an awareness that nearly everything that was once a part of their world is now absent or drastically changed (Jylha & Jokela, 1990). Pleasant and painful memories from the past are frequently evoked in the conditions of everyday life. Their stories reveal the distressing nature of loneliness, and they use various coping strategies to mitigate its unpleasantness in their everyday lives.

Participants who do not mention loneliness describe other subjective experiences characterized by boredom, somatization, and failed expectations. In their narratives, other subjective realities (terror, anger, rage, isolation) are more dominant than loneliness or sadness. Like those who talked about loneliness explicitly, these women report feelings of separateness from family and others in their ethnic group, as well as isolation from people in the larger culture.

Social needs approaches to understanding loneliness elaborated in Western psychology (Peplau & Perlman, 1982; Weiss, 1987) emphasize the importance of social relationships to individual well-being. The Western view of an independent, agentic self on which these approaches are based often attribute causes of loneliness to personality characteristics or to individual difficulties with interpersonal relationships. Similarly, cognitive perspectives on loneliness (Peplau & Perlman, 1982), which emphasize the importance of making social comparisons and evaluating present circumstances in terms of past expectations, assign responsibility to the perceptions of the individual. In these approaches, loneliness resides and is modified within the internal (private) environment of the self, where social behavior is motivated by the expression of one's private attributes, feelings, and thoughts (Markus & Kitayama, 1991).

In the lives of these Southeast Asian women, loneliness is associated with the loss of social relationships. At times, lonely feelings are connected with losses or separation from important people (the emotional loneliness referred to by Weiss). Others relate loneliness to a lack of meaningful work and activities. Many express feelings of helplessness about the conditions of their lives. They convey "depressive feelings, blended with boredom and painful yearning for a loved person" kin to the depressive type of loneliness differentiated by Mikulincer and Segal (1990).

Loneliness is also linked to disrupted relationships, lack of social ties, and the absence of community roles. Similar to the social isolation described by Weiss (1987) and the social estrangement subtype delineated by Mikulincer and Segal (1990), these women associate loneliness with feelings of being different from others in the environment, of not being able to connect with them and with unfamiliar social arrangements. Also characteristic of the social estrangement subtype, the women reveal a desire and longing to change the current situation, to be cared for by important others, and to perceive the obstacles involved.

Constrained by Western paradigms rooted in an independent view of the self that focuses on the internal feelings, thoughts, and behaviors of individuals, these concepts offer only a partial explanation of loneliness. Cultural norms influence individual beliefs about the relationship between self and others, particularly the degree to which the self is seen as separate or connected to others (Johnson & Mullins, 1987). How the self is construed, whether it is a more interdependent one that attends to others as the focus of behavior or an independent one that focuses on the private attributes of the self detached from their context, has important consequences for understanding the feelings, thoughts, and behaviors that determine individual experience (Markus & Kitayama, 1991). Our theoretical understanding of loneliness in these women elders' lives is constrained by a monocultural view of the self as independent and autonomous.

The interdependent nature of the self and relationships born in the context of Southeast Asian cultures provides the foundation for a distinct experience of loneliness in the lives of these refugees. In contrast to the autonomous, independent self of the West, the connected, interdependent self of the East is part of the wider social context in which it is embedded. This self is born and dies knowing its position in relation to others. Others are the focus of behavior, and the self is defined by its ability to accommodate and sustain these important relationships, ensuring interpersonal harmony within specific social situations (Markus & Kitayama, 1991). Developing a store of information about others and acquiring knowledge of the social surroundings is an important part of being able to occupy one's proper place in the world (Markus & Kitayama, 1991). Because the self is predicated on the presence of others, disruptions to role arrangements, their future uncertainty, and the experience of social estrangement may be more distressing and hold a distinctively different meaning for Southeast Asian elders than for older people in Western societies.

Forced from their cultural homelands where interdependent relationships based in reciprocity and mutuality are valued and supported, these refugees have resettled in a new context governed by an independent, autonomous system of relationships. The core loss defining the experience of loneliness in their lives is the discontinuity and disintegration of an entire relationship system that forms the basis for attachments and identity over the life course. No longer supported by the values of the culture, loneliness is related to the uncertainty of whether traditional principles of reciprocal obligations that structured relationships in the past will remain. In this study, loneliness is understood as part of the tension between continuity and change negotiated by individuals, families, and communities across the ecosystem.

Role expectations and responsibilities long established according to generational and gender hierarchies are now uncertain and fluid. Many describe their future status in the family as dependent on their children, but they are uncertain whether the reciprocity they always expected will be there. Although they want to retain the place in the family they expected would be theirs in old age, they are less than confident that mutual obligations will be fulfilled and more uncertain than ever about who will care for them in old age. The combined awareness of the dwindling esteem for old age, loss of place in the family, and the absence of relatives and familiar community supports create tremendous anxiety about the future. The cultural discontinuity central to the condition of loneliness is also contained in the unrealized expectations of old age.

The experience of loneliness in the lives of refugee elders extends beyond the domain addressed in most of the theoretical literature. The marginal social role and fragmented sense of identity that characterize the experiences of older Southeast Asian refugees in America are strikingly similar to the developmental characteristics of adolescence, a time in the life course when the incidence of loneliness is greatest (Perlman, 1988). For older refugees, losing the place they long expected to occupy threatens their sense of identity and disrupts the sense of self that has always sustained them.

Conclusion

The condition of loneliness appears to be a central part of the life experience of Southeast Asian women elders resettled in the United States during the two decades following the fall of Saigon. Their narratives reveal painful and persistent feelings of loneliness experienced in relation to isolating cultural conditions and discontinuity, family separation and reorganization, and individual aloneness and boredom. Experiences of loneliness for the refugee elders are stimulated by daily reminders that those things once important and central to identity are now missing from one's everyday world.

It is the experience of being uprooted, of being suddenly separated and cut off from one's cultural roots that frames the discourse on loneliness in this chapter. What follows this dislocation is the disintegration of an entire system of meaning. For not only are the social and family worlds of each of these women dramatically altered in the new culture, but the systems that govern these relationships have also changed. The cultural context no longer supports the relational self that has provided the basis for identity, family, and community over the life course. The extensive nature of cultural change, discontinuity, and family loss are influential in shaping the experience of loneliness. The situation of having experienced such profound loss, including the loss of one's cultural home, is one of the primary conditions of loneliness in the lives of these Southeast Asian elders.

Notes

1. The definition of old age differs across cultures. In Southeast Asian culture, status as an elder is determined by one's role and function in the family and community. Depending on accumulated life experiences, some persons become elders in the community at 40 or 45. In the United States chronological age (65) is the marker most often used to define the categories of old age. Because data collected among refugees granted asylum in the United States does not reflect these cultural distinctions, it is difficult to determine the percentage of "older refugees." About 3% of the more than 1 million Southeast Asian refugees in the United States are 65 years of age or older (Schwartz & Schlader, 1995).

2. Prior to beginning this investigation of loneliness, we were very familiar with narratives of both men and women in the larger study. The first author had previously written detailed case studies from each narrative summarizing each elder's story and the structure, culture, identity, and interaction of their families. The second author is principal investigator for the larger study on Southeast Asian Families with Elders (SAFE) funded by the Agricultural Experiment Station (No. MN 52668).

References

Atchley, R. C. (1989). A continuity theory of normal aging. *The Gerontologist, 29*(2), 183-190.

Brettell, B. C., & Simon, R. (1986). Immigrant women: An introduction. In R. J. Simon & B. C. Brettell (Eds.), *International migration: The female experience* (pp. 3-20). Totowa, NJ: Rowman & Allanheld.

Chung, R., & Kagawa-Singer, M. (1993). Predictors of psychological distress among Southeast Asian refugees. *Social Science Medicine, 36*, 631-639.

Cohler, B. (1982). Personal narrative and the life course. In P. Baltes & O. Brim, Jr. (Eds.), *Life-span development and behavior* (pp. 205-241). New York: Academic Press.

Detzner, D. (1992a, November). *The family life of Southeast Asian elderly refugees.* Paper presented at the National Council of Family Relations, Baltimore, MD.

Detzner, D. (1992b). Life histories: Conflict in Southeast Asian refugee families. In J. Gilgun, K. Daly, & G. Handel (Eds.), *Qualitative methods in family research* (pp. 85-102). Newbury Park, CA: Sage.

Dunnigan, T., McNall, M., & Mortimer, J. (1993). The problem of metaphorical nonequivalence in cross-cultural survey research. *Journal of Cross-Cultural Psychology, 24,* 344-365.

Gonsalves, C., Torres, T., Fischman, Y., Ross, J., & Vargas, M. (1993). The theory of torture and the treatment of its survivors: An intervention model. *Journal of Traumatic Stress, 6,* 351-365.

Good, B. J., Good, M. D., & Moradi, R. (1985). The interpretation of Iranian depressive illness and dysphoric affect. In A. Kleinman & B. Good (Eds.), *Culture and depression* (pp. 369-428). Berkeley: University of California Press.

Gozdziak, E. (1988). *Older refugees in the United States: From dignity to despair.* Washington, DC: Center for Policy Analysis and Research on Refugee Issues.

Hsu, F. L. K. (1985). The self in cross-cultural practice. In A. J. Marsella, G. DeVos, & F. L. K. Hsu (Eds.), *Culture and self* (pp. 24-55). London: Tavistock.

Johnson, P., & Mullins, L. (1987). Growing old and lonely in different societies: Toward a comparative perspective. *Journal of Cross-Cultural Gerontology, 2,* 257-275.

Jylha, M., & Jokela, J. (1990). Individual experiences as cultural—A cross-cultural study on loneliness among the elderly. *Ageing and Society, 10,* 295-315.

Kalab, M. (1990). Buddhism and emotional support for elderly people. *Journal of Cross-Cultural Gerontology, 5,* 7-19.

Kleinman, A., & Good, B. (1985). Introduction: Culture and depression. In A. Kleinman & B. Good (Eds.), *Culture and depression* (pp. 1-41). Berkeley: University of California Press.

LaRossa, R., & Reitzes, D. (1993). Symbolic interactionism and family studies. In P. Boss, W. Doherty, R. LaRossa, W. Schumm, & S. Steinmetz (Eds.), *Sourcebook of family theories and methods* (pp. 135-163). New York: Plenum.

Lofland, L. (1985). The social shaping of emotion: The case of grief. *Symbolic Interaction, 8,* 171-190.

Markus, H. R., & Kitayama, S. (1991). Culture and the self: Implications for cognition, emotion, and motivation. *Psychological Review, 98*(2), 224-253.

Marsella, A. (1985). Culture, self, and mental disorder. In A. Marsella, G. Devos, & F. Hsu (Eds.), *Culture and self: Asian and Western perspectives* (pp. 281-307). New York: Tavistock.

Marsella, A., Borneman, T., Ekblad, S., & Orley, J. (1994). Introduction. In A. Marsella, T. Borneman, S. Ekblad, & J. Orley (Eds.), *Amidst peril and pain: The mental health and well-being of the world's refugees* (pp. 1-13). Washington, DC: American Psychological Association.

Mikulincer, M., & Segal, J. (1990). A multidimensional analysis of the experience of loneliness. *Journal of Social and Personal Relationships, 7,* 209-230.

Mollica, R. F., Wyshak, G., & Lavelle, J. (1987). The psychosocial impact of war trauma and torture on Southeast Asian refugees. *American Journal of Psychiatry, 144,* 1567-1572.

Nicassio, P., & Pate, J. (1984). An analysis of problems of resettlement of the Indochinese refugees in the United States. *Social Psychiatry, 19,* 135-141.

Peplau, L., & Perlman, D. (Eds.). (1982). *Loneliness: A sourcebook of current theory, research, and therapy.* New York: John Wiley.

Perlman, D. (1988). Loneliness: A life-span, family perspective. In R. Milardo (Ed.), *Families and social networks* (pp. 190-220). Newbury Park, CA: Sage.

Perlman, D., & Joshi, P. (1987). The revelation of loneliness. *Journal of Social Behavior and Personality, 2,* 63-76.

Rosenblatt, P. C. (1983). *Bitter, bitter tears.* Minneapolis: University of Minnesota Press.

Rosenblatt, P. C. (1988). Grief: The social context of private feelings. *Journal of Social Issues, 44,* 67-78.

Rosenblatt, P., & Fischer, L. (1993). Qualitative family research. In P. Boss, W. Doherty, R. LaRossa, W. Schumm, & S. Steinmetz (Eds.), *Sourcebook of family theories and methods* (pp. 167-177). New York: Plenum.

Rumbaut, R. (1989). Portraits, patterns, and predictors of the refugee adaptation process: Results and reflections from the IHARP panel study. In D. W. Haines (Ed.), *Refugees as immigrants: Cambodians, Laotians, and Vietnamese in America* (pp. 138-182). Totowa, NJ: Rowman & Littlefield.

Schwartz, M., & Schlader, J. (1995). *Southeast Asian refugees—statistics 1975-1995.* Unpublished manuscript, Refugee Studies Center, University of Minnesota, Minneapolis, MN.

Seabloom, M. (1991). *Filial piety beliefs in Vietnamese refugee families: Perspectives of ten elderly refugees.* Unpublished master's thesis, University of Minnesota, Department of Family Social Science, St. Paul.

Seelbach, W., & Die, A. (1988). Filial satisfactions and filial norms among elderly Vietnamese immigrants. *Journal of Aging Studies, 2,* 267-276.

Smith-Hefner, N. (1993). Education, gender, and generational conflict among Khmer refugees. *Anthropology and Education Quarterly, 24*(2), 135-158.

Stokes, J. (1987). On the usefulness of phenomenological methods. *Journal of Social Behavior and Personality, 2,* 57-62.

Weinstein-Shr, G., & Henkin, N. (1991). Continuity and change: Intergenerational relations in Southeast Asian refugee families. *Marriage and Family Review, 16,* 351-367.

Weiss, R. (1987). Reflections on the present state of loneliness research. *Journal of Social Behavior and Personality, 2,* 1-16.

Widdershoven, G. (1993). The story of life: Hermeneutic perspectives on the relationship between narrative and life history. In R. Josselson & A. Lieblich (Eds.), *The narrative study of lives* (Vol. 1, pp. 1-20). Newbury Park, CA: Sage.

Wiseman, H. (1995). The quest for connectedness: Loneliness as process in the narratives of lonely university students. In R. Josselson & A. Lieblich (Eds.), *The narrative study of lives* (Vol. 3, pp. 116-152). Thousand Oaks, CA: Sage.

Yee, B. K. (1992). Markers of successful aging among Vietnamese refugee women. *Women & Therapy, 13,* 221-238.

❧ **7** ❧

Lost in the Fifties

A Study of Collected Memories

Janelle L. Wilson

*I*n this chapter, I intersperse secondary accounts and interview data in an effort to reconstruct the 1950s. As a sociologist, the method I used in the research that I present in this piece would be called *unstructured interviewing*. I am more inclined, however, to call this an oral history, as informants shared their recollections—their biographical narrative—of the decade in which they came of age.

Although my substantive topic is the 1950s, my approach is not historical, nor is it even sociohistorical. My approach is perhaps best viewed as interpretive/critical. By asking individuals about their recollections of the 1950s, I am seeking out their *meanings* of the decade in which they came of age. But also, by employing the concepts of *collective memory* and *collected memories* and exposing differences in recollections, I am offering a critical perspective on the way in which dominant American culture (namely, popular culture) reconstructs the past. I share informants' stories, providing a sense of what growing up in the fifties was like for them. My interpretation of and reaction to these stories are, of course, shaped by my age, race, and gender.

My Indirect Link to the 1950s

I begin by locating my place in this study of individuals' recollections of the 1950s. My conception of the 1950s is caught between two stories. On the one hand, my dad (Class of 1957) remembers the 1950s as truly being the "good old days": drive-in movies and drag races and driving a '57 Chevy, "the prettiest car ever built." He can produce "I like Ike" pins and voice his trust in and admiration for President Eisenhower. He identifies "real" heroes as Joe Dimaggio, Al Kaline, and Bobby Lane. The fifties were a time when there was "somebody you could really look up to." To him, the fifties were the conservative calm before the radical storm of the 1960s.

My colleague (Class of 1960) remembers the 1950s as a difficult, embarrassing decade in our nation's past. The images he retains from the period include McCarthy persecutions, rampant racism and sexism, bomb drills in school, the execution of the Rosenbergs, and the hypocrisy of the U.S. government. To him, the troubled fifties were washed away in the liberation of the 1960s.

Although I didn't actually experience life in the fifties (Class of 1986), I have a conception or view about what that decade was like. As a white girl, I grew up watching *Happy Days*, a 1970s situation comedy set in the 1950s. The title alone illustrates my picture of the fifties: Those *were* "happy days" with Fonzie, Richie, and the gang. Hanging out at Arnold's, going to Inspiration Point with your steady on a Friday night, competing in dance marathons—this was the picture.

When I was in high school, we had a "Fifties Day" each year. This was a day when we girls dressed in bobby socks, skirts (or jeans, rolled up at the bottom), and our mother's old high school sweater. Guys wore leather jackets (with the collar up) and black high-top basketball shoes, and they greased their hair back.

Music from the fifties has been part of my reality. I grew up knowing many of the "old" songs. One of the main reasons I have had a positive image of this decade is because of the rock music from that time. Its unintelligible "words" and its beat are uplifting and catchy. Some restaurants have capitalized on the popularity of the fifties' tunes and the fifties' scene. For instance, as an undergraduate student, I recall frequenting a restaurant called Flips, where the walls were covered with fifties items—for example, old Coca Cola signs and the old Coca Cola bottles, old albums, guitars, and so on. Waiters had names like Potsie or Richie, and waitresses had names like Gidget or Susie. The music playing was from the fifties and sometimes the employees performed dance routines to the songs. Also, on weekends, hula hoops were provided on the dance floor for patrons to use.

So here is an amazing thing: I have a nostalgia for this decade that I never actually experienced. In this chapter, I share recollections of individuals who came of age in the 1950s. Among those who, like my informants, grew up during the fifties, the stories presented may not be "news." However, my age at the time of conducting these interviews (26), my race (white), and my gender (female) were significant variables in the interactional dynamics of the interviewing process. My eagerness to hear individuals' stories was welcomed—and rewarded— by my informants. Some of my informants seemed almost to "adopt" me for an hour or two, sharing their recollections energetically and enthusiastically, often making comparisons of their coming of age in the 1950s with mine in the 1980s and 1990s. Certainly, some of the stories I share here *will* be news to people of my generation (Generation Xers —i.e., those of us born between 1964 and 1981). We learn that there was more to the fifties than poodle skirts, hula hoops, and sock hops.

I have set out to expose and explore individuals' recollections of the 1950s. By talking with 33 individuals who grew up during that decade, I attempt to reconstruct the fifties. The majority of my informants were teenagers/young adults in the fifties.[1] Those people whom I interviewed were not specifically selected because of special attributes or because they are well-known. Rather, they are "ordinary" individuals who, like all of us, have insights to offer. A number of participants felt that they had nothing to offer; they repeatedly would preface their comments with statements such as, "this is just the way *I* remember it," or "you might not get the same thing if you asked somebody else," or "you're just getting my opinion here." It is unfortunate that they felt it necessary to call into question their own life stories, but it is understandable when we consider how history is typically done (from the top down).

In effect, a major objective of mine is to listen for the unheard voices. We all have heard the dominant voices via the mass media. But what other stories are out there? I invite the discordant voices to be heard. As Stimpson (1987) aptly states,

> We must realize that no single memory of anything is suffi-cient, any more than any single method for the study of memory is adequate. Even to begin to represent the past, we must create a collage of recollections, which overlap and col-lide with each other. (p. 263)

A collage, by definition, juxtaposes fragments of disparate realities.

In recent years, a considerable amount of scholarly attention has been given to the fifties. The extant works which most closely mirror mine both substantively and methodologically, are Benita Eisler's (1986) *Private Lives: Men and Women of the Fifties* and Brett Harvey's (1993) *The Fifties: A Women's Oral History*. In the former, Eisler, who was herself a teen in the fifties, talked with 16 contemporaries, most of whom she found through snowball sampling. Her attempt, in this book, is to give a voice to the "silent generation." Indeed, she suggests that "we were not so much a 'silent generation' as a secretive, private one; a cohort of closet individualists, our 'real' lives were lived underground" (p. 7). Harvey interviewed 92 women who came of age in the fifties. These women talk about what they were thinking, feeling, and doing in the fifties. Harvey noted that they "seemed to feel almost ashamed they'd been so docile, so quick to submerge their identities into their husbands'. They needed to be reminded that they were hardly alone; that millions of American women were doing just what they were doing" (pp. xx, xxi).

I, too, used a snowball sample to locate my interviewees. I asked informants questions dealing with the fifties—for example, What did you do for fun as a teenager? What was the best thing about the 1950s? What was the worst thing? I asked participants to talk about what they were doing during the fifties. If, in the course of our interactions, they didn't touch upon social or political issues on their own, I probed and asked about notorious fifties events (e.g., the Rosenbergs, McCarthyism, the atomic bomb, the Korean Conflict).

Interviews were, on the average, an hour in length. Throughout this article, I intersperse secondary accounts with "a collage of recollections" (Stimpson, 1987). Both my informants and participants in other similar studies describe what it was like to grow up in the 1950s. From cruising and dancing to drinking at separate water fountains, these individuals remember, reconstruct, and relive the fifties.

A Sociological Approach to Memory

In my understanding and interpretation of the data I gathered, I am guided by two sociological concepts: Halbwachs's (1992) collective memory and Young's (1990) collected memories. For Halbwachs, who coined the term *collective memory*, the past is kept alive via membership in various social groups. He identifies collective memory as arising from our inclusion in social groups. Memories that individuals have, then, are not actually individual. Rather, they are a part of— and shared with—the other members of the social group that experienced the given event. Halbwachs represents my starting point. To suggest that American dominant ideology portrays a collective memory of the decade of the 1950s via memorabilia, bunny hops, movies like *Grease*, and programs like *Happy Days* is to take seriously Halbwachs's notion of memory as existing outside of the individual; here, memory is a social (and structural) entity.

I also embrace Young's (1990) concept of collected memories. With this term, Young emphasizes the point that memories vary from person to person and thereby allows for a more dynamic view of memory and time. Taken together, individuals' "discrete memories constitute the *collected*, not collective memory" (p. 70). Young's work guides my research on how real individuals recollect the past. To consider other faces of the fifties, as remembered, for example, by African Americans, is to acknowledge the importance of considering Young's idea of collected memories; here, individuals' memories are deemed worthy of representation. The collective memory provided by the dominant ideology fails to capture and give voice to individuals' unique memories.

Fun and Innocence in the Fifties

When I asked Shannon Norton what first comes to her mind when she thinks of the 1950s, she said, "Fun, fun, fun!" What did these teenagers do for fun? Well, Norton remembered, "there was a restaurant called Schwartz's Drive-In on Westnedge and you could park outside and scream and yell at all your friends. We had hamburgers and a Coke. It was just a fun thing to do." Most everyone I talked with who grew up in the Kalamazoo (Michigan) area mentioned Schwartz's. It was the place to go after football games; a place to cruise, a place to hang out.

For many of my informants, going to school was fun. There were a lot of activities to be involved in, and most of the people I talked with were really involved. Joni Wells recollected,

> I think of my fifties years—junior high and high school—as really, one of the best times of my life. I have tried to tell my kids that, and they say, "Ooooh, Mom!" But it was not like you got up in the morning and didn't want to go to school. We wanted to go to school. We had a good time in school.

Luther Parker, who grew up in the South, remembered some pranks he and his friends did for fun:

> We went to cafés and bus stations and changed the "colored seating" and "white seating" signs. At that time, we couldn't go to the drive-in theaters, because we were black. Many of the students were Creole, but they looked white. So we would take the back seat in the car out, and we dark boys would get in the trunk and put the seat up, and once we got into the drive-in movie, we'd watch it.

Another African American respondent, Brian Marcus, remembered, "On Halloween we would steal apples from orchards and put them on people's porches. They wouldn't know they would be there." He commented that, in a way, this could be viewed as a nice gesture, the giving of fruit. But, on the other hand, if the police saw the stolen apples on someone's porch, the people in that home would be held responsible. He said, however, that the biggest entertainment was going to the movies. Another big event was the weekend dances:

> The girls used to have their little white bobby sox; we'd be listening to Elvis; we'd have it in the gym. The black kids would be at one end of the gym and the white kids at the other. It would be a real big thing if a white kid and a black kid danced together.

Susan Allen Toth (1981), in her book *Blooming: A Small-Town Girlhood*, shared her memory of rinking:

> "Rinking" meant cruising aimlessly around town, looking for friends in their cars, stopping for conversations shouted out of windows, maybe parking somewhere for a while, ending up at the A & W Root Beer Stand or the pizza parlor or the Rainbow Cafe. (p. 52)

By and large, the fun things that these individuals remember doing in the fifties are the typical things that our culture associates with that decade: drive-in movies, house parties, cruising, and dancing. And, of course, there was the novelty of television. Every informant remembered when their family got a television set. In the majority of cases, individuals recalled the family in their neighborhood who first got a television—these were the neighbors to visit, as everyone gathered around to watch this magical black box—even spending time watching the test pattern. Tony Robinson, an African American informant, recalled,

> I remember *Amos and Andy*. I remember my mother getting real upset about my liking that show. My mom would get real mad, and say, "Do you know anybody that talks like that?" and I'd say, "no." But it was funny.

Brian Marcus grew up in Mississippi, and that's where he first saw a television: "I remember looking through this hardware store window. There would be a crowd of people looking through the window; there was this little movie thing happening. Everybody was just sort of laughing—that's going to be different!" Watching television in the fifties was, more or less, a family affair. George Myers has this memory:

> Saturday and Sunday evenings our family would be there by the TV. My dad would get out the big old iron skillet, put it on the gas stove in the kitchen, and pop up a couple of big bowls of popcorn, and get the Pepsi out. We watched *Ed Sullivan*.

Sharon Weiss remembered "black-and-white TV—getting our first one. They were so new and such a novelty, that we all watched it all the time—the test patterns and everything else."

Although watching television was "big," these individuals seemed to be more interested in going to watch a movie. As Brian Marcus said, "We spent a lot of time with other teenagers, and going to the movies was a lot more fun—you were away from parents."

A Time of Innocence

A prime example of just how innocent and naive a time the 1950s were is Sarah Owens's comment that "until I got to college, I didn't even realize there was a difference between the male and the female, body-wise."

Joan Weber described the fifties as a time of "naïveté, parochialism, and fun." Donna Wood felt that the best thing about the fifties was

> the innocence and the trust that you could have in people; the trust in the safety of the world—your own immediate world; the freshness. The image of the fifties today makes it look silly and nonsensical, but people were more real and genuine.

The majority of the people I talked with lamented the loss of innocence among today's youth. In her book, Toth (1981) said something that was evident in most of my informants' words as well:

> Does any girl today have the chance to grow up as gradually and as quietly as we did? In our particular crucible, we were not seared by fierce poverty, racial tensions, drug abuse, street crime; we were cosseted, gently warmed, transmuted by slow degrees (p. 3). . . . Yes, I saw provincial smugness, but I didn't realize what it was. I can report its effects now, but I didn't suffer from them then. (p. 5)

When her young daughter asks her what it was like in the old days, Toth describes how her mind begins to spin with images:

> I want to describe for her the tension of the noisy, floodlit night we won the state basketball tournament; how sweat dripped down my dirty bathing suit as I detasseled corn under a July sun; the seductive softness of my red velveteen formal; the marble hush of the Ames Public Library; the feeling of choking on the cold chlorinated water of Blaine's Pool when a boy cannonballed on top of me (p. 4). . . . If there was a world outside Ames, it was easy to forget about it. The world, I knew, was out there all right. It would just take a long time, a long way, to find it. I was in no hurry. (pp. 191-196)

The majority of my informants said that they lived sheltered lives. The fifties, indeed, was the era of overprotective parents. But this protection or sheltering of young people from what was going on seemed to be an outgrowth of a national obsession rather than a family's style of raising children.

It is significant to note that one of the informants, Cheryl White, said the innocence was the best thing about the fifties: "The whole country was somewhat innocent." When asked what the worst thing about the fifties was, she gave the same answer: "Innocence. Absolute denial that anything was wrong. You didn't make waves."

The Fifties: An Apolitical Time

Not in My Backyard

Although this phrase is hardly original, it aptly describes many of my informants' reactions when particular topics were broached. I asked Matt Lawson, "Do you remember feeling that the bomb was a real threat?" His reply:

> I think we felt that we were pretty isolated from it happening in our backyard, though it was during that time that people were building bomb shelters. I wouldn't have dug a shovel full of dirt to build a bomb shelter. I'd ride around and see these things in people's backyards, but I thought they were kind of dumb. It was sort of that grandiose thing of, it's not going to happen here.

The general consensus among these individuals was that war only happened in far-off places, and other events of the fifties, such as the execution of the Rosenbergs and the McCarthy hearings, did not affect their lives. Lawson commented on McCarthyism:

> My wife and I didn't agree with him [McCarthy]; it's a bunch of crock. But we wouldn't have stood up and said, "That's a crock, man, go back into your corner and do what you got to do, but don't do it in the middle of our lives, because we think you're off on this one."

Toth (1981) said, "In Ames [Iowa], in the 1950s, as far as we were concerned, nothing happened" (p. 8). Eisler (1986), who also grew up in the fifties, stated,

> to my shame, I recall a classmate trying to induce a group of us to come to a lecture on apartheid by a government professor recently returned from South Africa. As I would

do so often later in life, I paid my two dollars for a benefit ticket—in order not to "waste" an evening hearing about it. (p. 8)

She also recalled, in the mid-seventies, a former student activist asking her what she had been doing when he was occupying college administration buildings. Her reply to him: "Pushing a swing." She wrote,

> Were there really mothers sitting in playgrounds in those days of rage and confrontation? Even while cities burned, civil rights workers and national leaders were murdered; while a far-off war moved closer to home? You bet. Vast numbers of us peered at those events on television screens in disbelief and horror—tempered by distance. (p. 250)

Eisler quoted one of her contemporaries whose midwestern college town was still (in 1959) a Southern-sympathizing place, where restaurants didn't serve blacks: "I was mad about that. I *almost* went to a sit-in organized by the local Y" (p. 264). But she never did go. Another of Eisler's contemporaries said,

> The pied pipers of the sixties did more than release the life-affirming impulses of uptight elders. Suddenly "rebellion and defiance" were in. In the fifties, I learned to sit on those feelings. Because to express them was a death sentence, almost literally. (p. 264)

In her book, Harvey (1993) quoted one of her interviewees:

> I was so aware of not fitting in. I'd been in Europe when McCarthy got started and had a different slant on him from the people around me. I thought he was a joke, despicable. I was also beginning to be aware of the Civil Rights Movement, enough to get involved with Urban League kind of stuff. But I was afraid to go down to the John A. Brown Company and sit in on the lunch counter because I knew that would offend my family and friends. I'm ashamed of that now. (pp. 204-205)

Regarding McCarthyism and the Red Scare, one of my informants, Louise Brown, had this to say: "I probably was not smart enough to pay attention to it back then. We were so involved with our friends and getting a job or getting married that we really didn't pay much attention." Similarly, Joan Weber remembered that the fifties were a "very social time. We read the news, but we were not out there working for political parties. We were young; we were in school. If you had things that you enjoyed doing, it was a nice time." She reflected on the Korean Conflict:

> It was a decision that was made by the government, and it was a war that was out there, over there. It was the thing to do. We were always very pro-military and pro the government. We just never questioned during that era. We had very little news, just papers. It seemed to be off in a little country. I have to be very honest: It was a country that didn't matter, terrible to say, but that's the way it was. Who were they?

Weber said this of the fifties: "We hadn't become political; that was why it was such a good time."

When I asked Raymond Baker if there were social or political events of the fifties that stand out in his memory, he discussed *Brown v. Topeka Board of Education*, McCarthy, and the Rosenbergs. Then, he acknowledged,

> However, I don't want to sound like I was overly sensitive to it. This was when I was still in high school, and I was mostly concerned about the dance on Saturday night. I wasn't that politicized at that time.

Joni Wells remembered the fifties as just a wonderful time in her life:

> I don't remember how the state of the nation was in the fifties—whether it was a bad time or a good time. I just remember, for me, it was a good time. I had a lot of fun, a lot of friends, not a lot of tension in my life.

Many of my informants said they lived sheltered lives in the fifties. They acknowledged this not to indicate that they didn't do much or go out and have fun, but rather, that they were protected from "the real world," or anything that did not directly affect their lives. Rachel Anderson recalled,

> I was really a sheltered kid as far as world experiences— what was going on. It seems like I can remember seeing pictures on TV and talks of war. I guess I always had the feeling that wars were in a different world; couldn't be around where I lived. If I remember, my mom and dad would say, "Oh, you don't have to worry about that over here."

Matt Lawson described the fifties as a conventional time: "You do things because this is just kind of the way it's done. That's what the fifties was all about: going along, functioning." As he talked, I immediately thought of Kohlberg's theory of moral development. According to Kohlberg, there are three levels of moral development: preconventional, conventional, and postconventional. The conventional level is characterized by one doing one's duty, obeying authority. Perhaps an accurate way of viewing the fifties is that it was a decade stuck at level-two morality.

Although many of the informants recalled their life in the fifties as an apolitical time for them, a few individuals talked about John F. Kennedy. Raymond Baker, who teaches political science at a community college, said, "I think Kennedy's presidency might have turned me on to politics. He raised our expectations; you could see the power of what politics could do through him." Shannon Norton had this to say:

> John F. Kennedy being elected president was just a big thing, because he was like a sex symbol—to be president? He really appealed to young people and made you want to identify with government. He brought fun into the White House. I remember his inauguration speech; I remember sitting there with tears in my eyes, being very impressed with that. When he was shot, that was awful. That was probably the most

traumatic political event. The wars were nothing compared to that, because you felt like, "What are we going to believe in now? If someone in that elevated position could be shot and killed, what does that say for the rest of us?"

Similarly, Sarah Owens recalled,

> The first thing I remember politically was probably the assassination of Kennedy. I remember just being blown away over that one. That really scared me. For the first time, I became political. Shivers just went up and down my body and I'm going, "Oh my God, who's handling the country?" And that was a fear for me.

When I asked Susan Curtis about any social or political events that stand out in her memory, she reflected,

> The most terrible thing to realize was that a person could shoot our president. You had so much respect for authority, and to think that that could happen in our country, that was really mind-boggling to me. It's where we went from little kids to grownups to think that something like that could happen.

Among those who mentioned Kennedy and the assassination, there seemed to be a sense that, at that time, as Donna Wood said, "the nation really was together." Thus, the fear and tragedy of the event itself is stored in these people's memories, but these negative emotions seem to be joined with a nostalgia for a time when the United States was really united.

Why So Apolitical?

In her important book, *The Feminine Mystique*, Betty Friedan (1963) stated that, after World War II, Americans escaped facing problems: "It was easier, safer to think about love and sex than about communism, McCarthy, and the uncontrolled bomb" (p. 178). After commenting on the Korean Conflict, McCarthyism, and the explosion of the hydrogen bomb, Rosen (1973) then wrote, "still, we chiefly remember the fifties, not for the horror of civil defense drills or witch hunts, but for kitschy fads like hula hoops and poodle cuts and crinolines. For Lucy and Miltie and Howdy and Kukla" (p. 245).

Similarly, Eisler (1986) explained her generation's political apathy this way:

> Atomic stalemate told us that the world could be blown up at any minute. Exposure of spies, foreign and homegrown, signaled "subversion from within." It was an unsteady world out there, over which we could look forward to having no control. The promise, "I'll be his and he'll be mine/We'll love until the end of time/and we'll never be lonely anymore," might be the only certainty. (pp. 110-111)

In Harvey's (1993) oral history of women coming of age in the fifties, she described this fearful scene:

> Blackouts, air raids, warning sirens in the night, first aid courses in how to bandage the wounded, and, more than anything else, newsreels showing ruined cities, exploding buildings, endless lines of haunted-looking people trudging down muddy roads with their suitcases on their backs—these things created fear, uneasiness, a sense of vulnerability. (pp. xii-xiii)

In a 1972 issue of *Newsweek*, Rodgers quoted a 29-year-old photographer who decorated his duplex with old pictures of fifties' stars: "There were plenty of problems in the world but nobody cared. All we worried about were cars, records, who broke up with whom" (p. 78).

My informant Matt Lawson lamented his lack of activism but, in retrospect, understands it:

> I never took a Saturday and went to Detroit, I never took any time and stood alongside of and did things, because it

just did not enter as legitimate within the life of my social set, and it didn't cause us to be affected by these things. It was kind of a distant sort of thing. There were some people who were speaking about it, nationally; some people were, thank God, on top of it and aware—quiet sort of voices that were speaking out—but never got to where I was living in the southwest side of Grand Rapids [Michigan].

He closed the interview—that is, our conversation—with this significant reflection: "When I think back to the fifties, I feel a lot of anger. Where were the people who could have been instruments of change for the oppressed?"

The Fifties That *Happy Days* Failed to Depict

The Issue of Color

The fifties (as presented in our popular culture): the Cleaver family; the hula hoop and 3-D movies; Mantle, Mays, and Marciano; soda fountains, leather jackets, and circle skirts. Contrast Henry Louis Gates, Jr.'s (1994) recollections of the same decade:

> *Leave It to Beaver.* . . . was out of reach. . . . Beaver's street was where we wanted to live, Beaver's house where we wanted to eat and sleep, Beaver's father's firm where we'd have liked Daddy to work. These shows for us were about property, the property that white people could own and that we couldn't. About a level of comfort and ease at which we could only wonder.

These comments hint at a more complex and variegated picture of America in the fifties than has been transmitted through dominant media images.

The majority of my white informants remembered the fifties as a time of relative racial harmony. Many of these respondents could cite as least one specific instance of a black person being treated especially well or having done very well. For example, Roy Stevens said,

Most people were accepted. There weren't any black people
in power, but they were allowed free movement in the city
[Battle Creek]; I mean it wasn't "sit in the back of the bus"
or anything like that from in the South. I don't think the
Civil Rights Movement did much for those people because
it was already integrated.

Larry Fields offered this commentary:

If you were poor, you were poor; if you were black, you
were black. There weren't a lot of black people fighting for
equality. We lived next door to a black family, and it was no
problem. We got along well. There just didn't seem to be the
issues.

He also recalled that "one of the more popular cops in town was a
black cop." There was also a popular restaurant/night club that was
run by "a black fella."

There seemed to be a general acceptance of "the way things were."
It sounds as if racial harmony was the result of the separate races
leading separate, albeit unequal, lives. Rachel Anderson explained,

It was like the blacks kept to themselves and we kept to
ourselves. They had their own way of living and we had our
own way of living. I don't really think that anyone felt that
the whites were better than the blacks. I don't remember
there being any tension. I think our homecoming king was a
black person—and a very nice black person. They all seemed
to be very thoughtful and kind.

Marge Scott put it succinctly: "They were on their side of town;
we were on our side." Shannon Norton said that there were no racial
problems in her high school: "Friday night after a game, we didn't go
to a black person's home—didn't party together." Donna Wood, who
grew up in the South, said that she only now is finding out what
happened in the South: "I did not grow up with that feeling of
prejudice. I didn't know that was an issue." She knew that her black

friend went to an all-black school instead of her school, but "that was just the way it was."

There was one respondent who said that there were racial problems in her school (Battle Creek, MI). Cheryl White said that there were race riots in the fifties: "We had a terrible race problem." She was scared to death of people with black skin.

Another informant, Maureen Hunter, also shared recollections of events which did indeed demonstrate the troubled times between the races. She recounted a job she had—not during the 1950s, but in 1966—in Georgia: She worked at a motel that wouldn't give rooms to blacks. She was told that when she answered the phone, if the voice sounded like that of a black person's, then she was to say that they had no vacancy. If she made a mistake, and someone called who was black but she guaranteed them a room, then she was to put them in the back room. She also was instructed to try to keep them from using the pool. This job really bothered her, and she finally ended up quitting. She recalled, too, that she grew up (in Kalamazoo, MI) with black neighbors—the only blacks in the area. When her family was ready to move, they were told not to sell the house to a black family. Yet, no white people would buy it because of the black family next door. Finally, because otherwise it would not sell, they did sell it to a black family, and they had to hide their heads in shame because of this.

Hunter also talked with me about the marriage of her cousin to a black man in 1957. She remembered that they weren't allowed to visit her or have anything to do with her. Furthermore, when this couple went to the courthouse to get married, they weren't given a marriage license. "The racism," she said, "was supposed to be in the South. There was subtle racism here, but it wasn't talked about." Her mother had told them to be nice to the one black boy in school, but they weren't to go to his house, or kiss him, and so on.

A few of my informants grew up in areas where there were no African Americans. When I asked Doris Rice about racial relations, she said, "None. We did not think of it." She went on to tell me the story of her trip down South just after she had gotten married:

They had two water fountains: One said "colored" and one said "white." And this is how ignorant I was—I thought, oh, colored water! So I went over there, and the water wasn't colored! My husband yelled at me, "Get over here."

Howard Conrad remembered when the Harlem Globetrotters came to his all-white town:

They went to the Dohorty Hotel afterward, and they wouldn't let them stay there. They had to go to Mount Pleasant [Michigan]. Everybody loved 'em, they were just the greatest thing that ever happened, they were thrilling, and yet, "You can't stay here."

A couple of white women I talked with indicated that this issue of race relations has become a very personal one. Sarah Owens confided in me,

Two of my grandchildren are mixed, and if it hadn't been for my friend helping me get through that whole thing, I probably would not have handled that well at all. My sisters and brothers have not accepted it. We don't talk about it.

When I asked Rachel Anderson about race relations in the fifties, she said,

This is a really hard issue to separate for me right now because my daughter dates black guys. It's hard for me to see my daughter with a black person, but then I think, if it's a person who is warm and loving and wants to make something out of their life, that's the main thing. But it's hard because there are people who just will not accept it.

The African Americans I talked with obviously painted me a picture of what it was like to be a black person growing up in the 1950s. When I asked Tony Robinson what first comes to his mind when he thinks of the fifties, he said,

> 1954—I was 7 years old and I remember the decision of
> the Supreme Court, *Brown v. Topeka Board of Education.*
> I wasn't sophisticated enough to know the details of it, but
> I knew how my family talked about it. It was also about that
> time that I began to have my first experiences of being called
> a "nigger."

Robinson grew up in Michigan City, Indiana, and he said that most of the black people in that town lived in a section called "the patch." He remembered that "in the mayor's office, there was a map of the city, and there was this black patch."

Brian Marcus grew up in Mississippi. He said that schools were very segregated. He remembered walking to school—about two and a half miles one way: "I remember seeing the white kids ride past us because they got picked up by school buses. They all went to school uptown. Only the black kids went to school in the rural areas." He recounted an instance that really demonstrated to him that blacks could be arbitrarily beaten and killed:

> One of my memories was this guy we knew was dumped
> across the road from our house from a police car one night.
> He had been in a fight uptown and had gotten his throat slit
> with a knife, and rather than the policemen taking him to
> the doctor, they just dropped him off on the side of the
> road. If we hadn't found him, he probably would have bled
> to death. If the police had dropped someone off like that,
> you weren't supposed to take him to the doctor.

Marcus remembered that his mother was constantly telling him that, if he were walking or hitchhiking, to never take rides from white people: "If I was walking down the road and saw a carload of white people making noises, I was to take off running to the woods because it was dangerous." He said that getting arrested was probably one of the worst things that could ever happen to a black person. "You feared white people, but the white people you feared most were the police, because of so many horror stories—people getting beat in jail, killed, people going to jail and nobody ever hearing about them again." Marcus had this to say about segregation:

Segregation never made sense to me, and I always thought
it was something that was stupid. I thought it was fundamentally incorrect and, as far as I could see, fundamentally illegal. I never could figure out how it was that people could get
away with it. No adequate explanations for these kinds of
contradictions. You just realized that you had to live with
them, but there was always a real sense that something was
wrong. But it didn't appear that white people cared that
much that something was wrong.

Regarding the *Brown v. Topeka Board of Education* decision, he said,
"people finally decided they were going to start paying attention to
what was going on between blacks and whites in the South."

Because Marcus moved from Mississippi to Michigan in the fifties,
I asked him about the degree of segregation in the North:

Of course [there was segregation], but we didn't think about
it. Like the school dances—the white end and the black end.
I remember occasionally we would get some courage and go
down to the white end and ask some white girl to dance.
But we always thought white people danced funny, so we
couldn't figure out how we was going to do it; like how do
you get in rhythm with 'em?

Luther Parker, who grew up in Louisiana, also has indelible
memories of Jim Crow:

As a boy, I could not go to the public library. I could not
try on a shirt in any store downtown. I had to estimate.
I couldn't try on shoes; if I put my foot in a shoe, I had to
buy it. Now, you can't tell me that doesn't do something to a
person's self-esteem.

He recalled efforts in the fifties, albeit isolated, at desegregation:

You read about them, and you wondered about them. There
were never any protests or assemblies or militant stance
taken in our schools. Anybody who did so was so severely
punished until you just didn't want to risk that. I can remem-

ber coming out of New Orleans, and the police would stop you if they could see that you were black. They would stop me and ask, "Whose car is this?" They'd push us around.

Resistance to integration was, he said, the worst thing about the fifties: "It was very hurtful to find out that so many people resisted our very being. It puts a distrust inside you that's not easily washed away." Parker did acknowledge that there was a comfort in segregation—"a comfort in being with people whom you feel comfortable with." However, "it taught you that you were inferior, and if you didn't accept it, you were punished."

Emma Brooks grew up in Kalamazoo. She said that the segregation seemed worse there than in the South, because "down South it was open, and here it was under the surface." She lamented the narrow range of jobs available to blacks. They never worked in positions where they were seen by the public. Rather, they could work in factories, or stock shelves, and so on. Supposedly, there was no segregation in the restaurants in Kalamazoo, but "it was there." She remembered going to lunch with a friend at a restaurant on the north end of town: "We sat there until we finally realized we wouldn't be served. You could walk in and buy something and then walk out, but you couldn't sit down and eat. And rather than open the counter up, they just closed the counter."

Lynette Cole grew up in the North. In 1959, she and her baby went to the South for the first time (to spend time with her mother-in-law). While they were there, her baby got sick. Cole recounted her experience of seeking medical treatment:

> We went to the doctor. It was a nice office, but at that time, the blacks and whites were separated, and we went in the back door of this office, which was filthy. They had windows where you could look over in the white part. It was clean and plush. But they didn't even clean this little place. It scared me to death. I'd never seen anything like that. There was a sign over the door, "Blacks Enter Here." And the other door, "Whites Only."

Cole wouldn't let the doctor see her child. She figured that "if they can do this to you, he's not gonna care whether my baby is sick or not." She also remembered seeing "the little white kids in the other part, up on their knees, looking over and laughing at you, and the whites were snubbing their noses."

In the course of our interview, Cole made a powerful comment to me: "Here you are, sitting here talking to me, but back then, there's no way you would ever talk to me, because I would be beneath you."

Returning to the recollections of Gates (1994), who grew up in Piedmont, Virginia, he said that, "all things considered, white and colored Piedmont got along pretty well in those years, the fifties and early sixties" (p. 27). However, he went on to state the conditions:

> At least as long as colored people didn't try to sit down in the Cut-Rate or at the Rendezvous Bar, or eat pizza at Eddie's, or buy property, or move into the white neigh- borhoods, or dance with, date, or dilate upon white people. Not to mention try to get a job in the craft unions at the paper mill. Or have a drink at the white VFW, or join the white American Legion, or get loans at the bank, or just generally get out of line. Other than that, colored and white got on pretty well. (pp. 27, 28)

The majority of my informants, then—in particular, the white individuals—remembered race relations in the 1950s as nonproble- matic. In fact, their recollections could, in general, be viewed as nostalgic. Those who didn't experience the discrimination remem- bered the 1950s as a time of "separate, but equal." But, for those who wore "colored" skin, things looked very different. African Americans' recollections are highly personalized and selective on this issue. An important point to make, however, is that although African American informants certainly had indelible memories of the effects of Jim Crow in the 1950s, they did indeed express some nostalgia for this decade. The nostalgia was for the strong community and church ties that they recalled in their black neighborhoods.

Growing up Female in the Fifties

Although some of the women I talked with recalled that there were more opportunities and activities available for men in the fifties than for women (e.g., in school), a very small minority could recall really feeling negatively about it. As women would tell me, for instance, about the limited sports activities in school for girls ("the only things we had were swimming and cheerleading"—Shannon Norton), they would also state that they didn't feel limited as women. A common statement was "you didn't think of it then." That is, these women accepted the sexism of the time because "that's just the way it was."

Yet, there were a few women I talked with who had a bit more to say about being female in the fifties. Donna Wood had a job in the fifties that "women had not been allowed to do before": working for the Department of Defense. I asked her if men had trouble with her working there. Her response:

> I think because we were young, they really didn't. It was male chauvinistic.
> Once I had gotten married and had a child, I would get comments like, "Well, why aren't you home with your child?" After my divorce, I applied for jobs and employers would ask me if I would be able to work evenings, even though I had a child. There was a lot of discrimination. It's interesting when I see today that women fight those issues. I was really angry and frustrated about it, but I just never really dwelled on things. I just went to something else.
> I ended up working in the state library.

Betty Richards, a nurse, shared with me how structured the fifties were. I asked her if, as she looks back on the fifties now, she feels that she was overly restrained. Her reply:

> Absolutely. I would have done things that you wouldn't have thought of. Let me just tell you how it worked: When I had children in 1958, I had to quit my job, and I had to start back at the beginning—at the bottom salary—so every time after I had a child, I had to start back at the minimum salary,

and then I was not guaranteed my job, and I had to quit each time. Doctors were like gods—you didn't question anything they did. Like if you thought that something they did was not ethically right, you didn't say anything. You had no avenue for questioning.

She went on to talk about sexual restraint in the fifties, and shared a story:

I'm 59 years old and have never used any form of birth control. This is very unusual in this day and age. [In the fifties], I wouldn't have intercourse—no way in hell. I'd be too afraid of losing my parents, the church, everything. We might go almost all the way, but we'd never have sexual intercourse; I mean, my God, we'd be struck down from heaven. I can remember [in 1956], we had a lady admitted to the hospital who had a diaphragm. She had put it in the drawer. I called every nurse in the place, 'cause we had never seen one. We would sneak in at night with a flashlight to look at it.

Betty also recalled that a friend of hers got pregnant in high school, and she was going to give her a shower. She said, "I was called in and told that I would not graduate from high school if I gave that girl a shower."

Cindy Rogers, a registered investment adviser who grew up in Stockton, California, views her generation as a "transitional or bridging generation from my mother's generation to my children's generation, when it comes to women's rights." She said,

I think it's my generation that was the first generation to say, "I'm not going to stay in a marriage if I hate this person, and it's not working; I am going to get out on my own." I think our mothers stayed in those relationships because they didn't want to go out and be independent on their own, and I think our generation said, "That's not good enough for us, and I'm going out on my own." I almost see in some of the older women who have stayed in relationships that they've not been happy in, resentment of the younger women because maybe they would have been happier people if they had done that, but because of the constraints of society at the time and where women were, not being able to have good jobs, maybe they settled to compromise in areas that they regret.

Two men also had comments on the sex discrimination in the fifties. At the end of our interview, Brian Marcus had this to say:

The thing that strikes me, as I stop and think about it, is the real emphasis on the old value of women being virgins when they got married; sexually conservative; the fact that women wore long dresses. Real strong emphasis on gender-specific roles.

And Matt Lawson said,

I think of the mindless injustices that were a part of the fifties—the male-female roles that were unquestioned, the inequities of sexual roles and identity. And, upon reflection, all that means is that there was just more work to do later— work which, in some places, has still never gotten done.

Thus, for at least a few of these women, the restraints they experienced because of their sex was important. Yet, the variable of sex did not emerge as a master status in the way I anticipated that it might. My interviews with African Americans demonstrated that race did emerge as a master status. The memories that African Americans had of the fifties were systematically different than the memories of the white informants. The latter remembered racial relations in the fifties in a nostalgic fashion. The African Americans, on the other hand, remembered the segregation and the feeling of the color of their skin being a disgrace to others.

Historian David Halberstam (1994) commented on this "other" side of the fifties when he said that "we've ended up remembering what is attractive about it and forgetting the rigidity, the narrowness." He added that we've forgotten how much pain there was and how much less freedom. "There were vast parts of the United States where blacks could not legally have the rights of whites." And furthermore, "we've forgotten what women could not do then." Certainly a major reason for this condition of amnesia that Halberstam is talking about is what followed the fifties. As Gitlin (1987) said, "The Fifties were, in a sense, rewritten by the Sixties, as the Sixties have been rewritten by the Eighties" (p. 12).

Joan Weber, at the end of the interview, said, "You picked the fifties, but the sixties is when everything happened!" It is significant to note that one of the participants, Tony Robinson, when asked what the best thing was about the fifties, said "the sixties." Although he laughed as he said this, it is very telling. That succinct response hints at what it must have been like to be a black teenager in the fifties.

The Birth of Rock 'n' Roll and Revolutionaries

Considering recollections by many of my informants, we can see a challenge to the collective memory of the 1950s, which depicts this time as a time of innocence, fun, and consensus. Another specific area where this challenge is apparent is in the emerging youth culture in the latter part of the 1950s.

Rock 'n' roll and the cool, tough image of James Dean represented this generation's attitude toward the establishment—an attitude that would be more associated with the 1960s. *Rebel Without a Cause* (1956) touched upon topics that we may not typically associate with the fifties: dysfunctional families and adolescent angst. After a confrontation with her father, Judy (Natalie Wood) angrily leaves the room. Her mother tells her husband, "It's just the age when nothing fits." Similarly, when Jim (James Dean) is having problems, his dad says: "Every boy goes through it; there's a lot of others going through the same thing."

Bill Haley's hit, "Rock Around the Clock" (1955) was hailed as a genuine revolutionary phenomenon: "Whether or not they were aware of it, when teenagers bought this 45, they were taking a stand against the established order" (Pielke, 1986, p. 29). Belz (1969) claimed it was Haley's style that made "Rock Around the Clock" revolutionary: He shouted his lyrics, and the guitars and saxophones were allowed in the foreground (p. 37). The song has been called "an iconic fifties street gang anthem" (Eliot, 1989, p. 54). The 1955 movie *Blackboard Jungle*, which featured this song, generated youthful excitement. As Gillet (1972) said,

> Youngsters who had previously listened to the music only in places where they could dance proceeded to tear out the seats of the movie houses and to dance in the aisles. The excitement caused by the song was reinforced by the content of the film, which included several scenes in which school students defied or beat up their teachers. (p. 278)

The movie itself depicted youth as quite different from Richie, Potsie, and Ralph Malph. A police officer in the movie referred to youth as "problem kids" who grew up without direction. With "father in the army, mother in the defense plant, no church life, no home life, no place to go," the kids formed street gangs. "Gang leaders are taking the place of parents." The officer also said, "The kids today are like the rest of the world: mixed-up, suspicious, scared." It is especially interesting to note that the mass media themselves, through movies such as *Blackboard Jungle* and *Rebel Without a Cause*, depicted the fifties as not such an innocent, fun time. Gitlin (1987) identified rock and roll as "the opening wedge" of dissent, which hollowed out "the cultural ground beneath the tranquilized center" (p. 29). He referred to it as "the noise of youth submerged by order and affluence, now frantically clawing their way out" (p. 37). He provided an interesting interpretation of the nonsense syllables that characterize many of the popular fifties rock songs. He suggested that "these devices could be heard as distrust of language, distrust of the correct, distrust of practicality itself." Gitlin wrote convincingly, "With a catch in its collective throat, rock announced to unbelievers: Before your very ears we invent a new vocabulary, a generation's private language. Distrusting the currency, we coin our own" (p. 41).

Eisler (1986) wrote about one of her contemporaries who talked with her about his love for race music in the fifties. He loved dancing to this music, which got him into trouble with his parents because, he said, "we were not allowed to listen to this music openly" (p. 69). He elaborated,

> I was always getting into trouble at school proms for "suggestive dancing." It all came from Elvis—all of his hip wiggling, pelvis gyrating. Our parents were scared that Elvis encouraged sexuality. But to the degree they disliked him, they emphasized the forbidden fruit aspect of both sex and Elvis. They were just telling us, if they thought it was so bad, it must be something great. (p. 72)

Cheryl White was a big Elvis fan. She remembered that his movies would be released at the theaters at midnight: "That was a big deal. Though that was past curfew, we were allowed to see opening Elvis movies."

Brian Marcus stated that the best thing about the fifties was "the rebelliousness of it." He recounted what he remembers:

> I can remember watching the Jimmy Dean movies; Elvis hitting the scene; the white cats wearing their shirt collars up, the Ricky Nelson haircuts—ducktails. Even in small towns like Vandalia and Cassapolis [both in Michigan], this start of youth rebelliousness was there—at odds with authority figures; questioning why people had to do certain kinds of things. I think it was just that unfolding sense of rebellion against what we saw as arbitrary rules; people trying to tell you how to live your life. There was this arrogance of youth saying that we knew what was best. Movies like *Rebel Without a Cause* fed the rebelliousness; I remember we saw that movie not once, but several times. That was always one of my favorites.

Matt Lawson feels that the fifties were fun because in some ways, there was the beginning development of a kind of counterculture. People were starting to say, "Well, maybe the way we're doing it isn't just always the best for everything and everybody." There were some dissident voices.

The rampant racism and sexism of the 1950s are virtually absent in our culture's collective memory of that time period. The voices—the stories—of African Americans especially have been silenced. Although the birth of rock 'n' roll is very much a part of the collective memory of the 1950s, the association of the fifties with rebellion and revolution is not. And yet, the rebelliousness and counterrevolutionary forces that we associate with the sixties were actually begun in the fifties—that seemingly quiet, complacent decade.

Summary and Conclusions

The interspersing of my interview data with secondary accounts of the 1950s represented an attempt to reconstruct the 1950s by drawing upon the reconstructed memories of real individuals who grew up during that time. This reconstruction, as presented here, demonstrates that we cannot treat the fifties as a monolith—for example, as a wonderful time for everyone. There are many sides to the 1950s. Juxtaposed to the memories of the innocence and fun, there is also mention of the fear (of Communists, of the atomic bomb, etc.) and the racism. By letting informants speak for themselves, we gain insight into what life was like for them during that important decade in their lives.

It is significant to note that when I asked Raymond Baker if he would consent to an interview with me about the 1950s, he said, "You know, they weren't 'the fifties' then!" Certainly, the dominant culture has presented the fifties in a particular way. This presentation is bound to affect one's actual memory of that decade. Although there were a number of informants who did not go so far as to say that the 1950s, as they experienced those times, were really like *Happy Days*, the majority did recollect the fifties as a time of fun, innocence, and rock 'n' roll. To what extent have these individuals internalized this collective memory, and to what extent did they really experience the fifties in the way they described? Although answering this question is beyond my scope, asking it is important. It is significant to acknowledge, too, that, in a sense, our interactional conversations helped to "reconstruct" the fifties. That is to say, my role as interviewer (and, specifically, the fact that I am white, female, 26 years old, etc.) must be taken into account in the interpretation of what my informants said. The easy rapport established during actual interviews was, I believe, largely a function of my age and gender. Informants did not view me as a threat. Their recollections catapulted me back to an era that I can only know in this second-hand way. Together, we got into a time machine and traveled to the 1950s. In some cases, I was taken back to a comfortable, fun, easy time in which to grow up. In other situations, I felt the restraint, the powerlessness, and the desire to return to the modern era.

The realization that not everyone has the same recollections of the fifties is a significant one. This is where the utility of the concept collected memories is demonstrated. Young's (1990) point, in introducing this concept, was to draw attention to discrete memories that may not "fit" with the collective memory. If one ignores these discrete or different memories (i.e., if we "collect" people's memories of an event), then we get a simplified, albeit incomplete, picture of the past.

I invited these too-often-unheard voices to speak out. Talking with males and females, white-collar and blue-collar workers, northern folk and southern folk, white people and African Americans, I was able to get a more accurate and complete—and different—image of the 1950s than our caricatured collective memory of that decade allows.

My study was guided, then, by both Halbwachs's (1992) concept of collective memory and Young's (1990) notion of collected memories. I began with collective memory and, as people gave me their local narratives, the concept of collected memories became ever more useful and appropriate in understanding and interpreting their responses. Both white and African American informants expressed collected memories. That is to say, although white informants' recollections were more consistent with the collective memory of the 1950s than were African American informants' recollections, they were not necessarily monolithic and homogeneous.

I found my informants to seem to be at a time in their life when reflection and commentary came naturally, and the interview, I think, was an enjoyable exercise for them. The unfortunate aspect of this exercise is that it is difficult—and perhaps not appropriate in a scholarly format—to capture how valuable and meaningful it was for me to talk with these individuals. I owe a great deal to them for their allowing me to come into their homes (or meet them in restaurants) and talk with them about what it was like to be a teenager in the fifties. Through this project, I was able to meet many wonderful people. This study is the result of our collaborative efforts.

A discussion of my conception of the 1950s—caught between my father's and my colleague's conceptions—was my starting point. It is only fitting, then, that I return to this in closing. My *Happy Days* vision of the fifties was a comfortable inviting image to sustain. Listening to and making sense of recollections of the fifties that fail to match that version complicates and casts doubt on the view I grew up with. Yet, even with a greater awareness of the troubles and fears that abounded in the fifties, it is difficult to eschew my quixotic vision. Part of the reason for this is national tradition and romanticism, part of it is some seemingly natural urge to view the past as somehow better, part of it is an appreciation for popular trends from an earlier era, and a big part of it is the picture painted by the dominant ideology as well as people like some of my informants. Yes, I hold onto this mythologized view, but now it is juxtaposed alongside other, additional views. For me, the fifties will never be the same.

Appendix: Brief Introduction of Informants

Let me introduce my informants. True to the promise of anonymity, none of the interviewees' real names are used.

Emma Brooks (Class of 1957)—Black female, married, employed at a university library, Pentecostal, grew up in Kalamazoo, Michigan.

Larry Fields (Class of 1955)—White male, married, a school administrator, Catholic, grew up in Mattawan, Michigan.

Joan Weber (Class of 1953)—White female, married, a college professor, Protestant, grew up in Holland, Michigan.

Brian Marcus (Class of 1961)—Black male, married, a college professor, childhood years were spent in Mississippi and teen years in Cassapolis, Michigan.

Tony Robinson (Class of 1962)—Black male, divorced, a clinical psychologist, Taoist, grew up in Michigan City, Indiana.

Cheryl White (Class of 1958)—White female, divorced, administrative assistant, grew up in Battle Creek, Michigan.

Raymond Baker (Class of 1954)—White male, married, community college instructor, Congregational, grew up in Ostego, Michigan.

Joni Wells (Class of 1960)—White female, married, vice president and controller of a business, Protestant, grew up in Kalamazoo, Michigan.

Roy Stevens (Class of 1957)—White male, single, college assistant professor, grew up in Battle Creek, Michigan.

Luther Parker (Class of 1948)—Black male, single, college professor, who lived in Louisiana in the fifties.

Matt Lawson (Class of 1952)—White male, married, a retired campus minister, Protestant, grew up in Grand Rapids, Michigan.

Louise Brown (Class of 1957)—White female, married, self-employed in a blue-collar position, Catholic, grew up in Kalamazoo, Michigan.

George Myers (Class of 1958)—White male, married, owner and operator of an automobile shop, Baptist, grew up in Kalamazoo, Michigan.

John Spencer (Class of 1959)—White male, married, retired General Motors worker, Baptist, grew up in Mattawan, Michigan.

Maureen Hunter (Class of 1961)—White female, divorced, child care provider, Presbyterian, grew up in Kalamazoo, Michigan.

Sarah Owens (Class of 1959)—White female, divorced, housekeeper, Baptist, grew up in Grand Rapids, Michigan.

Marge Scott (Class of 1960)—White female, married, legal secretary, Baptist, grew up in the Detroit area.

Marilyn Hamilton (Class of 1957)—White female, married, administrative assistant, Presbyterian, grew up in Muskegon, Michigan.

Donna Wood (Class of 1956)—White female, married, works in real estate sales, Church of Christ, grew up in Virginia.

Rachel Anderson (Class of 1965)—White female, married, cosmetologist, nondenominational, grew up in Kalamazoo, Michigan.

Shannon Norton (Class of 1960)—White female, divorced, Realtor, Baptist, grew up in Kalamazoo, Michigan.

Cindy Rogers (Class of 1962)—White female, divorced, registered investment adviser, Catholic, grew up in Stockton, California.

Sharon Weiss (Class of 1960)—White female, divorced, rancher/ditch tender, grew up in Merced, California.

Mary Sanders (Class of 1957)—White female, married, middle school teacher, Protestant, grew up in Fresno, California.

Doris Rice (dropped out of high school at age 15)—White female, married, health care analyst, Protestant, grew up in Clare, Michigan.

Howard Conrad (Class of 1958)—White male, married, disabled (but used to work in a factory), Protestant, grew up in Clare, Michigan.

Gary Simmons (Class of 1950)—White male, married, veteran of the Korean War, retired chemical process operator, grew up in Farwell, Michigan.

Carrie Barkley (Class of 1953)—White female, married, housewife, grew up in Farwell, Michigan.

Gail Powers (Class of 1954)—White female, married, reading tutor, grew up in South Haven, Michigan.

Al Shattuck (Class of 1953)—White male, married, manager at extermination company, Episcopalian, grew up in Midland, Michigan.

Lynette Cole (Class of 1954)—Black female, married, typist clerk, grew up in Cassapolis, Michigan.

Susan Curtis (Class of 1954)—White female, married, nurse, grew up in Lake Odessa, Michigan.

Betty Richards (Class of 1954)—White female, married, director of nursing, grew up in St. Clair Shores, Michigan.

In terms of the aggregate demographics of my informants, I talked with 12 men and 21 women. Of the participants, 28 were white and 5 were African American; 24 were married (9 men, 15 women), 7 were divorced (1 man, 6 women), and 2 were single (both men). Fourteen informants had occupations that the sociologist would label professional; six had skilled jobs; another six had semiskilled jobs; and seven worked (or had retired from) unskilled occupations. The majority of my respondents (26) were in Michigan during the 1950s. I also talked with three people who grew up in California, one in Virginia, one in Louisiana, one in Indiana, and one who spent part of the decade in Mississippi before moving to Michigan.

Note

1. Please see the appendix for demographic information on my informants. True to the promise of anonymity, none of the interviewees' real names are used. I give them fictitious names.

References

Belz, C. (1969). *The story of rock*. New York: Oxford University Press.

Eisler, B. (1986). *Private lives: Men and women of the fifties*. New York: Franklin Watts.

Eliot, M. (1989). *Rockonomics: The money behind the music*. New York: Watts.

Friedan, B. (1963). *The feminine mystique*. New York: Dell.

Gates, H. L., Jr. (1994). *Colored people: A memoir*. New York: Knopf.

Gillet, C. (1972). The black market roots of rock. In R. S. Denisoff & R. A. Peterson (Eds.), *The sounds of social change* (pp. 274-281). Chicago: Rand McNally.

Gitlin, T. (1987). *The sixties: Years of hope, days of rage*. New York: Bantam.

Halberstam, D. (1994, May 5). Interview on *"Eye to eye with Connie Chung."*

Halbwachs, M. (1992). *On collective memory*. Chicago: University of Chicago Press.

Harvey, B. (1993). *The fifties: A women's oral history*. New York: HarperCollins.

Pielke, R. G. (1986). *You say you want a revolution: Rock music in American culture*. Chicago: Nelson-Hall.

Rodgers, J. (1972, October 16). Back to the '50s. *Newsweek*, pp. 78-82.

Rosen, M. (1973). *Popcorn Venus: Women, movies, & the American dream*. New York: Coward, McCann & Geoghegan.

Stimpson, C. (1987). The future of memory: A summary. *Michigan Quarterly Review*, 26(1), 259-265.

Toth, S. A. (1981). *Blooming: A small-town girlhood*. Boston: Little, Brown.

Young, J. E. (1990, Winter). When a day remembers: A performative history of *Yom ha-Shoah*. *History & Memory*, 2(2), 54-75.

❧ 8 ❧

Adolescence, Gender, and the Development of Mental Health

Phame M. Camarena
Pamela A. Sarigiani
Anne C. Petersen

$\mathcal{F}$rom the earliest beginnings of the scientific study of adolescence, the transition from child to adult has been framed in terms of challenge and distress (Freud, 1925/1961; Hall, 1904). Although it is now known that most adolescents cross this phase of the life span without major psychological difficulties and the "storm and stress" model of adolescence has largely been discarded, it continues to be recognized that adolescence represents a time of substantial developmental challenge and potential psychological vulnerability (Petersen, Compas, Brooks-Gunn, Stemmler, Ey, & Grant, 1993). Psychological difficulties in adolescence cannot be assumed to be transitory; rather, they usually persist and are unlikely to disappear spontaneously (Petersen, 1993). Of particular significance, increasing evidence reveals that girls are more likely than boys to experience the challenges of adolescence in ways that may have negative implications for their mental health (e.g., Brooks-Gunn, 1991; Petersen, Sarigiani, & Kennedy, 1991).

AUTHORS' NOTE: The authors wish to acknowledge assistance in the narrative analysis from Rachel Gordon, Diane Koehl, Kim Scanlan, Katherine Waskiewicz, and Janine Zweig.

Yet, relative to work on adult mental health, research focused on adolescent mental health in general (Kazdin, 1993), and female adolescent mental health in particular (McGrath, Keita, Strickland, & Russo, 1990), has been scant. Still, a good body of work has begun to emerge in both positivist-quantitative and narrative-qualitative research traditions that informs the issues surrounding the gender differential experience of mental health across the adolescent years. However, to date, these two lines of work have largely been conducted independent of, and sometimes in opposition to, each other. As Huffman and Hauser (1994) assert, however, advancing our knowledge of affective processes in adolescence may be best facilitated by combining assessment modes, including both qualitative and quantitative approaches. To the degree that both research traditions tap different aspects of the same phenomenon, the integration of the two may lead to important insights into how mental health develops in both girls and boys across the adolescent years. This study represents a partial bridge in this gap as it attempts to explore the connection between young women's and men's quantitatively assessed mental health trajectories across adolescence with narrative representations of personal experience across the same period of time.

Gender and Adolescent Mental Health

Quantitative Traditions

Adolescent mental health research conducted from the positivist tradition has typically focused on assessing mean level scores, patterns of development, and factors linked to various mental health indicators. Although the findings vary somewhat across studies, the pattern of results clearly indicates that, relative to boys, adolescent girls are more likely to experience greater subjective distress and to exhibit related internalizing disorders (e.g., depression, anxiety, and eating disorders; Leadbeater, Blatt, & Quinlan, 1995). Within this body of literature, the domain of mental health that has received the most attention in research on gender and adolescence has been depression. This research has shown that, in comparison to boys, adolescent girls are at greater risk for depressive episodes and generally report more depressed affect (Ge, Lorenz, Conger, Elder, & Simons, 1994; Petersen et al., 1993). The significance of this trend is underscored by the fact that these patterns of difference represent a reversal from childhood experience and that they carry on into adulthood (e.g., Leon, Klerman, & Wickramaratne, 1993; Nolen-Hoeksema & Girgus, 1994).

Explanations for why adolescent girls are at greater risk for depression and other related mental health indicators have centered on a range of factors such as hormonal influences (e.g., Brooks-Gunn & Warren, 1989) and girls' greater likelihood of experiencing stressful life events (e.g., Petersen et al., 1991), including sexual victimization (Cutler & Nolen-Hoeksema, 1991). Other explanations suggest that expectations for adolescent girls to conform to restrictive social roles (Nolen-Hoeksema & Girgus, 1994) and socialization toward interpersonal relationships (Gore, Aseltine, & Colten, 1993) may contribute to gender differences in mental health outcomes.

Within this research tradition, an alternate set of explanations has suggested that the ways in which boys and girls interpret or make sense of their personal experiences may be, in part, responsible for gender differences in psychological well-being. For example, Rutter (1987) identifies the ways in which the style of *cognitive framing* of life experience can put girls at greater risk for psychopathology. Likewise, Nolen-Hoeksema (1987) indicates that women are more likely to cope with stressors using a ruminative style that amplifies depressed mood, whereas men are more likely to employ distracting behaviors that reduce depressed mood.

Narrative Tradition

Like this cognitively oriented work but building from a different set of assumptions, research studying adolescence from the narrative tradition has emphasized gender differences in the way adolescents interpret their world and experiences. Most notable in this regard is the work of Carol Gilligan and colleagues, who have explored the features of adolescent experience that distinguish between boys' and girls' stories of development (Gilligan, 1988; Gilligan, Ward, & Taylor, 1988). Gilligan specifically contrasted how the traditional theoretical perspectives of "successful" detachment and autonomy were more reflective of boys' stories. In contrast, although detachment and autonomy also were reflected in girls' stories, they were more likely to be framed in problematic terms. For girls, the dilemma became one of balancing self-integrity with caring for others.

Rogers, Brown, and Tappan (1994) point to the importance of the adolescent developmental period in understanding the significance of relational issues for the development of ego in girls. They report that a loss in ego development across adolescence was a common occurrence in the girls in their longitudinal study. However, the meaning of this ego regression varied. For some girls it represented increased evidence of adherence to societal conventions for relationships, a pattern of developmental vulnerability. In contrast, for others it represented resistance to conventional relationships and was characterized by a movement toward more authentic relationships. Note that while this body of work has not explicitly examined psychological well-being or mental health as typically assessed in quantitative empirical research, it is clear that gender differences emerge in domains that are relevant for understanding mental health in adolescence and beyond. In addition, as suggested by the Rogers et al. (1994) work, the meaning of psychological measures and assessments can be significantly informed by the narratives that surround them. It is important to note that the narrative study that most directly examined issues of adolescent mental health did not contrast the experience of boys and girls directly (Hauser, 1995). The study did, however, reveal that different experiences of psychological adjustment (e.g., psychologically resilient vs. vulnerable) were reflected in different types of narratives. Some noteworthy aspects of the resilient adolescents' narratives included their self-reflection, self-efficacy, and self-complexity.

Quantitative and Qualitative Integration

Although it is true that research from both the positivist and narrative perspectives has been tapping aspects of adolescent experience from different epistemological perspectives, data from each have identified the differential challenges and responses of girls and boys across this period of time. Both agree that adolescence is a time of important developmental challenge but that girls, especially, experience this time of transition in ways characterized by feelings of distress. What remains unclear, however, is the ways in which the findings from each of these perspectives are related. That is, although each tradition has provided valuable insights into adolescent experience, each has typically worked independent of the other. It is likely, however, that an examination of the commonalities and contradictions between positivist quantitative and narrative qualitative data on the same phenomena will lead to a richer and more complete story of both girls' and boys' experience.

The Adolescent Mental Health Study

The Adolescent Mental Health Study was begun as a longitudinal investigation of the gender-differential experience of early adolescence (Petersen, 1984). Through a series of successive follow-ups, this project continued to examine the factors that explain gender divergence in mental health across the adolescent years (e.g., Petersen et al., 1991). So far, the data from this study have indicated clear gender-typed differences in adjustment across adolescence. For example, the project data indicate that although the general affect and self-evaluation of both boys and girls increase across the early adolescent years, the level of emotional tone plateaus for girls after middle adolescence but continues to rise for boys across the late adolescent years. In addition to differences in the reported rates of depressive episodes, gender-differential associations of stressors and supports for depression have also been found. For example, girls were more likely than boys to link reports of depressive episodes to stressful family experiences. By 12th grade and continuing into young adulthood, consistent gender differences had emerged on a range of mental health indicators including depressive mood and self-image (for overview see Petersen, Sarigiani, Camarena, & Leffert, in press).

Although the majority of the work on the project has clearly centered within the positivist-quantitative tradition, there has always been an awareness of and appreciation for work being conducted in the narrative tradition. In fact, because data collection techniques paired psychometric assessments with semistructured personal interviews at each phase of the study, narrative information from the interview files was often used to clarify the meaning of statistical analyses or to explore possible directions for future work.

For example, Sarigiani (1987) examined the link between parent-adolescent relationships and adolescent psychological adjustment. A lack of closeness with parents was linked to psychological adjustment indicators, such as depressive mood. In particular, the quantitative results suggested that it would be useful to further explore the father-daughter relationship to better understand adolescent girls' adjustment. The narrative information from the interview files suggested that girls who scored low on father closeness perceived their fathers to be emotionally distant, strict, and unavailable.

From this background of work, it was agreed during the planning for the young adult follow-up (age 21) that the potential to integrate longitudinal assessments with participants' subjective reflections of the same experience represented a "once in a lifetime opportunity." To that end, efforts were made to design a data collection strategy that would fit within the constraints of the larger project but allow for an explicit examination of our study participants' subjective perspectives on their personal experience.

The primary tool for assessing personal experiences of well-being was developed as an adaptation of Runyon's (1980) Life Satisfaction Chart and Gergen's (1988) Graphic Story Line method. The Psychological Well-Being Chart was included as the final task of the study to be completed after the other traditional psychological assessments. This form of the measure began by stating that the overall project was designed to study adolescent mental health and then explained,

> As researchers, we have our own ideas about what psychological well-being is, how it changes over the years, and what things influence its development. Now that you are a young adult and have a greater ability to reflect on yourself and

your life, we want to know *what you think* is important in understanding psychological well-being in *your* life.

Participants were then directed to draw a line representing their psychological well-being "as they recalled it from the past into the future" on the chart provided and to "label the chart in as much detail as possible in order to explain the graphed line." On separate pages, participants were then asked to define what they meant by the term *psychological well-being* and to summarize what they believed to be most important for understanding their personal experience of psychological well-being across the adolescent years.

Because the Self-Image Questionnaire for Young Adolescents (SIQYA; Petersen, Schulenberg, Abramowitz, Offer, & Jarcho, 1984) had been the primary tool used in the assessment of psychological well-being from the beginning of the study, it was chosen as the indicator of the basic pattern of girls' and boys' mental health across the period of the study. Although the SIQYA measure includes a number of subscales that tap different dimensions of self and social functioning, the total score was used as a generalized assessment of overall psychological well-being.

Statistical analysis of the data confirmed that this overall score is highly correlated with other indicators of psychological adjustment included in the data set (e.g., depression, substance abuse, self-esteem).

In order to allow for the connection of the narrative data to these quantitative data, the sample used in the analyses for this study was drawn from those participants that had completed both the Psychological Well-Being Chart and the SIQYA measure at both the age 11 and 21 waves of data collection. This subset of participants included 103 women and 76 men.

Although a number of different analytical strategies were used in the analysis of various portions of these data, the major results presented here focus on the interpretive exploration of the descriptions, definitions, and explanations of psychological well-being across adolescence contained in the chart measure. This particular set of analyses draws from grounded theory techniques (Strauss, 1987; Strauss & Corbin, 1990) to identify the core constructs contained within these data.

The first set of analyses were conducted separately by gender with consideration of the core constructs within each set of reports. The initial constructs developed on the first half of the data set were then confirmed in the second half of the data, as independent coders reviewed the entire data set for all of the themes within both the men's and women's reports. It is important to note that this study did not ask explicitly for a *story* of experience; however, we quickly discovered that in most personal reports, a clear story of experience was contained within the chart, definition, and explanation data. The importance of these stories for understanding gender and adjustment across adolescence was reflected in both the particular gender-typed themes identified and the quality of the stories constructed.

Gendered Themes

Although the evidence for gender-differential adjustment experiences across adolescence was compelling, there were a number of content elements that were consistent across both men's and women's reports. For example, although most participants did not comment on adolescence as a life stage generally, when it was directly noted, it was described in terms reflecting distress. Both women and men described adolescence, especially early adolescence, as a "hard time" with "growing pains" and "too many changes at once." Similarly, both men and women consistently identified the significance of relationships with others, especially family, peers, and romantic relationships for the experience of psychological well-being across the adolescent years.

Men's Themes. The development of core constructs to represent the men's data was significantly informed by ideas generated from both developmental concepts and the words of participants themselves. At the concept level, a category for *coping/adjustment* was initially used to represent descriptions of how men responded to specific challenges across adolescence. For example, in descriptions of normative transitions, such as starting a new school or losing friends who moved away, men often described an adjustment period where they worked to "get back" to previous levels of well-being. Furthermore, in defining the nature of psychological well-being, men consistently included comments about the importance of being able to "cope with life's problems" and "deal with things in a calm, reasonable manner."

From the in vivo codes, men consistently referred to *stable* and *stability* as key elements of well-being. In fact, four of the first five narratives examined included one or more specific uses of these words. For example, in describing his story line over time, one of these men concluded: "Basically, I've been pretty stable without any negative event happening—thank God." Even in the absence of the word *stable*, many men communicated the connection of stability to mental health by acknowledging that "mood swings" or other "fluctuations" away from stability were indicators of poor psychological well-being. Combining both the concept and in vivo codes, it soon became apparent that maintaining stability was an essential component of how men were describing psychological well-being during their adolescent years. Coping and adjustment merely serve the function of getting a person back on track so that stability is restored. As one man explained,

> The most important aspect for understanding psychological well-being is to realize it exists. If one understands it, he can always keep it toward the top by adjusting to situations. If one is down because of something, he should react accordingly to counter these feelings and get back toward the top.

Although somewhat less pervasive and obvious as a core construct or theme, a considerable number of men's narratives described the importance of keeping perspective. Throughout the course of analysis, this theme was manifest in a number of different ways. Some men described the importance of "being aware of personal strengths and weaknesses" whereas others noted the need to remain "focused on internal goals and directions." At a higher level of focus, some men described how "perceptions of the world" or a "purpose in life" were essential for healthy functioning. Similar importance was attached to "having a positive mental attitude" or "remaining optimistic" in the face of challenge.

It is important to note that although perspective was valued by the men in this sample, most men did not explain where this set of optimistic attitudes came from. Whereas one man explained how the death of his father had made him "aware of the beautiful things in life," few men described the source of their perspective on life and adjustment. This disconnection between lived experience and perspective was most clearly described by one young man who focused on the need to "exercise the mind." He simply noted that "psychological well-being to me is independent of life experience." In contrast, most men were quite clear about why keeping perspective mattered.

Drawing the two primary themes together, it was evident that while many men acknowledged the role of supports and other active coping methods in promoting psychological well-being, the primary strategy for maintaining stability was to keep perspective on the challenges and processes of life. Sometimes the blending of these two themes was woven implicitly through descriptions of adolescent experience. For example, on a chart where an early dip in well-being was attributed to "feelings that life was purposeless and cruel," positive adjustment in young adulthood was reflected in an "increase in stabilization" stemming from a "change in perception of the world and my role in it."

A number of men also explicitly defined the connection between the two themes. These statements are especially noteworthy because of the richness and clarity of description. Although most of the men's responses were not well-elaborated or clearly articulated, descriptions joining the stability and perspective themes were often well-developed.

> Psychological well-being to me means that I have the ability to see things—namely things that have a potential of creating stress, emotional strain, or strong negative feelings—in an optimistic way. The ability to clear away the "commentary of life" and understand that things are never irreversible. To me the most important value a person can have is the value of life itself, and in hard times, it's remembering the big picture of life that will pull you through.

In an even more descriptive vein, another man explained,

> Every time I get down, I think of the street dwellers in
> India who are actually happy to be alive. Or I think of our
> tiny spaceship Earth in the vast galaxy, and how small I am.
> It makes me just want to forget about all the trivial troubles
> in my life because that is what they are.

Women's Themes. The factors identified in past empirical research as central to adolescent girls' mental health were evident in the reports of these young women. Similarly, the relational focus of self developed in previous narrative work was evident as well. However, all these issues proved to be most useful as a backdrop for the narrative themes that emerged in these women's descriptions and explanations of psychological well-being across adolescence.

Like the men's explanations, the women's descriptions of psychological well-being typically began by referring to a generalized happiness or satisfaction. However, for women, but not men, the focus of the definition and explanation quickly moved to an emphasis on *self-acceptance*. As one woman clarified, "happiness can be deceiving. . . . More important is understanding that every person is important and worthwhile, and that we all have faults. Loving oneself is very important." Although this orientation toward well-being was manifest in a number of different ways, consistent references to liking, loving, and being satisfied with oneself were found across the women's reports.

The reason for the focus on self-acceptance was quite apparent as women discussed the influence of social expectations and the pains of trying to "measure up." Some women framed this challenge in general terms. For example, after completing the graph one woman was surprised to "realize" that her graph really reflected how much "time I spend worrying about myself and the way that others perceive me."

For most women, however, a clear source of pressure was identified with family and peers playing the most central roles. A woman who defined psychological well-being in terms of self-confidence, self-worth, and self-value explained that "I was always being over-shadowed by my family" but now realize that "I count." Similarly, the standards of peers presented a number of women with significant challenges across adolescence. The long-term effects of such peer comparisons were clearly noted:

> I have always lacked self-confidence in myself in school and appearance because of my "friends" in junior high. This carried on with me into my later years. It took a while for me to realize that I was just as good as anyone else and I could let a part of my guard down.

This example also alludes to the second core theme of the women's reports. For the women in this sample, but not the men, psychological well-being was something that develops because of experiences across adolescence. The theme of growing from experience was consistently reflected as women incorporated both specific experiences and general life lessons into explanations of how their psychological well-being had developed across adolescence. Unlike the men, who described efforts at "maintaining control" across personal experience, the women in this sample were considerably more likely to describe how their past experience with both the "very high points and very low points" was used to build the foundation of current psychological well-being.

This openness to learning from experience was consistently reflected in both how women integrated particular events into their story of adolescent adjustment and in generalized assessments of the importance of self-reflection and assessment. For example, a woman who described a number of major family disruptions across adolescence concluded, "I did mature a lot faster psychologically. . . . However, I will use this later in life when situations occur that I can't prevent." In contrast, another woman did not mention any outstanding challenges across adolescence, but she similarly concluded that "it's important to *think* about things and try to *mentally learn* from bad experiences, and gain strength and knowledge from good experiences."

For many of these women, learning and growing from experiences across adolescence appeared to be the specific catalyst for self-development. Although the particular lessons and subsequent changes varied across individuals, by far the most consistent lesson learned was the need to accept oneself.

That is, similar to the integration of men's themes, the connection of these two primary themes in the women's responses typically formed the basis of the strongest stories told.

Some women described the growth to self-acceptance as a slow and gradual process leading to profound changes in the experience of psychological well-being. As one woman explained,

> Over the years, I've had several yardsticks of well-being: my family's standards, my friends' standards, etc. It takes a lot of self-exploration, however, to realize that personal well-being is an individual evaluation. I've realized that some of the ideas and experiences that make me feel comfortable with myself don't match up with those of the people who surround me. Slowly I am learning that I will live with *me* for the next 60 to 70 years and that I will constantly be coming up against various measurements of well-being. Mine is the only one that will endure, so I better be satisfied with it.

Others linked the growth to self-acceptance more directly to particular experiences. This was illustrated in the story of a young woman who, over the course of adolescence, experienced the divorce of her parents and the suicide of her brother. In her story, she attributed the growth to her work with a therapist and a semester abroad. Each provided an opportunity to learn how to integrate the negative life experiences in more positive ways. The end result was a more confident person. As she reflected in her summary, "I think that's the key—once you learn to love yourself, others will love you too. . . . and because I've overcome a lot of obstacles. . . . I know I can handle any situation I'm faced with." Although the peak of challenges described by women in these narratives generally occurred or began during early adolescence, the period of growth and awareness was more typically associated with late adolescence and young adulthood as women moved into new situations away from family and old peer groups.

Adjustment Group Contrasts

Although these themes do not reflect an exclusive story of either men or women, the recognition that they are generally descriptive of a qualitatively different experience of psychological well-being across adolescence is clear. As suggested by the previous work on our project, however, the reports of the "average" experience often inflate gender differences and mask important within-group variability (Petersen, 1988). Therefore, an additional set of analyses was performed to separate the boys and girls who had experienced the most and least distress across adolescence as measured by total self-image score (SIQYA Total).

Drawing from the means and slopes (change scores) of SIQYA data at ages 11 and 21, groups were developed to represent different patterns of psychological adjustment across the adolescent years. The positive adjustment group included everyone who scored in the top third (within gender) of self-image and had an increase in score from age 11 to 21. The negative adjustment group included everyone who scored in the bottom third of self-image and had a decrease in score from age 11 to 21.

Men's Contrast. In comparing the reports of these men from the negative ($n = 20$) and positive ($n = 20$) adjustment groups, it quickly became apparent that the basic themes identified within the previous analyses remained consistent across groups. There were, however, indications of important distinctions in both the nature of events included in stories and the tone of the "perspective" described.

Counter to our expectations, the men in the negative adjustment group did not generally describe nonnormative life events or special challenges that might lead to problems in psychological well-being. Although a few men did mention the death of close family members or problems with moving across the country, for the most part, they described normal adolescent transitions such as "starting at new school" or "first serious girlfriend." What is distinctive about their descriptions, however, is that these men often acknowledged the problems they had in controlling and mastering their experience across these transitions.

This pattern is noted in the way that two different men described their school experience. The first explained that he was "anticipating college" and "hit the ground running" but soon became "dissatisfied with what school offers" and with his "ability to stand up under fire."

The second reported consistent problems in adapting to the "stresses" of high school and college. Although he claimed to have "adapted well" and kept "a positive outlook" through these challenges, he described the transition out of college in less than confident terms: "As I come to graduation, I am very excited and scared. I end one part of my life that went well and begin another step of my life which worries me because I don't want to fail at it."

As suggested by this example, even though men in the negative adjustment group typically expressed some optimism about life, their descriptions reflected a more jaded and alienated perspective. Consistent with this more negative perspective, men in this group often admitted to loneliness and appeared to be resigned to the boredom and routine of life. Even the most thoughtful in this group tempered his optimistic perspective with ironic pessimism:

> One must be able to look ahead at things; to be able to look to the future. This may sound optimistic, but that's how I am. And I think it's a good thing to be a bit optimistic. It seems I talk to a lot of my friends and it's like they are always down on themselves and their lives. That's bullshit, cuz it doesn't get them anywhere. Yes, I've had really horrible things happen and they bum me out and I still think of them, but life goes on. . . . your life is just that—*your life!* You can die and the whole world won't even bat an eye. It's dismal almost but it doesn't get me down cuz that's just how it is. So I'm pretty much having fun while I'm able to. You got to.

In contrast to the experience and perspective of the negative group, the men in the positive adjustment group reported more significant life events but always framed perspective in more confident and positive terms. However, these descriptions of perspective and stability did not necessarily reflect a subjective experience of psychological strength or depth.

For about a fourth of the men in this group, the experience of life challenge was connected to the development of their life and self-perspective. One young man who had to adjust to the simultaneous divorce of his parents and moving to a new community commented on the value of "bad times" to "build character" and "reconstruct foundations" of self. Another reflected on how the death of his father forced him to "mature much earlier" and led to an appreciation of how "fragile" and "precious" life is.

For the majority of these men, however, their descriptions of adolescence revealed perspectives that indicated an attempt to avoid or control the potentially painful experiences of life. As one of the men who scored the highest on self-image across time explained, "even if a tragedy comes along, don't let it affect life too much. Have and show feelings, but don't let it interfere with your life." This perspective of control and avoidance is also reflected in the description of a young man who experienced the death of several family members during early adolescence when he explained that it is important to be "strong-willed and thick-skinned. . . . to cope with life's problems and tak[e] them in stride."

Even by their own admonition, these men often did not know where their perspective came from or what sense to make of their experience. As one young man who described the challenges of his sister's psychiatric hospitalization and the effects of her problems on the family acknowledged, "I ignored the situation and denied its existence" and "still really don't understand" the significance of this experience. In a different vein, another man who describes his adolescence as a constant struggle to maintain "certainty" and "control" explained that although some of his self-confidence probably came from his parents' "praise and compassion," he also believed that it is simply a personality trait that is also "just inherited." He somewhat quizzically concludes, however, that although his sisters are "tremendously successful" and received the same parental encouragement, they "do not possess the self-assuredness."

Women's Contrast. Similar to the situation in the men's comparison, the two primary gender-typed themes were consistently identified across both the negative and positive adjustment groups. That is, in their discussions, the women in each sample described the need to accept oneself and to grow from experience. Those distinctions that did emerge in this adjustment group contrast seemed to reflect differences in quantity rather than quality.

Compared to women in the positive adjustment group, women in the negative group described their reaction to challenges as being more intense. This was primarily reflected in the tone of description used. For example, whereas a woman in the positive adjustment group described adolescence as a "nervous" and "unsettled" time, a woman from the negative adjustment group described a similar period as being "a seesaw from 'tops' to 'rock bottom.' " Similarly, although a comparable proportion of women in each group noted parental divorce as a challenge during adolescence, women in the negative adjustment group were more likely to describe a chain of negative effects emerging from this experience. One woman who remained with her father after the divorce claimed that the divorce proceedings had "changed the course" of her life. Another described how the divorce led to her feelings of worthlessness and anorexia. As revealed in this last woman's comments, the greater intensity of challenge was also manifested in the report of additional personal problems.

Whether these problems were considered a cause or consequence of psychological well-being within individual stories varied. It was clear, however, that these experiences were more characteristic of the negative adjustment group and that these experiences reflected gender-typed crises. For example, in addition to the difficult school transitions, deaths, and family moves described by men in this sample, women in the negative adjustment group indicated that they had also struggled with an eating disorder, were sexually victimized, or had dealt with an unplanned pregnancy. Whereas only one woman in the positive adjustment group reported any of these experiences, almost a third of the women in the negative adjustment group indicated one or more of these crises across adolescence. This was reflected in the summary of a woman from the negative adjustment group:

> I have had numerous family difficulties. My father died at age 7, I was sexually abused for 5 years, my grandmother died, my mother is an alcoholic, I have a bad ending to a long-term relationship, and I have been bulemic for the last 6 years.

Not surprisingly, given the difference in intensity of challenges reported, women in the negative adjustment group were more likely to describe their growth and self-acceptance as a work in progress. A woman who described the struggle of learning to accept herself in the face of an overly critical father reported that

> there was no one there to stand up for me except me.
> I had to learn to be strong that way but when I wasn't up
> to defending myself, my spirit was broken a little more and
> a little more.

Similarly, a woman who acknowledged the importance of self-acceptance explained,

> It's sometimes a struggle between what I want as an individual and what I want for myself. . . . I think it is a problem, at least for me to be social as well as self-reliant. As I enter into "adulthood," I sometimes find it difficult to balance independence with commitment to others.

These comments stand in stark contrast to many of the women in the positive adjustment group who describe the lessons learned as complete and life-transforming. For example, a woman who described a difficult adolescence noted,

> It is important to know that during adolescence I was extremely unhappy. Because of that period in my life, I have changed drastically as a person. Never again will I allow my life to bottom out as it did then. I am a stronger person and have created and forced myself to develop into a happy and satisfied person. Now that I am the kind of person who likes myself, I am content with the direction my life is taking!

Similar sentiments about the strength of the lessons learned were acknowledged by a woman who sought counseling while at college to deal with long-standing family problems:

> With 4 months of counseling, I picked up the pieces of my life and have been on an upward climb ever since. I have let my family rely on themselves. I don't mediate any longer.

> I don't struggle for perfection any longer. I recognize all of
> my feelings and I no longer lock them up inside. I'm no
> longer an emotional island that supports everyone else.

For the women in the positive adjustment group, adolescence was
generally a time of distress and change. They, more than any other
group, however, used these challenges as a source of growth and
development of mental health.

Lessons

We began this investigation with the purpose of examining what
the participants in this study could tell us about gender, the experience
of psychological well-being across adolescence, and the meaning of
our quantitative mental health assessments across this 10-year period.
The lessons we learned have affected the way we understand the data
from our own project and have given us a new appreciation of the significance of narrative perspectives for informing traditional positivist-
quantitative research.

At the most basic level, the themes that emerged in the gender
comparisons suggest that psychological well-being may not have the
same meaning for boys and girls across the adolescent years. In the
case of these data, the boys' focus on stability and the girls' focus on
self-acceptance clearly reflect qualitative differences in both experience and perspective. Similarly, the gender contrasts also give clear
indications that the significance of adolescence for the development
of mental health is not the same for the boys and girls in this study.
Based on the reports of these women and men, it does appear as
though girls experience greater challenge and distress across the
adolescent years. It is striking, however, that whereas the women
describe the value of using these challenges for growth and learning,
the men appear to be "riding out" the challenges of this time by using
perspective to distance themselves from potentially painful feelings.

Given previous quantitative and qualitative research, none of these
themes should be surprising. At the quantitative level, these themes
and the stories they reflect are consistent with research that has

examined gender-related differences in adolescents' self-evaluation processes, relational orientations, and interpretive styles (e.g., Gore et al., 1993; Nolen-Hoeksema, 1987; Ruble, Greulich, Pomerantz, & Gochberg, 1993). At the qualitative level, these themes are also reflected in work that has identified the challenges that adolescent girls confront in balancing autonomy with connection and the growth that comes from confronting this challenge (e.g., Gilligan, Lyons, & Hanmer, 1990; Rogers et al., 1994). In this regard, it is interesting to note that there is less narrative work that examines how adolescent boys make sense of their experience across this time of transition.

The significance of these basic gender-typed themes is further highlighted by the contrasts that allowed us to examine how the quantitatively assessed patterns of psychological well-being were reflected in the personal stories of the participants. Although the same gender-typed themes were reflected in both the positive and negative adjustment groups for both women and men, the distinctions between the groups suggest that the quantitative data is only telling one part of the story.

For example, although both the women and men in the negative adjustment groups were having difficulty in integrating adolescent experiences in healthy ways, the men did not typically connect their more lonely and alienated perspectives to specific events or issues. In contrast, the women described significant and dramatic adjustment challenges that emerged from their experience as girls and women but still remained committed to using these experiences for personal growth.

Furthermore, while the men in the positive adjustment group reflected an attitude of confidence and control, their narratives were typically simplistic and reflected a general lack of depth and insight. This is similar to Josselson's (1992) finding that, in comparison to women, men's descriptions of experience are not only less relational, they are also less complex. Given the data here, our interpretation of this pattern is not that these men were unwilling to self-disclose negative feelings to us; rather, we believe that they were unwilling to admit negative emotional experiences to themselves (e.g., Chevron, Quinlan, & Blatt, 1978). Similarly, we do not interpret these findings to suggest that the psychometric assessment is invalid; rather, it is this very interpretive style that protects these young men from emotional distress and allows them to score high on these assessments (Gore et al., 1993; Nolen-Hoeksema, 1987).

In contrast, the women in the positive adjustment group acknowledged significant adjustment challenge across adolescence. These women, however, were more likely to describe a rich narrative that identified how they had worked to integrate a new appreciation and understanding of themselves to build a new foundation for the development of psychological well-being. Like the description offered by Hauser (1995) of the *resilient narrative*, these women created quality stories that reflected self-reflection, self-complexity, persistence, and self-esteem. In comparison to the men in the positive adjustment group, these women appear to have developed a solid foundation of mental health because of how they have confronted adolescent experiences.

The importance of these patterns for our understanding of adolescent mental health more generally was suggested by Gilligan (1982) when she noted that the externally imposed standards and definitions of researchers may not adequately reflect the experience of both boys and girls equally. The problem in defining mental health adequately is further suggested in a study that contrasted male and female psychotherapists' conceptualizations of mental health. In an outcome similar to the themes in our women's and men's descriptions, these researchers found that whereas male therapists were more likely to value affective control, female therapists prioritized self-acceptance as a key component of mental health (Haugen, Tyler, & Clark, 1991). In addition, the nature of adolescence as a complicated, transitional period of development with natural "perturbations of adaptation" also complicates the assessment of mental health of boys and girls at this time (Kazdin, 1993, p. 127).

As Powers, Hauser, and Kilner (1989) noted, it is important to both identify what "mental health" is and to describe the "variety of profiles of healthy development" across the adolescent years that might exist—varieties that include a recognition of the differential experience and strengths of both girls and boys (p. 201). For at least in these data, mental health does not have the same meaning across gender, and the pathway to positive mental health over the period of adolescence does not appear to be the same.

These important insights from our project would not have been possible with analyses of either quantitative or qualitative data exclusively; rather, it was the combination of the two that led to these findings. To that end, we believe that neither research tradition alone, positivist-quantitative or qualitative-narrative, is adequate for examining the issues of gender and adolescent mental health. We believe the two must increasingly be brought together within individual studies and broader programs of research to clarify the complex issues of how adolescent experience shapes the development of mental health in both girls and boys (see Sechrest & Sidani, 1995, or Pugliesi, 1992, for discussion of qualitative-quantitative integration issues).

With careful consideration of the biases inherent in psychometric assessments, it is possible to continue to identify the factors that explain and predict which girls and boys will use adolescent challenges to develop a foundation of mental health for positive functioning in adult life. Our ability to predict how boys and girls will respond to the challenges of adolescence is undoubtedly essential for developing effective responses to the needs of each. At the same time, it is important to understand how adolescents understand what mental health is and how they make sense of their own adolescent experiences. For as young adults reflect on the significance of their adolescent experience for their future choices, they do not consider their scores on a measure or test—it's the story of their experience that matters. The nature of that story should also explain and predict who will succeed in the transition to adulthood. As one of our study participants summarized,

> Regardless of our upbringing—whether it be pleasant or unpleasant, most important is to develop the understanding and memory of our past that is most helpful in allowing us to be happy with ourselves and to achieve in other areas as adults. What I am saying about myself is that my understanding of my past is an understanding which has allowed me to move on and achieve as an adult. I am very grateful for this advantage.

References

Brooks-Gunn, J. (1991). How stressful is the transition to adolescence for girls? In M. E. Colten & S. Gore (Eds.), *Adolescent stress: Causes and consequences* (pp. 131-149). New York: Aldine de Gruyter.

Brooks-Gunn, J., & Warren, M. (1989). Biological and social contributions to negative affect in young adolescent girls. *Child Development, 60*, 40-55.

Chevron, E. S., Quinlan, P. M., & Blatt, S. J. (1978). Sex roles and gender differences in the expression of depression. *Journal of Abnormal Psychology, 87*, 680-683.

Cutler, S. E., & Nolen-Hoeksema, S. (1991). Accounting for sex differences in depression through female victimization: Childhood sexual abuse. *Sex Roles, 24*, 425-438.

Freud, S. (1961). Some psychical consequences of the anatomical distinction between the sexes. In J. Strachey (Ed.), *Standard edition* (Vol. 19). London: Hogarth. (Original work published 1925)

Ge, X., Lorenz, F. O., Conger, R. D., Elder, G. H., & Simons, R. L. (1994). Trajectories of stressful life events and depressive symptoms during adolescence. *Developmental Psychology, 30*, 467-483.

Gergen, M. (1988). Narrative structures in social explanation. In C. Antaki (Ed.), *Analyzing lay explanation: A casebook of methods* (pp. 94-112). Newbury Park, CA: Sage.

Gilligan, C. (1982). *In a different voice: Psychological theory and women's development.* Cambridge, MA: Harvard University Press.

Gilligan, C. (1988). Adolescent development reconsidered. In C. Gilligan, J. Ward, & J. Taylor (Eds.), *Mapping the moral domain* (pp. viii-xxxix). Cambridge, MA: Harvard University Press.

Gilligan, C., Lyons, N. P., & Hanmer, T. J. (Eds.). (1990). *Making connections.* Cambridge, MA: Harvard University Press.

Gilligan, C., Ward, J. V., Taylor, J. M. (Eds.). (1988). *Mapping the moral domain.* Cambridge, MA: Harvard University Press.

Gore, S., Aseltine, R. H., & Colten, M. E. (1993). Gender, social-relational involvement, and depression. *Journal of Research on Adolescence, 3*, 101-125.

Hall, G. S. (1904). *Adolescence.* New York: Appleton-Century-Crofts.

Haugen, M. L., Tyler, J. D., & Clark, J. A. (1991). Mental health values of psychotherapists: How psychologists, psychiatrists, psychoanalysts, and social workers conceptualize good mental health. *Counseling and Values, 36*, 24-36.

Hauser, S. T. (1995, March). Exceptional outcomes: Negotiating a perilous adolescence. In S. T. Hauser & J. Brooks-Gunn (Chairs), *Resilience beyond adolescence: Longitudinal studies of transitions from adolescent to young adult years.* Symposium conducted at the biennial meeting of the Society for Research in Child Development, Indianapolis, IN.

Huffman, L. C., & Hauser, S. T. (1994). Afterward: Reflections and future directions. *Journal of Research on Adolescence, 4*, 657-662.

Josselson, R. L. (1992). *The space between us.* San Francisco: Jossey-Bass.

Kazdin, A. (1993). Adolescent mental health: Prevention and treatment programs. *American Psychologist, 48*, 127-141.

Leadbeater, B. J., Blatt, S. J., & Quinlan, D. M. (1995). Gender-linked vulnerabilities to depressive symptoms, stress, and problem behaviors in adolescents. *Journal of Research on Adolescence, 5*, 1-29.

Leon, A. C., Klerman, G. L., & Wickramaratne, P. (1993). Continuing female predominance in depressive illness. *American Journal of Public Health, 83*, 754-757.

McGrath, E., Keita, G. P., Strickland, B. R., & Russo, N. F. (Eds.). (1990). *Women and depression: Risk factors and treatment issues.* Washington, DC: American Psychological Association.

Nolen-Hoeksema, S. (1987). Sex differences in unipolar depression: Evidence and theory. *Psychological Bulletin, 101*, 259-282.

Nolen-Hoeksema, S., & Girgus, J. S. (1994). The emergence of gender differences in depression during adolescence. *Psychological Bulletin, 115*, 424-443.

Petersen, A. C. (1984). The early adolescence study: An overview. *Journal of Early Adolescence, 4*, 103-106.

Petersen, A. C. (1988). Adolescent development. *Annual Review of Psychology, 39*, 583-607.

Petersen, A. C. (1993). Presidential address: Creating adolescents: The role of context and process in developmental trajectories. *Journal of Research on Adolescence, 3*, 1-18.

Petersen, A. C., Compas, B. E., Brooks-Gunn, J., Stemmler, M., Ey, S., & Grant, K. E. (1993). Depression in adolescence. *American Psychologist, 48*, 155-168.

Petersen, A. C., Sarigiani, P. A., Camarena, P. M., & Leffert, N. (in press). Resilience in adolescence. *International Annals of Adolescent Psychiatry.*

Petersen, A. C., Sarigiani, P. A., & Kennedy, R. E. (1991). Adolescent depression: Why more girls? *Journal of Youth and Adolescence, 20*, 247-271.

Petersen, A. C., Schulenberg, J. E., Abramowitz, R. H., Offer, D., & Jarcho, H. D. (1984). A self-image questionnaire for young adolescents: Reliability and validity studies. *Journal of Youth and Adolescence, 13*, 93-111.

Powers, S. I., Hauser, S. T., & Kilner, L. A. (1989). Adolescent mental health. *American Psychologist, 44*, 200-208.

Pugliesi, K. (1992). Women and mental health: Two traditions of feminist research. *Women and Health, 19*, 43-68.

Rogers, A. G., Brown, L. M., & Tappan, M. B. (1994). Interpreting loss in ego development in girls: Regression or resistance? In A. Lieblich & R. Josselson (Eds.), *The narrative study of lives: Vol. 2. Exploring identity and gender* (pp. 1-36). Thousand Oaks, CA: Sage.

Ruble, D. N., Greulich, F., Pomerantz, E. M., & Gochberg, B. (1993). The role of gender-related processes in the development of sex differences in self-evaluation and depression. *Journal of Affective Disorders, 29*, 97-128.

Runyon, W. M. (1980). The life satisfaction chart: Perceptions of the course of subjective experience. *International Journal of Aging and Human Development, 11*, 45-64.

Rutter, M. (1987). The role of cognition in child development and disorder. *British Journal of Medical Psychology, 60*, 1-16.

Sarigiani, P. A. (1987). *Perceived emotional closeness with father, mother, and a friend: Gender differences in links to adjustment in early adolescence.* Unpublished master's thesis, Pennsylvania State University, University Park, PA.

Sechrest, L., & Sidani, S. (1995). Quantitative and qualitative methods: Is there an alternative? Special Feature: The quantitative-qualitative debates. *Evaluation and Program Planning, 18*, 77-87.

Strauss, A., & Corbin, J. (1990). *Basics of qualitative research: Grounded theory procedures and techniques*. Newbury Park, CA: Sage.

Strauss, A. L. (1987). *Qualitative analysis for social scientists*. Cambridge, UK: Cambridge University Press.

❦ **9** ❦

In Search of Resilience in Adult Survivors of Childhood Sexual Abuse

Linking Outlets for Power Motivation to Psychological Health

Jacquelyn Boone James
Joan Huser Liem
Joan Gateley O'Toole

Childhood sexual abuse (CSA) and its aftermath must be dealt with by about one out of every four females in the United States (Russell, 1986). Although many studies point to devastating psychological consequences (see, for example, Beck & Van der Kolk, 1987; Patten,

AUTHORS' NOTE: Parts of this chapter were presented at the American Psychological Association conference, Psychosocial and Behavioral Factors in Women's Health: Creating an Agenda for the 21st Century, May 11-14, 1994, Washington, D.C. This research was supported by the College of Arts and Sciences Faculty Development Grant to Joan Liem from the University of Massachusetts at Boston and grants to Jacquelyn James from the President's Fund at Radcliffe College and from the Spring Foundation for Research on Women in Contemporary Society. The authors also gratefully acknowledge the assistance of Ana Abrantes and Evelyn Liberatore in the preparation of this report.

Gatz, Jones, & Thomas, 1989; Sachs, Goodwin, & Braun, 1985), seldom are survivors who seem less psychologically distressed seen as the focus of inquiry. Yet, within samples of children who have been abused, fully 30% appear to be asymptomatic (Kendall-Tackett, Williams, & Finkelhor, 1993). Studies of adults reveal subgroups who make positive adjustments, as well (Haugaard & Reppucci, 1988; Liem, James, O'Toole, & Boudewyn, in press). Still, little is known about the processes by which some individuals adapt to a childhood stressor such as sexual abuse better than others and appear resilient, in spite of their childhood trauma.

Indeed, resilience in the face of childhood trauma of all kinds has been a topic of increasing interest over the last two decades (see Cicchetti & Aber, 1986; Garmezy, 1970, 1981 for examples). There is growing evidence that resilience may be based on a sustained perception of one's own worth as a person alongside the confidence that one can "successfully cope with life's challenges" (Rutter, 1990, p. 206). How these outcomes are possible or by what processes they are accomplished in the aftermath of a specific stressful life event like CSA is less clear.

One line of inquiry sorely missing from research about the aftermath of childhood stressors in general and CSA in particular is the concern with power that would seem to flow logically from abuses of power by trusted adults. Although theoretical models on the effects of CSA are multifaceted, one dominant and consistent factor included in the most widely cited models (e.g., Briere, 1992; Browne & Finkelhor, 1986) is the role of power in the lives of survivors. Yet little empirical work has been aimed in this direction. In two previous studies (Liem, O'Toole, & James, 1992, 1996), we found that individuals with histories of CSA injected themes of power and influence into Thematic Apperception Test (TAT) stories more often than did individuals who had not experienced CSA. CSA survivors' TAT stories indicated a stronger need for power (n Power; Winter, 1973).

A high need for power, according to Winter (1988), can have both positive and negative consequences. For example, it can be satisfied by assuming socially responsible leadership positions and caring for others, as well as by aggression, drinking, gambling, and exploiting others. We hypothesized that having or creating socially acceptable outlets for the need for power might be one source of resilience in survivors of CSA. Thus, among the questions posed in this chapter are: How do survivors understand their own adaptive processes, that is, their resilience? And are these processes linked to what we know about healthy adaptation for those who manifest a high n Power motive profile?

Resilience

The meaning of *resilience* is a matter of some complexity and the focus of much debate. First of all, it has been acknowledged that factors involved in resilience are multiple and interactive (see Hauser, Vieyra, Jacobson, & Wertlieb, 1985; Mrazek & Mrazek, 1987; Neiman, 1988). Clearly, there are important aspects of the person, the environment, and the stressful event itself that combine to determine both positive and negative outcomes (see, for example, Garmezy, 1991). Thus, the study of resilience has generally involved a focus on those who manage reasonably well in the face of known risk factors for developmental impairment (Hauser et al., 1985; Neiman, 1988; Werner, 1984; West & Prinz, 1987). Wolin (1991), for example, defines resilience as the "capacity of children in troubled families to prevail, grow, be strong, and even thrive despite their daily lot of hardship" (p. 3).

Rutter (1990) has cautioned, however, that resilience must not be seen as a "fixed attribute of the individual. If circumstances change, the risk alters" (p. 184). Moreover, says Rutter, such definitions may characterize some as resilient for whom the impact of the stressor is indirect. Most important, the study of resilience is meaningless without attention to the processes or mechanisms by which resilience is obtained. "Is it chance, the spin of the roulette wheel of life, or did prior circumstances, happenings, or actions serve to bring about this desirable state of affairs?" (Rutter, 1990, p. 183). These are the questions that, if answered, provide suggested avenues for prevention and intervention.

Recognizing Resilience When We See It

With its primary focus on children, resilience has sometimes been assessed in terms of behavioral manifestations such as competence in social and school realms (see Garmezy, 1983; Rutter, 1979, 1983; Werner, 1984). Anthony (1987), suggesting that there are many kinds of resilience among children, defines the truly resilient as those who cope well and who are capable in relationships (love), work, and play. It would seem that these would be behavioral manifestations of resilient adults as well. Because the participants in our study were all college students who ranged in age from 21 to 50, it could be said that all of our subjects were resilient in that a certain level of functioning is required for college entrance. This is especially noteworthy because the prevalence rate of sexual abuse appears to be lower among college students (Haugaard & Reppucci, 1988).

Thus, we searched for other strategies for identifying resilient survivors among a group of study participants believed to be already quite resilient.

Resilience as Adjustment

Resilience has sometimes been ascertained on the basis of measures that assess psychological well-being. Thus, individuals who have been exposed to known stressors but do not reveal psychological symptoms may be identified as resilient (Kendall-Tackett et al., 1993; Lyons, 1991). As empirical research often reveals differences between abused and nonabused subjects on many of these adjustment measures, it is conceivable that a subgroup who report high levels of adjustment might be deemed resilient. Liem et al. (in press), for instance, found that a sample of sexual abuse survivors who were relatively free of depression and had higher than average self-esteem differed from their counterparts in several ways. Survivors deemed resilient were older and further from the abuse experience; came from larger families, and were more likely to attribute control over future outcomes to themselves. They were more likely to have had a life course characterized by few early childhood stressors—families less disrupted by divorce and/or physical abuse—and to have experienced somewhat less physi-cally coercive sexual abuse, but they were no less likely to seek help in coping with the abuse nor less likely to encounter subsequent adult challenges.

These findings, although interesting and informative as a starting point for understanding resilience, tell us very little about how the survivors of CSA in our study understand their own emotional health or whether they see themselves as resilient. Thus, moving beyond survey data became necessary in order both to examine the qualities of resilience in people's lives and to begin to ascertain some of the mechanisms by which it might be obtained. Extending our earlier work, this study was conducted to learn more from survivors' own narration about the meaning and experience of resilience and the role that power-related concerns might play in it.

Resilience as Having Outlets for the Power Motive

As we have seen, survivors of CSA are more likely to have high n Power than those who have not experienced CSA (Liem et al., 1992, 1996). What is the relevance of this finding in the lives of survivors?

According to Winter (1988), n Power is

> a concern for having impact on others, arousing strong emotions in others, or maintaining reputation and prestige. N Power predicts a wide range of actions involving leader-ship and social power, acquiring prestige, and several "vicarious" or profligate, impulsive actions (drinking, gambling, sexual exploitation). (p. 510)

The evidence suggests, however, that resilience requires more than the presence of the need for power per se; it also requires access to the feeling of powerfulness or "outlets" for the need. McClelland (1977) has shown that alcoholics who, in addition to their regular treatment program, learn about the n Power motive, participate in experiences designed to examine the affective response to being powerful or powerless, and incorporate self-determined outlets for the motive were more likely to recover from alcoholism than those who were in the regular treatment program alone.

Other effective outlets for the power motive, discovered mostly in studies of college students, have been: office holding and organizational activity; the pursuit of power-related careers such as psychology and therapy, journalism, business management, and clergy; acquiring prestige and visibility in terms of a concern with appearance (diet, exercise, clothes, etc.), and participation in social movements (Winter, 1988). Lips (1991), however, has pointed to the many forms that the expression of a need for power can take, depending on the cultural and social context of the power seeker: "Depending on the situation, a person can achieve feelings of power by winning, by gaining respect and liking, by accomplishing an important task, by giving away possessions, or even by being pointedly self-sacrificing and modest" (p. 55).

To create an outlet for the power motive, then, means to identify and have access to ways of having an impact on one's environment that provides an emotional "charge." Two of the coding categories for n Power in TAT stories are statements indicating *instrumental activity* toward power goals and/or statements concerning *blocks* in attaining power goals. It may be that victims of sexual abuse who have high n Power and who develop numerous socially acceptable outlets for the power motive are more resilient than those high in n Power who do not locate these outlets.

If this is true, then the exercise of power in socially acceptable ways may be "neutralizing" (see Rutter, 1990) the negative impact of sexual abuse and serving as a source of resilience in survivors. Whether or not the power motive is a source of resilience is the focus of our analysis of the four in-depth interviews that follow.

Aims of the Study

Our purpose is to use interview materials to expand our understanding of resilience in the face of CSA by addressing the following questions:

1. How do CSA survivors currently assess their own emotional health?
2. Are they able to identify sources of comfort and strength in the face of childhood adversity?
3. If, in their view, healing has occurred over time, what do they view as instrumental to their healing process?
4. Finally, given that CSA involves an experience of powerlessness and betrayal by powerful others, is there evidence that creating socially responsible outlets for power and influence in their own lives is in any way curative?

Methods

The Original Studies

The original sample consisted of 687 volunteers (253 men, 434 women) from undergraduate courses at two urban universities recruited for two studies reported elsewhere (Boudewyn & Liem, 1995a, 1995b; Liem et al., 1992, 1996). Students on these campuses are racially and ethnically diverse, are often working as well as attending school, and are substantially older than the typical undergraduate (the average age of incoming freshmen on these campuses is 26).

Participants in both studies were given several measures, including: (a) The Life Experiences Survey (Boudewyn & Liem, 1995a, 1995b; Liem et al., 1996)—an inventory of stressful childhood events; (b) the Beck Depression Inventory—Short Form (BDI; Beck & Beck, 1972); and (c) the Rosenberg Self-Esteem Scale (RSE; Rosenberg, 1965) as well as other measures.

To separate CSA experiences from exploratory sexual experimentation or consensual sexual activity with peers, we defined CSA (using a definition employed by Wyatt, Guthrie, & Notgrass, 1992) as unwanted sexual contact before the age of 14 involving either (a) a 5-year age difference between the victim and perpetrator or (b) overt coercion (the use of verbal or physical threats, physical force, or violence by the perpetrator). On the basis of this definition, 145 individuals (16% of the men and 24% of the women; 21% of the entire sample) were identified as having histories of CSA, whereas 503 individuals (79% of the sample) were identified as having no history of CSA.

Forty of the 145 CSA survivors (28%) reported virtually no evidence of depression as adults and self-esteem ratings that were more positive than the mean rating for the entire sample (see Liem et al., in press, for a full description of the sample, measures, and procedures). Because depression and low self-esteem are frequently reported long-term outcomes of CSA (Browne & Finkelhor, 1986), and because we had data from the BDI and RSE for the entire sample of 687 participants, we focused on these measures for our working definition of a resilient adult outcome. We then examined our data for characteristics of people, their early and later family environments, CSA experiences, and subsequent adult outcomes associated with this definition of resilience as healthy adjustment. The results, as summarized above, revealed meaningful differences between survivors of CSA who were relatively free of depression and had higher than average self-esteem in contrast to less resilient survivors. These findings inspired us to learn more from our respondents' own words about the meaning and experience of resilience in the face of CSA.

Resilience Interview. A subsample of sexual abuse survivors was recruited from the first study ($N = 169$; 43 women with CSA histories) for in-depth interviews about their experience. The average interview was about 3 hours. Participants were identified from a question on the Life Experiences Survey tapping willingness to participate in an interview about their experiences. Whereas 10 students with histories of CSA volunteered to be interviewed further about their experiences, only 4 could be reached when we called to make the arrangements. Although the number is small, these interviews provide in-depth information, from a nonclinical sample representing a range of ages, about coping mechanisms used by the survivor, aspects of the family situation in which the abuse took place, the family's response, and the survivor's own sense of power and efficacy. As such, these interviews provide compelling portraits of adaptation to CSA and suggest new lines of inquiry.

All three authors worked together to develop and pilot the interviews; each of us did at least one of the interviews used for these analyses. Although we are similar in age and all female, we represent different relationships to our participants and knowledge of their experiences. Two of us were teaching psychology classes from which participants in the study were recruited. One of us has a long history of conducting studies of social stress; another has a rather new interest in the study of human motivation and in promoting research that seeks to understand the development of competencies as a correction for overattending to the development of psychopathology. Two of us have clinical practices where CSA is sometimes the focus. Thus, our collaboration was rich with varied experiences and perspectives.

All of us, however, were struck by the richness of these interviews. Participants spoke with surprising openness and ease of expression. From our surveys, we already had a great deal of data about the occurrence of CSA and other childhood stressors and their psychological concomitants, but we had little on how they understood their experiences and evaluated them in relation to other aspects of their lives.

In the course of the interviews, we asked respondents to tell us about their experiences of sexual abuse. These experiences were extremely painful to hear. Explicit and graphic in detail, the stories are horrible; they speak volumes about abuses of power in our society. But our intention here is not to provide portraits of the experience; this has been done elsewhere (Bass, 1988; Herman, 1981, 1992). For our purposes, much was revealed about resilience from responses to questions about the high points and low points in our respondents' lives. These accounts were emotionally charged and varied. They presented the sexual abuse as one chapter in a full life story, one that was a central and important chapter, but that did not fully define nor overwhelm other chapters. We turn now to these transcripts in an attempt to illuminate the various psychological processes operating for CSA survivors at this point in time.

Results

Table 9.1 provides a brief description of each interviewee and her experience of abuse. Three of our interviewees seemed to have dealt

TABLE 9.1   Brief Portraits of Interviewees and Their Experiences of
Childhood Sexual Abuse

Connie: A 22-year-old, newly married student, Connie believes she has been molested by her father. Clearer memories, however, center around a rape perpetrated by the older brother of a girlfriend when Connie was 11. After walking her home from school, he asked for something to drink and, once inside her home, forced himself upon her. When she was 13 and at a party with peers, she was invited outside to talk in the backyard. There she was pinned to the ground and forced to perform oral sex. Now, she is having flashbacks that include similar acts on the part of her father, both before and after his divorce from her mother.

Betsy: Single by choice in her mid-forties, Betsy remembers living with the pressures of her mother's life-threatening illnesses and her father's alcoholism. As an 8-year-old, she was molested repeatedly and eventually forced to perform oral and genital sex by an older boy (16) who lived next door and who was a close friend of the family. When she tried to tell her mother, she was referred to the family priest. She still sees the perpetrator at family functions. She is now in the process of changing careers, from nursing to business.

Mary: A very bright student who made nearly all A's throughout high school, Mary has served in the Marine Corps, has pumped gas, has entered (and left) a convent, and has now entered college at the age of 31 to complete a major in psychology. She was abused by two male relatives from the time she was 7 until she was 14. Her uncle, then in his thirties, would ask her to go hit golf balls with him; after the golf, he would molest her behind a building, demanding oral sex and attempting vaginal penetration. She felt she could not tell her parents because they would think she was "bad."

Karen: A high school dropout turned entrepreneur, Karen owned several hair salons in New York City and lived on the fast track of business, night life, drugs, and alcohol by the time she was 23. She is now 34. It has been 7 years since she gave up the drugs that were shielding her from pain (both past and present) and has entered college with the intention of completing a double major in psychology and art. Her sexual abuse perpetrator was her older sister and her sister's friends, who had orgies in her room when her parents were away. Karen does not remember the details of the sexual activity, but her sister has confirmed her suspicions that sexually abusive activities were visited upon her regularly during her childhood.

---

with their past experiences, to have gained an adult perspective on their childhood trauma, and to be functioning well in a variety of roles. One of the three spoke of herself quite pointedly as resilient and indicated that resilience was what she gained from her painful experiences of sexual abuse. One of the women, whom we refer to as

Connie (none of the names are real), seemed to be in the midst of adult recognition of childhood maltreatment, of facing the hard questions of whether to confront someone (and whom to confront) about her past, and of considering the potential of psychotherapy for dealing with some of her confusion around the events of her childhood.

It is interesting in light of our earlier finding that resilience was related to age and distance from the event that Connie is the youngest of our four interviewees. At 22, she is beginning to face aspects of her past that have troubled her for a long time; she has not had the distance from those experiences to evaluate them in a therapeutic way. Encouraged by information presented in several courses she had been taking, she is actively seeking ways to move beyond her distress and expressed, during the interview, relief that she now has the insurance coverage that she needs to enter treatment. Yet, referring to her experience of confiding to a friend about her past, she revealed her ongoing anguish: "This is too confusing for people. . . . I'm still struggling to come to terms with it. . . . I know I'm angry. I know I've been abused, but I'm still trying to sort it all out."

It is clear from these interviews that time alone does not heal. All four of the women who told us their stories described many paths to healing; all four had sought or were seeking clinical treatment, often of more than one sort. Perhaps with the exception of Connie, all told stories of overcoming challenges, of having beaten the odds. Seeing themselves as efficacious, they presented as having beaten the odds. If there was a central theme in their narratives, it was that of mastering adversity.

It is important to note that each of these women described many difficult family dynamics in addition to her experiences of abuse: Connie's father, an alcoholic, physically abused her mother and her older sister. Connie's mother eventually divorced her father but remained in conflict with and afraid of him and had great difficulty taking action to protect herself and her children from him. Connie still lives in a working-class culture that is not supportive of her efforts to be an efficacious adult with rights to her own body. Mary's father had multiple sclerosis; her brother was on medication for hyperactivity; and her sister had life-threatening asthma. Karen divulged the overwhelming intrusiveness of her sisters' problems on her well-being—one sister became pregnant at 14 and left home (accompanied by Karen's mother); another sister had a nervous breakdown. In addition, Karen recounted acid, pot, and sex orgies orchestrated by her sisters in her bedroom at times when they were responsible for her care in the absence of their parents. Betsy described a family troubled by the illness and their worry about the impending death of her mother and the alcoholism of her father. Still, all described strengths they developed in the midst of these difficulties.

Betsy, our self-avowed resilient survivor (and our oldest interviewee, in her mid-forties), described it this way:

> I think I'm very resilient, from, uhm, the kind of childhood that I had. . . . I was always able to say—I'll think of that tomorrow, and things will look better in the morning, and uhm, I was always able to have a vision, or fantasize, you know, I used to call it my little fantasies. . . . I don't know, I always had that capacity, I was always able to use humor, . . . uhm, I don't know, I think some of that helped.

And Karen remembered,

> I've always been creative all my life. I mean, that's what I did to take care of myself. I isolated with doing art projects. And—so I tried those. And then I tried some hotter stuff, math and English and psychology, and now I'm a psych and an art major, and I make films and make documentaries, and my average is 3.8 and . . .

Begging her parents to put her into a foster home to no avail, Karen turned to drugs and alcohol as an escape from her abusive childhood family environment. Even that, however, Karen has reframed:

> I don't regret anything at this point in my life that has happened. I have a lot of sadness about a lot that happened, but I don't regret it. I needed every drink and drug that I took to get to where I am today. I needed every life experience in my family to become who I'm becoming. . . . Like I think I'm

okay. . . . I feel good about the work I've done on myself in
recovery. . . . I wish my childhood were different, but it
isn't . . . and you know, I had some fun when I was on drugs.
In the beginning, of course, you know, it starts off as fun.
But my goals are much different now. I didn't have any goals
or dreams before recovery.

Mary, the daughter of an illiterate father (an assembly line laborer
with a fourth-grade education), took refuge in books. She enthusiastically spoke of her love of reading as an escape when she was being
abused by her uncle (at age 7 or 8):

> Rather than face what was going on with me and my uncle
> and my family, and tell somebody or do something about it,
> it was easier to sort of be all these other people in books.
> 'Cause when you're reading a book, for the amount of time
> that you're in the book, you can be that main character; and
> you don't have to be yourself. I could be Nancy Drew, or I
> could be one of the Hardy boys, or I could be any one of a
> number of [characters in] children's books that I read, or
> adult books that I happened to get my hands on. And I
> didn't have to be me, I didn't like being me.

Although some might quibble with the escape from self as adaptive, it
would seem that her love of reading was indeed so. Mary was an
exceptional student in school. All her life, she valued education and
ended up in the top 10% of her class in high school, all while taking
a full load of honors courses. Even Connie, who was not functioning
as comfortably as Mary, mentioned the inspiration she currently
gleans from reading and the strength she drew from getting good
grades in school.

Thus, we can see how the use of humor, fantasy, creativity, reading, and school success developed as sources of resilience for our
interviewees during childhood (similar to Sanford, 1990; see also,
Vaillant, 1993). Other perceived sources of healing came later in the
adult process of making sense of childhood events. Each of the women
we interviewed internalized self-blame for the experience, and all

emphasized the importance of psychotherapy for its role in overcoming shame and guilt about the past while providing new perspectives on the here and now. Karen, who had used drugs and alcohol as an escape from her childhood misery, gave great weight to the importance of the 12-step recovery process for overcoming her past. Not surprisingly, because all of our subjects are college students, all valued their ongoing education as a continuation of their recovery process.

Each also mentioned the importance of empathic and supportive (and not so supportive) relationships. For several, it was lessons learned from early commitments that helped them move forward in their lives. Two of our interviewees are lesbian; the other two are straight. Mary recounted the painful break with her first live-in lover, a woman, early in her 20s. She said that she used this experience to call out for help; on a self-destructive journey (cutting her arms with razor blades), she said, "I wasn't trying to commit suicide. I just wanted attention; I wanted help." In addition to psychotherapy, the help she got came in the form of encouragement from her new lover, to whom she is now permanently committed.

Similarly, Karen, also lesbian, described a series of relationships from which she drew the lessons of intimacy. In each relationship she described an increasing ability to communicate, to trust, to be less controlling, and to "stay with" sexual encounters (as opposed to "leaving her body" as she did during abusive episodes). When asked about her goals now, in her present relationship, she answered:

> I'd like to be in a healthy, committed relationship. I'd like to be—have greater comfort in my loneliness and grieving process. I want to make movies, and get a Ph.D. in psychology. I want my dog to have puppies. I will have a baby next year, hopefully. I want to stay sober. I want to live in a unity that I feel safe and comfortable in. I want to be able to continue to put my art into the world and challenge myself in areas that I was too afraid to go into. . . . I've been a very—I've been a very controlling person all my life, and it doesn't serve me any longer in my relationships. . . . And I made some changes that will help me. Because my goal is to be closer to people, not further [away].

Similar themes were echoed by Betsy, who fell in love and carried on an intense affair with a married man well into her forties. The conclusion of the relationship, according to Betsy, catapulted her into her current program of study at the university and taught her that she should

> try new fields, tread new waters, [use] that drive that I have to try new things. . . . I [have also] chosen to stay single and you know, rather than get into a relationship for the sake of just getting married, or something like that, you know, [my priority is] going to school.

Although each of our interviewees derived different lessons from different experiences, all pointed to the importance of lessons learned from postfamilial relationships in coming to terms with their past and learning to find meaning in the present. Other important perceived sources of resilience in adulthood were psychotherapy and recovery programs, education, and successes in the workplace.

Yet, we still cannot see with any certainty just how these sources of healing were curative. Were they simply helpful coping mechanisms? Did they represent new arenas for success that compensated for the disappointing family arena? Was it just their good fortune that they happened upon these resources? What was the neutralizing effect (Rutter, 1990) of these experiences? We wondered to what extent evidence of creating/finding outlets for the power motive would correspond with these themes and provide some explanation for why these women perceived the sets of experiences described above as helpful in their recovery process.

The Power Motive

The "drive" that Betsy referred to in the quotation above seems remarkably indicative of the power motive that we have found to be higher in survivors of sexual abuse (Liem et al., 1992, 1996). Less a drive than a response to a "natural incentive," McClelland (1987) describes the natural incentive of the power motive as "the production of effects upon the environment" (p. 148). Similar to White's (1959) notion of effectance, the impact incentive involves assertiveness and personal causation. The power motive, then, involves deriving intrinsic pleasure from "having an impact on others, arousing strong emotions in others, or maintaining reputation and prestige" (Winter, 1988, p. 510).

When asked about the high points of her life so far, Betsy knew right away—a high point was gaining the position she held 5 years ago as administrative director for a developing retirement community.

> It [this position] had always been held by men and by ministers, and I was the first woman, nonreligious person. . . . It was a first, and I felt, uhm, I felt in this job that I got a lot of kudos, uhm, a lot of recognition and a lot of it I didn't even have to work hard for. . . . I hadn't really realized that I could influence people so easily.

One of the things she reported enjoying most about this was that it came naturally—it was part of her personality to be able to easily affect people—and the realization of this was new to her. Pleasure in getting recognition (kudos), having prestige (director), presenting a dramatic presence (the only woman), and being influential are all experiences that can be seen as outlets for the need for power. Although it may seem to Betsy as if getting pleasure from power-related experiences comes "naturally," it is probably more complicated than that.

Although there are many known correlates of high n Power, there is no simple one-to-one relationship between having high n Power and one's actions. The need for power, as well as other motives, interacts with a person's skills or habits and values and is shaped over time in the context of one's environment (McClelland, 1987). Moreover, as we have seen, there can be both positive and negative ways to satisfy the need for power.

There are, moreover, many motives for behavior, and people tend to vary on the extent to which they are high in one or the other. Generally, no one of the motives in and of itself is more indicative of psychological health, but the power motive is the least socially sanctioned, especially for women. Therefore, one aspect of having a high need for power (as do many of our survivors), and coming to terms with that motive, has involved making the "need" for power socially acceptable.

Professionals who use the analysis of motives as a method for increasing self-understanding actually instruct clients about the ingredients of the motive (McClelland, 1987), the feelings it inspires (Steele, 1973, 1977), the dangers that lurk around it—for example, drinking (McClelland, Davis, Kalin, & Wanner, 1972) and aggression (McClelland, 1987)—and constructive outlets for it (Boyatzis, 1974; deCharms, 1976; Fersch, 1971). Thus, we hypothesized that survivors of CSA who manifest a high need for power might show more resilience if they had access to socially acceptable feelings of powerfulness. We first assessed the themes of "feeling powerful" in relation to our interviewees' own understanding of what had helped them cope with such adversity.

Betsy felt powerful (during childhood) in that she could create a new vision of tomorrow, use a fantasy of a better day to get through a series of bad days. Mary used a similar strategy but employed her love of reading to embolden her fantasy of being a character who makes an impact, for example, Nancy Drew or the Hardy boys. Karen accessed her creativity—at first through art, then trying some "hotter stuff" (power-infused vocabulary)—and is now involved in the production of films and documentaries (gaining prestige and visibility). Both Mary and Karen noted the importance of good grades (more highly correlated with n Power than n Achievement; Costa & McClelland, 1971) in paving the way toward a brighter future. Even Connie, who was by her own assessment not doing very well at the time of our interview, said that "getting good grades" in college helped her to move forward and deal with her troubles.

In addition, all of our interviewees are involved in the pursuit of careers more typical of those high in n Power, those that provide opportunities to be influential such as teaching, psychology, business, and journalism (Winter, 1973). We found it noteworthy, however, that Connie, while majoring in psychology, does not have a job that satisfies her need to have influence or impact but recognizes its importance to her. Currently working in a nursing home as a kitchen aide, she recalled other experiences.

I worked in some business jobs, some temporary agencies . . . [doing] data entry, customer service, and it was good. The people were nice, but the job itself was boring. I couldn't sit behind a desk for the rest of my life. Then I got a job at a social mental health [setting] working with the autistic and mentally ill. I loved it. I could see something going on with everyone. Every day is different.

Mary described a rather unusual career path, moving from service in the Army to gas station attendant to restaurant manager to service as a nun. Working part-time in order to complete her college degree and prepare for further graduate training, she is working as a nursing assistant at a geriatric/psychiatric facility in the "locked dementia unit." Karen, in pursuit of a double major in psychology and art, is already involved in making documentaries and networking to get them "shown." Betsy, a business major, was most articulate about her intrinsic pleasure in having influence and will be described in further detail later in the chapter. Thus, it would appear that the three more resilient interviewees described sources of their well-being and recovery that may have to do with satisfying their n Power motive, both in terms of the coping strategies they used during childhood and in terms of present-day strivings as well.

The women also revealed evidence of having some of the known difficulties that go with high n Power. Both Karen and Betsy articulated their process of coming to terms with the use of drugs and alcohol, related to n Power, perhaps because alcohol consumption facilitates feeling powerful for some (McClelland, 1987). In her own words, Karen said that these were used to "help me cope" but, in the end, only impeded her success.

I owned my own hair salon when I was 23. . . . And it wasn't successful because I was on drugs . . . it would have been successful because, I mean, I did good hair. . . . And as far as like high points, there really weren't any high points other than getting sober, and then everything [went better] after that.

There are also certain relationship issues associated with high n Power that we saw running through the narratives in our interviews. McAdams, Healey, and Krause (1982) have shown that the "high n Power individual tends to experience friendships in an agentic manner, understanding them in terms of opportunities to take on dominant, controlling, organizational roles" (cited in McClelland, 1987, p. 286). All of our interviewees described having some relationship problems. They described the problems in the past tense and emphasized their mastery over them. Both Connie and Karen, however, have sisters with whom they are not on speaking terms. Karen, as quoted earlier, described a history of overcoming her need to be controlling in relationships. And Betsy told of leaving a position of employment that she loved because of her involvement in a very problematic relationship triangle.

> I got myself into one of those wonderful triangles, uhm, between my boss and the developer [a married man with whom she was having an affair]. . . . the developer would tell me, you know, things [such as] that my boss was very intimidated by my standing in the organization . . . and was trying to sabotage my . . . position . . . and I had been going down the road [thinking] that my boss and I had a working relationship based on trust, even though, I mean, sometimes the boundaries would get mushy.

But then the relationship with the developer went sour, as well, and Betsy told the interviewer why this was such a low point in life for her.

> Betsy: I fell in love with a married guy, and he . . . was a developer and I worked with him. We went away a couple of days when I was supposed to be working . . . we went in town to a hotel . . . so, that was kind of scary . . . that I . . . just lost control of my emotions.
>
> Interviewer: Is that what made this such a low point for you . . . not being in control?

Betsy: Yeah, yeah, I wasn't in control, and uhm, he didn't . . . he
     was exciting and he was challenging, and I loved him, and I
     thought he was being truthful, but he was just, in a way, using
     me to get ahead with his business ventures and everything, you
     know . . . when I found out about that, that he was using me
     . . . that was another low point for me.

Her lover (of 6 years) left her when she became pregnant. After much
anguish, she decided to have an abortion. The traumatic conclusion
of that relationship, she asserted, was the impetus behind her decision
to begin her current program of study at the university where she is
now experiencing considerable success. She has a few close friends to
whom she is very committed but has remained single by choice (as
noted in the earlier quotation above). Her goals, which she seems quite
sanguine about, are to get a place of her own, to pursue a Ph.D. by
continuing some research she has been working on, and to become
financially solvent.

   Betsy, in fact, provides our most vivid example of one who derives
great pleasure and well-being from her capacity to find outlets for her
power needs. Winter (1973) has shown that people high in the need
for power not only like recognition, but also attend to status, both
symbolic and real. Betsy clearly was energized by these manifestations
of importance:

        I remember this one time in a board meeting, this man
        that . . . inwardly, I was intimidated by, I'll never forget
        it. . . . He's a partner in this big law firm in Boston and we
        were on the top floor in this conference room and I just
        said, "Wow! I can't believe I'm standing here talking to this
        group." There was only one other woman there . . . (and she
        was recording the minutes) and I felt like. . . . "Wow, I can't
        believe I'm here!" And I was standing up and I was present-
        ing a budget and I was nervous because that's not my back-
        ground. And I was kind of winging it.

When people in high positions of power responded favorably to her
presentations, she was ecstatic. In the end, she told the interviewer,

"Actually, I'm more comfortable in a leadership role than . . . [when I'm] not in a leadership [position]."

Betsy was the only one of our interviewees who actually described herself as resilient. Perhaps this match between motive and outlets is one of the reasons. Only further empirical research that operationalizes outlets for the power motive will tell. We believe this to be a very promising new direction for research about the role of power and influence in the lives of adults who have experienced CSA.

Discussion

From our analyses of four in-depth interviews with volunteers from a nonclinical sample representing a range of ages, we have attempted to demonstrate that victims of sexual abuse who have high n Power and who have numerous socially acceptable outlets for the power motive see those outlets as sources of their recovery and well-being, and in one case, self-defined resilience. Our observations suggest that exercising power in socially acceptable ways may be neutralizing (see Rutter, 1990) the negative impact of sexual abuse by restoring power where power and status have been denied (see Winter & Stewart, 1978) and, in this way, serving as a source of resilience in survivors.

Three of our four interviewees reported that at this time in their lives, they are doing well psychologically. There is evidence from all four of our interviewees that having outlets for power and influence in their own lives is beneficial. Clearly, Connie, who appears to be doing least well, appeared to have the fewest outlets for the power motive; Betsy, who defines herself as resilient, had the most.

With reference to her childhood abuse, Betsy informed us,

> I actually don't think about it as much as I used to. It's not that up-front in my mind any more. I guess I've kinda let it go. You can never let it rest completely, but I've come to a good place with some of it. I mean . . . if you can come to a good place with that type of thing . . . you know it's over, it's done, you are who you are because of your experi-

> ences . . . and I just feel I have made such headroads into
> not feeling guilty, or remorseful, or having to explain why
> I chose not to be places if he [her abuser who is still a close
> family friend] is around. . . . Because our families are so
> intertwined, there are going to be things—wakes, funerals,
> and all that he is going to attend, but I don't have to be nice
> to him. I feel real good about that, that I have come to the
> point in my life where I can do that.

Connie, in strong contrast, remains preoccupied with her CSA because it is consistent with and serves as a representation of her current experiences of victimization. Still not in a supportive environment, she reported that some of her friends see her as complicit in both rape experiences and are unwilling to affirm her definition of them as rapes. She noted that at times, she found it easier to think of herself as a "whore" than to recognize how little she mattered to the young men who raped her. In her words,

> It's so much easier to say, "I must be a whore, I had sex
> with some guy I didn't know. So what's the big deal?" than
> to say, "Listen, wait a minute, there's a big problem here.
> He doesn't like me and he is not making love to me. He is
> raping me and he doesn't like me at all. He doesn't even see
> me as having human emotions."

Referring to her efforts to stop her abusers from raping her, including her father, she told us, "To this day, I don't know why I speak to these people because it's going to happen anyway. That's just so frustrating." Her experience, repeated with each of her three abusers, involved trying unsuccessfully to tell them to stop, being ignored by them—in fact, being told to shut up and being forcefully restrained—and dissociating as she was raped.

Neither Connie's mother nor her sister has been able to help her with her confusion about her sexual abuse. She characterized her mother as being in total denial and her sister as blaming her. She reported the following response by her sister to her disclosure of abuse by her father:

> Maybe they [Mom and Dad] weren't having sex before the
> divorce, and he had to get it somewhere. You wanted to go
> on vacation with him, so hey, whatever happened happened.
> It wasn't repeated or I would have known about it.

Connie became preoccupied with her childhood abuse after getting married about 6 months before the interview. She had flunked out of school the semester after her marriage but now was back taking courses, doing better grade-wise, and hoping to get into therapy. She was having flashbacks, had ongoing problems in her sexual relationship with her husband, and reported alternating between being anxious, angry, and depressed. She was talking more with friends and with her husband about her past and about her current needs, but she was far from seeing herself as efficacious. Connie appears to be in the early stages of a recovery process. She may someday appear resilient but did not at the time of our encounter.

Betsy, years ahead of Connie in terms of real time and in terms of perspective on her childhood, is assertive and engaging. She enjoys leadership positions in several social organizations. She is a self-conscious, purposeful actor with strong desires and future aspirations and the capacity to devise cognitive and behavioral strategies to overcome momentary threats to her agenda.

All four women who shared their experiences with us seem quite cognizant of their coping processes. Each one described more than one form of coping and source of strength. Each credited aspects of her person (ability to be creative, to become someone else in fantasy, to think about tomorrow), aspects of relationships with important others (trusted friends, teachers, relatives), and aspects of help-seeking (psychotherapy and trauma groups) not just for her survival, but for her growth. Each seems realistic in her appraisal of her current functioning.

We believe that, with further confirmation of the link between the availability of outlets for the power motive and well-being, interventions that focus on the power motive and its expression could prove useful in treating CSA survivors. Women with histories of CSA might benefit from being made more aware of their need for power and their particular affective responses to feeling powerful or powerless. They might benefit even further from opportunities to express the power motive in social arenas through assertiveness training or leadership development programs or other self-defined power outlets.

In conclusion, we believe that at least three of the survivors of CSA presented here have, to borrow a phrase from Lillian Smith, "taught the terrors of their nature[s] and their world to sing" (cited in Hauser et al., 1985, p. 83). We have suggested that important ingredients in the "teaching" process for them were coming to terms with the discovery of the feeling of being powerful rather than powerless, recognizing the intrinsic pleasure inherent in personal agency and causation, and accumulating knowledge of ways to acquire power and influence that are both personally and socially edifying. Some of their success could be attributed to personality and to having the good fortune to come upon and take advantage of opportunities for satisfying needs for power in positive ways. Much of it, however, was due to deliberate and focused efforts toward overcoming their hardships by *finding* ways to restore a feeling of powerfulness.

References

Anthony, E. J. (1987). Risk, vulnerability, and resilience: An overview. In E. J. Anthony & B. J. Cohler (Eds.), *The invulnerable child* (pp. 3-48). New York: Guilford.

Bass, E. (1988). *The courage to heal: A guide for women survivors of child sexual abuse.* New York: Harper & Row.

Beck, A. T., & Beck, R. W. (1972). Screening depressed patients in family practice: A rapid technique. *Postgraduate Medicine, 52*, 81-85.

Beck, J. C., & Van der Kolk, B. (1987). Reports of childhood incest and current behavior of chronically hospitalized psychotic women. *American Journal of Psychiatry, 144*(11), 1474-1476.

Boudewyn, A. C., & Liem, J. H. (1995a). Childhood sexual abuse as a precursor of depression and self-destructive behavior in adulthood. *The Journal of Traumatic Stress, 8*(3), 445-459.

Boudewyn, A. C., & Liem, J. H. (1995b, March). *The effects of childhood sexual abuse on adult self- and social-functioning: An attachment theory perspective.* Poster presented at the meeting of the Society for Research in Child Development, Indianapolis, IN.

Boyatzis, R. E. (1974). *Power motivation training workbook.* Boston: McBer & Company.

Briere, J. (1992). *Child abuse trauma: Theory and treatment of the lasting effects.* Newbury Park, CA: Sage.

Browne, A., & Finkelhor, D. (1986). Impact of child sexual abuse: A review of the research. *Psychological Bulletin, 99*(1), 66-77.

Cicchetti, D., & Aber, J. L. (1986). Early precursors to later depression: An organizational perspective. In L. Lipsitt & C. Rovee-Collier (Eds.), *Advances in infancy* (pp. 87-137). Norwood, NJ: Ablex.

Costa P., & McClelland, D. C. (1971). *Predicting rank in class from motivational, social class, and intelligence measures.* Unpublished manuscript, Harvard University, Department of Psychology and Social Relations.

deCharms, R. (1976). *Enhancing motivation: Change in the classroom.* New York: Irvington.

Fersch, E. A. (1971). *Inward bound: The motivational impact of a combined Outward Bound-Upward Bound program on adolescents from poverty families.* Unpublished doctoral dissertation, Harvard University.

Garmezy, N. (1970). Vulnerable children: Implications derived from studies on an internalizing-externalizing symptom dimension. In J. Zublin & A. M. Freedman (Eds.), *The psychopathology of adolescence* (pp. 212-239). New York: Grune & Stratton.

Garmezy, N. (1981). Children under stress: Perspectives on antecedents and correlates of vulnerability and resistance to psychopathology. In A. I. Rabin, J. Aronoff, A. M. Barclay, & R. A. Zucker (Eds.) *Further explorations in personality* (pp. 196-269). New York: John Wiley.

Garmezy, N. (1983). Stressors of childhood. In N. Garmezy & M. Rutter (Eds.), *Stress, coping, and development* (pp. 43-84). New York: McGraw-Hill.

Garmezy, N. (1991). Resiliency and vulnerability to adverse developmental outcomes associated with poverty. *American Behavioral Scientist, 34*(4), 416-430.

Haugaard, J. J., & Reppucci, N. D. (1988). *The sexual abuse of children: A comprehensive guide to current knowledge and intervention strategies.* San Francisco: Jossey-Bass.

Hauser, S. T., Vieyra, M. B., Jacobson, A. M., & Wertlieb, D. (1985). Vulnerability and resilience in adolescence: Views from the family. *Journal of Early Adolescence, 5*(1), 81-100.

Herman, J. L. (1981). *Father-daughter incest.* Cambridge, MA: Harvard University Press.

Herman, J. L. (1992). *Trauma and recovery.* New York: Basic Books.

Kendall-Tackett, K. A., Williams, L. M., & Finkelhor, D. (1993). Impact of sexual abuse on children: A review and synthesis of recent empirical studies. *Psychological Bulletin, 113*(1), 164-180.

Liem, J. H., James, J. B., O'Toole, J. G., & Boudewyn, A. (in press). Assessing resilience in adults with histories of childhood sexual abuse. *Journal of Orthopsychiatry.*

Liem, J. H., O'Toole, J. G., & James, J. B. (1992). The need for power in women who were sexually abused as children. *Psychology of Women Quarterly, 16,* 467-480.

Liem, J. H., O'Toole, J. G., & James, J. B. (1996). Themes of power and betrayal in sexual abuse survivors' characterizations of interpersonal relationships. *Journal of Traumatic Stress, 9*(4), 745-762.

Lips, H. M. (1991). Responsibility vs. dominance? Women, men, and the need for power. In H. Lips (Ed.), *Women, men, and power* (pp. 36-55). Mountain View, CA: Mayfield.

232 THE NARRATIVE STUDY OF LIVES

Lyons, J. A. (1991). Strategies for assessing the potential for positive adjustment following trauma. *Journal of Traumatic Stress, 4*(1), 93-111.

McAdams, D. P., Healey, S., & Krause, S. (1982). *Relationships between social motives and patterns of friendship.* Unpublished manuscript, Loyola University, Department of Psychology.

McClelland, D. C. (1977). The impact of power motivation training on alcoholics. *Journal of Studies on Alcohol, 38*(1), 142-144.

McClelland, D. C. (1987). *Human motivation.* New York: Cambridge University Press.

McClelland, D. C., Davis, W. B., Kalin, R., & Wanner, E. (1972). *The drinking man: Alcohol and human motivation.* New York: Free Press.

Mrazek, P. J., & Mrazek, D. A. (1987). Resilience in child maltreatment victims: A conceptual exploration. *Child Abuse and Neglect, 11,* 357-367.

Neiman, L. (1988). A critical review of resiliency literature and its relevance to homeless children. *Children's Environments Quarterly, 5*(1), 17-25.

Patten, S., Gatz, Y., Jones, B., & Thomas, D. (1989). Posttraumatic approach to assessment of perceived control. In H. Lefcourt (Ed.), *Research with the locus of control construct.* New York: Academic Press.

Rosenberg, M. (1965). *Society and the adolescent self-image.* Princeton, NJ: Princeton University Press.

Russell, D. (1986). *The secret trauma: Incest in the lives of girls and women.* New York: Basic Books.

Rutter, M. (1979). Protective factors in children's responses to stress and disadvantage. In M. W. Kent & J. E. Rolf (Eds.), *Primary prevention of psychopathology: Social competence in children* (Vol. 3) (pp. 49-77). Hanover, NH: University Press of New England.

Rutter, M. (1983). Stress, coping, and development: Some issues and some questions. In N. Garmezy & M. Rutter (Eds.), *Stress, coping, and development in children* (pp. 1-42). New York: McGraw-Hill.

Rutter, M. (1990). Psychological resilience and protective mechanisms. In J. Rolf, A. S. Marten, D. Cicchetti, K. H. Nuechterlein, & S. Weintraub (Eds.), *Risk and protective factors in the development of psychopathology* (pp. 181-214). New York: Cambridge University Press.

Sachs, R., Goodwin, J., & Braun, B. (1985). The role of childhood abuse in the development of multiple personality. In R. Kluff & B. Braun (Eds.), *Multiple personality & dissociation.* New York: Guilford.

Sanford, L. T. (1990). *Strong at the broken places.* New York: Random House.

Steele, R. S. (1973). *The physiological concomitants of psychogenic motive arousal in college males.* Unpublished doctoral dissertation, Harvard University.

Steele, R. S. (1977). Power motivation, activation, and inspirational speeches. *Journal of Personality, 45,* 53-64.

Vaillant, G. E. (1993). *The wisdom of the ego.* Cambridge, MA: Harvard University Press.

Werner, E. E. (1984). Resilient children. *Young Children, 40,* 68-72.

West, M. O., & Prinz, R. J. (1987). Parental alcoholism and childhood psychopathology. *Psychological Bulletin, 102*(2), 204-218.

White, R. (1959). Motivation reconsidered: The concept of competence. *Psychological Review, 66*(5), 297-331.

Winter, D. G. (1973). *The power motive.* New York: Free Press.

Winter, D. G. (1988). The power motive in women—and men. *Journal of Personality and Social Psychology, 54,* 510-519.

Winter, D. G., & Stewart, A. J. (1978). The power motive. In H. London & J. Exner (Eds.), *Dimensions of personality* (pp. 391-447). New York: John Wiley.

Wolin, S. J. (1991, November). *The challenge model: How children rise above adversity.* A plenary address delivered at the annual meeting of the American Association of Marriage and Family Therapists, Dallas, TX.

Wyatt, G. E., Guthrie, D., & Notgrass, C.M. (1992). Differential effects of women's child sexual abuse and subsequent sexual revictimization. *Journal of Consulting and Clinical Psychology, 60,* 167-173.

Index

Ego development, 185
Eisler, B., 150, 156, 161, 174
Ekblad, S., 113
Elder, G., 184
Elias, N., 16
Eliot, M., 174
Empowerment, 55
    criminal reform and, 84-85
Epic narration, 3
Erikson, E. H., 22, 74
Ethical issues, privacy,
        62-63
Ey, S., 182

Face, xii, 9-12
Falk, N., 40
Family history, 4, 24
Family relationships, in Southeast Asian
        culture, 119-120
Feeney, T. J., 104
Female genital mutilation, 55-56
Fersch, E. A., 223
Fifties recollections, xv, 147-181
    fun and innocence, 152-156
    informants, 178-180
    political awareness, 156-162
    popular culture, 147-149, 153-154,
        162, 173-175
Finestone, H., 62
Finkelhor, D., 208, 214
Fischer, L., 120
Fischer-Rosenthal, W., 22, 23
Fischman, Y., 133
Fish, R., 15
Folklore, life story narration and, 5
Franz, C., 86
Freud, S., 11, 12, 14, 15, 17,
        182
Friedan, B., 160
Fromm, E., 101

Gabison, R., 105
Garmezy, N., 208, 209, 210
Gates, H. L., Jr., 162
Gatz, Y., 208
Ge, X., 184
Geertz, C., 11
Geis, M. L., 8

Gender:
    adolescent mental health and, xv,
        182-186, 189-203. *See also*
        Adolescent mental health
    coping/adjustment themes,
        189-199
    mikvah attendant perspectives, 52-56
    1950s recollections, 170-173
    peer standards and, 192-193
    psychotherapist mental health
        conceptualizations, 202
Generativity script, 86
Genital mutilation, 55-56
Georges, R. A., 5
Gergen, K., 6
Gergen, M., 6, 187
Giddens A., 62
Gillet, C., 174
Gillett, G., 7
Gilligan, C., xvi, 96, 100, 184-185, 201,
        202
Girgus, J., 184
Gitlin, T., 173, 174
Glaser, B., 24
Glueck, E., 65
Glueck, S., 65
Gochberg, B., 201
Goffman, E., 9, 73, 98
Gonsalves, C., 133
Good, B. J., 116, 125
Good, M. D., 116
Gore, S., 184, 201
Gottfredson, M., 65, 67
Gottlieb, A., 42
Gozdziak, E., 116, 127
Grant, K. E., 182
Graphic Story Line, 187
Greenberg, D. F., 60
Greimas, A. J., 15
Greulich, F. 201
Grice, H. P., 8
Gross, R., 40
Groves, W. B., 78
Gubrium, J. F., 1, 2, 41
Guthrie, D., 213

Habermas, J., 100, 101
Halberstam, D., 172

About the Contributors

Pertti Alasuutari, Ph.D., is Professor of Sociology at the University of Tampere, Finland. His recent books include *Desire and Craving: A Cultural Theory of Alcoholism* and *Researching Culture: Qualitative Method and Cultural Studies* (Sage, 1995).

Jane A. Bennett is a Ph.D. student in the Department of Family Social Science at the University of Minnesota and in the Marriage and Family Therapy clinical program. She is currently exploring identity and the social and family worlds of lesbians in later life.

Phame M. Camarena is Associate Professor of Human Development and Family Studies at Central Michigan University. Previous research has focused on gender and adjustment across adolescence. He is currently working on research and applied projects to explore how adolescents interpret personal experience to shape their own developmental trajectories.

Daniel F. Detzner is Professor of Family Social Science at the University of Minnesota and Director of its Refugee Studies Center. He is currently writing a book on the resettlement of Southeast Asian families in the United States and developing a model bicultural parenting curriculum for family life educators. He has long-standing

interests in intergenerational relationships, aging, and life-history research and uses life-history methods in both teaching and research.

Jacquelyn Boone James is Assistant Director of the Henry A. Murray
Research Center at Radcliffe College. She has focused her research on
the meaning and complexity of gender, adult development, and
motivation. Her most recent work, *Multiple Paths of Midlife Development*, with coauthor Margie Lachman of Brandeis University, is an
edited volume compiling 12 studies examining different aspects of
midlife development using data from the Radcliffe Murray Research
Center archive. She received her doctorate in personality psychology
from Boston University.

Ruthellen Josselson is Professor of Psychology at Towson State University and on the faculty of The Fielding Institute. Recipient of the
APA Henry A. Murray Award (1994) and a Fulbright Research Fel-
lowship (1989-1990), she has also recently been Visiting Professor at
the Harvard Graduate School of Education and Forchheimer Professor of Psychology at the Hebrew University in Jerusalem. She is author
of *Revising Herself: The Story of Women's Identity From College to
Midlife* and *The Space Between Us: Exploring the Dimensions of
Human Relationships*.

Amia Lieblich is Professor of Psychology at the Hebrew University of
Jerusalem, where she served as chairperson from 1982 to 1985. Her
books have presented an oral history of Israeli society, dealing with
war, POWs, military service, and the kibbutz. Recently she has published two psychobiographies of female writers: *Conversations with
Dvora* (about Dvora Baron) and *Towards Lea* (about Lea Goldberg).

Joan Huser Liem is one of the founding members of the Ph.D. program
in clinical psychology at the University of Massachusetts, Boston, and
is currently Graduate Program Director. She received her Ph.D. in
clinical psychology from Boston University and took postdoctoral
training in social psychiatry at Harvard Medical School. Her research
interests focus on individual and family responses to stressful experi-

ences, most recently the long-term consequences of childhood physical and sexual abuse.

Ruth Linn is Senior Lecturer at Haifa University's School of Education, specializing in the study of moral decisions and transitions. Her books, *Not Shooting and Not Crying—Psychological Inquiry into Moral Disobedience* and *Conscience at War—the Israeli Soldier as a Moral Critic* focus on the phenomenon of resistance among Israeli reserve soldiers who assumed a posture of selective conscientious objection during the wars in Lebanon and the Intifada.

Shadd Maruna is a Ph.D. candidate in Northwestern University's Human Development and Social Policy program and is a graduate fellow at the Northwestern/University of Chicago Poverty Center. He is currently collecting the life stories of ex-convicts in Liverpool, UK, on a Fulbright Grant.

Joan Gateley O'Toole is practicing social work at a multiservice agency in Boston and has coauthored several articles examining the role of power in adult survivors of childhood sexual abuse. She has a special interest in research that explores the development of strength and resiliency rather than psychopathology in victims of trauma. She is a summa cum laude graduate of the University of Massachusetts at Boston.

Anne C. Petersen is Senior Vice President for Programs at the W. K. Kellogg Foundation. A past president of both the Society for Research on Adolescence and the Developmental Division of the American Psychological Association, she has worked to advance research on the developmental significance of adolescence. A primary focus of her extensive research program has been on gender and mental health across the period of adolescence.

Gabriele Rosenthal received her Dr. rer. soc. in sociology from the University in Bielefeld, the Federal Republic of Germany, in 1986. In 1993, she completed her thesis on *Experienced and Narrated Life* at the University of Kassel. She presently teaches as Professor for Social Therapy at the University of Kassel. Teaching and research interests address interpretive sociology, qualitative methods, and biographical research. She is currently investigating the Shoah in the family history and the family dialogue of three-generation families in Israel and West and East Germany.

Pamela A. Sarigiani is Associate Professor of Human Development and Family Studies at Central Michigan University. She received her Ph.D. from The Pennsylvania State University. Current research interests include adolescent mental health, children under stress, and the significance of personal relationships for development.

Susan Starr Sered is Associate Professor of Anthropology at Bar Ilan University in Israel. She is the author of *Women as Ritual Experts: The Religious Lives of Elderly Jews in Jerusalem* and *Priestess, Mother, Sacred Sister: Religions Dominated by Women.* Her recent projects include a study of religion and gender in Okinawa and a study of the experiences of Israeli women who have had breast cancer.

Janelle L. Wilson is an Assistant Professor in the Department of Sociology-Anthropology at the University of Minnesota, Duluth, where she teaches courses in popular culture, social psychology, and deviance. She received her Ph.D. at Western Michigan University in Kalamazoo. Her most current research interests are in the sociology of nostalgia and Generation X.